Towards a Critique of E
Essays of Thomas T. Sekine

STUDIES IN SOCIAL SCIENCE AND PHILOSOPHY

VOLUME 1

Towards a Critique of Bourgeois Economics

Essays of Thomas T. Sekine

EDITED BY JOHN R. BELL

Owl of Minerva Press

Author's website:
dx.doi.org/10.4444/34

Publisher's website:
www.owlofminerva.net

Owl of Minerva Press, Berlin
First edition 2013

doi: 10.4444/34.20
ISBN 978-3-943334-00-5 (Hardcover)
ISBN 978-3-943334-01-2 (Paperback)
BID 002

Table of Contents

Introduction by the Editor   vi

I. Methodological Essays

Uno's Method of Marxian Economics   2

The Dialectic, or Logic that Coincides with Economics   12

The Dialectic of Capital: An Unoist Interpretation   23

An Essay on Uno's Dialectic of Capital   34

II. Theoretical Essays

Uno School Seminar on the Theory of Value   80

The Necessity of the Law of Value,
    Its Demonstration and Significance   101

The Transformation Problem,
    Qualitative and Quantitative   114

The Law of Market Value   139

Arthur on Money and Exchange   163

General Equilibrium and the Dialectic of Capital   185

Marxian Theory of Value, What We Might Learn from It   216

III. A New Essay

Towards a Critique of Bourgeois Economics   238

Appendix

Bibliography   278

Introduction by the Editor

John R. Bell (formerly Professor, Seneca College)

Thomas (Tomohiko) Sekine completed his doctorate at the London School of Economics and Political Science and then began his teaching career in Canada at Simon Fraser University in 1966-68 before accepting a position in the Economics department at York University in Toronto where he spent the bulk of his teaching career (1968-1994). After retiring from York, he returned to Japan and completed his teaching career at Aichi-Gakuin University.

Until 1973-4, Sekine worked mainly in the area of neoclassical monetary theory and its application to international economics, but he never really felt at home with that sort of enterprise. Fortunately, a Marx Renaissance was then taking hold in North America, and this gave him a welcomed opportunity to teach Marxian economics. He thus changed the focus of his research to Marxian economics and, more specifically, to the work of Kôzô Uno (1897-1977), who had been by far the most impressive and influential teacher that Sekine came into contact with during his undergraduate studies in Japan. His *Journal of Economic Literature* article on Uno-Riron (1975) was his first publication after his intellectual reorientation; it was soon followed by his translation into English (1980) of Uno's condensed *Principles of Political Economy* (1964). (The original *Principles*, published in 1950-52, was a much longer, two volume work.) Sekine subsequently published *The Dialectic of Capital, a Study of the Inner Logic of Capitalism*, 2 vols. (1984 and 1986), and *An Outline of the Dialectic of Capital*, 2 vols. (1997), in which he expanded and elaborated upon his mentor's *genriron* (or the pure theory of capitalism). All of the twelve essays collected in this volume were written and published during Sekine's 35-year research career, during which he single-mindedly devoted himself to the appropriation, reformulation and exegesis of Uno's unique approach to economics.

The essays in this volume are, however, not arranged in the chronological order in which they were written. The first four items are grouped together under the heading of *I. Methodological Essays*. The following seven items are classified into *II. Theoretical Essays*. The last essay is simply called *III. A New Essay,* since it has been drafted afresh and specifically for this volume. Among the four methodological essays, the fourth is the earliest dated, and retains most vividly Sekine's old interest in, and concern with, the scientific method. He read Popper and Logical Positivists on the one hand, and Engels, Lenin and the Dialectical Materialists on the other; yet he felt that neither was compatible with Uno's approach. He discovered instead that Hegel's *Logic* was much more congenial to Uno, even though the latter had never quite professed his intellectual affinity with it. The awakening to this fact launched Sekine into a characteristic research career of his own, as the other three methodological essays will bear witness. Just as Hegel's "logic coincided with metaphysics", the logic of capital must coincide with economic theory. For, according to Sekine, it is only in this way that the "dialectic" can be made "materialist" and be released from Hegelian idealism. Moreover, it is in this light that Sekine rejected the natural-scientific pretensions of bourgeois economics, which he viewed as nothing more than a covert invitation to conform to the existing social order, the significance of which he elaborates further in the last (or new) essay.

The fifth paper, which opens the section entitled *Theoretical Essays,* having been written under stringent space limitations, turns out to be a rather excessively condensed summary of Marxian theory of value. The latter constitutes the very core of the dialectic of capital, which, in a nutshell, is nothing more than "the definition (or specification) of capitalism by capital itself". The reader may be relieved, to some extent, after the extremely dense nature of the first contribution to be able to turn to three more expansive articles that supplement and expand upon the first: the sixth, on the "meaning of the law of value", the seventh, on the "transformation problem" and the eighth, on the "law of market value". Together, they explicate the thesis that the existence and viability of capitalism hinge upon the validity of the labour theory of value, and that capitalism itself cannot even be defined objectively, unless "labour-power" is recognized as the sole factor that produces the specifically capitalist category of value, as distinct from use-values, where labour is, of course, recognized as only one of three factors of production in any society. The remaining three articles of the section are comparatively new.

The ninth paper is a rebuttal of Chris Arthur's critique of the Unoist approach to value-form theory. Marx's treatments of the "value expression by the commodity seller" and of "the measure of value function of money" were both unsatisfactory because he allowed the "exchange process" to intervene between the two. The commodity seller must find a way to express the value of his commodity in a money price before an exchange ever takes place. Value form theory thus begins with the commodity expressing its "moneyness or value" in the use-value of another commodity and only ends when one commodity emerges as the general equivalent or money. This is a point that Uno had made quite clear many years ago in Japanese, but it understandably escaped Arthur's notice.

The tenth essay advances the view that the dialectic of capital is a "general equilibrium theory" that is much more general and defensible than the one made much of in the bourgeois tradition. For one thing, it is subject only to the "fundamental constraint of the capitalist market", which says that the workers do not save, and not to Walras' law, which says that no one saves (and, thus, confines general equilibrium theory to a stationary state). As in many other essays, Sekine is quite averse to Sraffian Marxism. Yet, he recognizes the importance of Sraffa's work, which shows that, in a system of many interrelated capital-goods, there exists a unique standard commodity, in terms of which many Marxian theorems can be reformulated more adequately. He also emphasizes the fact that the micro law of value can, and must, be founded on the macro law of relative surplus population in the dialectic of capital, although the "micro-foundation of macro-theory" that bourgeois economics seeks is a chimera.

The last essay, which has been written specifically for the present volume, and which shares with it the same title, recapitulates Sekine's fundamental argument that only the Unoist approach to economics renders the latter scientifically defensible in the light of a materialist copy-theory, which does not copy its object, capitalism, so much as it reproduces in theory the process of self-abstraction and self-synthesis that capital employs to organize itself, while simultaneously managing the reproduction of material or substantive economic life. The dialectic of capital thus reveals how capitalism actually operates, whereas bourgeois economics merely dictates what capitalism ought to be (the image of which it imposes by means of arbitrarily concocted models) as the ideal, norm or "ought" that should guide the operation of any economic life. In other words, only Marxian economics, as reformulated by Uno, constitutes an objective knowledge of capitalism, whereas bourgeois economics is essentially a religious faith that glorifies capitalism with esoteric adornments.

Throughout all these essays, there are certain recurrent themes, which delineate the Uno-Sekine approach to economics. They may be summarized as follows: (1) Economics is a social, and not a natural, science. Society, as the object of study, is quite unlike nature; thus, the application of the natural scientific method to economics amounts to a humbug, a smokescreen to hide a rabid ideology behind a "scientific" appearance. If the knowledge of nature is bound to be "partial", since we are not its Creator, that of society must be "total", since we ourselves compose it. (In other words, there cannot be an "unknowable thing-in-itself" of any human society.) Therefore, just because empirical and positivist methods make a good fit with research in the natural sciences, it does not follow that such methods are suitable for social science, including economics. Social science does not seek a predictive knowledge, but only one that is "post-dictive", or, as Hegel would say, "grey", knowledge. Otherwise, we will allow ourselves to be deprived of the freedom to choose to reform or remake our own society, and will be easily coaxed into "conforming" to the existing social order. (2) True economic theory cannot be obtained by arbitrarily constructing a subjective "model" (or an ideal type) of what economic life seems to us to be, but, rather, by uncovering the "definition of capitalism by capital itself". Here, "capital" is the Economic Man, or the "economic motive", present in all human beings, "made infinite"; and "capitalism" means a "use-value space" (or real economic life of society) "subsumed under" commodity-economic logic, or the capitalist principle. This subsumption, however, is never complete because "use-values" (representing the concrete-specific, material and heterogeneous substance of wealth) always resist "value" (representing the abstract-general, homogeneous and mercantile form of wealth). There is, therefore, a "contradiction" (meaning either an incongruity, tension, conflict, gap, stress, cleavage, or the like) between the commodity-economic and the real-economic. Capitalism is always an uncertain union between these two sides of the economy. This makes capitalism a historical, transient and once-and-for-all economic order, not a permanent and eternal one, as liberal-bourgeois ideology falsely claims. (3) Capitalism consists of the process of cyclical accumulation of capital, in which the widening (or extensive) phase, with the organic composition of capital held constant, and the deepening (or intensive) phase, involving its elevation, alternate. From the point of view of the capitalist market, the same process appears as the alternation of prosperity and depression in business cycles. The phase of prosperity consists of the sub-phases of recovery, average activity and precipitancy (or over-heating). Only in the sub-phase of average activity do the demand for and the supply of labour-power tend to be equalized, thus determining its value. It is also in this sub-phase that rates of profit tend to be equalized in all industrial sectors. In other words, the micro-law of value (which appears in the capitalist market as the law of average profit) is founded on the macro-law of population (which, by innovating techniques, substitutes capital-goods for labour-power).

The twelve essays assembled in this volume were each written on different occasions to suit the house-style of the original publisher. Therefore, differences from one essay to another in the spelling of the same word, in the use of punctuation methods, etc. cannot be avoided. The author and the editor are in agreement that it is appropriate to retain such differences in the original writing, rather than enforcing uniformity throughout the chapters, although all footnotes are changed to endnotes, and shown at the end of each essay under "Notes and References". Quite apart from these issues related to editorial matters, the author himself changed his writing style over time. For instance, he used such terms as "commoditize, commoditization" before "commodify, commodification" became the more common usage. He also frequently used the term "political economy" in the sense of "non-bourgeois economics" in his early writings, which usage he later abandoned as "political economy" came to be recognized as an independent branch of political science. On the other hand, the qualifiers Marxian and Marxist are both used throughout but in different senses; the former means, for Sekine, "in the intellectual style of Marx", while the latter connotes "an ideological sympathy with Marx". Sekine presumably aims to maintain Uno's clear distinction between "Marxian economics (marukusu-keizaigaku)", to which his own economics belonged, and "Marxist economics (marukusu-shugi keizaigaku)", which refers to the economics advanced and defended by politically and ideologically motivated Marxists.

The editor wishes to express his thanks to the original publishers of the essays for the permissions granted for reprinting them in this collection. The original sources are listed in the bibliography at the end of this volume.

I. Methodological Essays

Uno's Method of Marxian Economics

Two kinds of Marxism

In order to highlight the nature of Uno's approach, I would like to begin by characterising Marxism in two distinct types. All forms of Marxism contain, and stand on, a critique of capitalism. There are, however, two ways of criticising capitalism.

The first type, which I would call the conventional type, denounces capitalism as an "unjust" society, in which a large number of propertyless workers are exploited by a handful of greedy and repressive capitalists. The latter monopolise the means of production, while the former have nothing but their own labour-power to sell. Hence, there is a war, a class struggle, between haves and have-nots, between exploiters and exploited, and it will end in a proletarian revolution. This version is so well known that it hardly bears repetition. In short, it is an ideology that opposes the economic exploitation and political repression of the working classes by the capitalist class.

There is, however, another type of critique of capitalism, the alternative type. This one criticises capitalism as a market economy, which is "upside-down" or "inverted" in the sense that human priorities are subordinated to the market priorities of capital. Human relations in capitalist (or civil) society are "reified", i.e., translated into relations among things, called commodities. That is viewed as anti-human or dehumanising because, in principle, they exclude direct I-Thou relation among persons. Human beings can be liberated from the spell and sway of capital, only when capitalist society is superseded by a more human-centered society, according to the second type of critique.

Marx's writings contain elements of both arguments. Most Marxists, however, have followed the first approach. Even though some of them pay lip service to the second type of critique, they demonstrate very limited understanding of its importance. Only the Unoist approach brings out its full implication, and that is what makes Unoism unique.

I include in the conventional type both the old party-line, Soviet Marxism and the Western Marxism which developed later after the discovery of the *Paris Manuscripts* in the 1930s. The former, of course, is more economistic, deterministic and scientistic, and, hence, more fanatical, arrogant and hypocritical. The latter is perhaps more humane, environment-friendly and voluntaristic. Yet both share the Judeo-Christian eschatological outlook, and see in Marx the arrival of a prophet. Now that the prehistory of mankind is about to end, there will be an inevitable Armageddon, after which the kingdom of freedom, namely, a socialist society free from class antagonisms, will replace the kingdom of necessity in which drudgery, misery and hardships, as well as alienation and repression, must be endured. They derive this incredibly optimistic outlook from *the materialistic conception of history (historical materialism),* which says that capitalism is the last class-antagonistic society, and will inevitably break down to give way to a socialist paradise.

At first sight, paradoxically, conventional Marxism has always avoided a serious study of *Capital,* which objectively defines or specifies capitalism. It has never understood what the "critique of political economy" really means. And that is one reason why it has proven to be so fragile today, i.e., vulnerable to the breakdown of the Berlin Wall and the recent resurgence of neo-conservatism. I wish to emphasise that Marx's critique of political economy means a critique of "liberal" (i.e., bourgeois and capitalist) social science. Indeed, modern social science, of which economics forms the core, is an offspring of the capitalist age. Before the evolution of capitalism there was not even a clear enough concept of society (actually the word "society" appeared in the English language only in 1531). Modern social science is without any doubt liberal, bourgeois and capitalist. It is so out and out, through and through, so much so that we are not even conscious of the fact that it is one-sided. To some extent, it is true, the bourgeois bias in social science has been criticised from the point of view of landed property. But that kind of criticism has always been partial and half-hearted. A truly radical critique of capitalism and of the social science to which it has given rise was undertaken only by Marx. This is the point that the alternative approach to Marxism values, especially so in the case of Unoism.

Actually, the conventional approach which reduces Marxism to a litany of secular eschatology does not need an economic analysis of capitalism at all. It only needs historical materialism. That is why we find that few Marxists today are professionally trained economists. Those few Marxists who happen to be trained in economics suffer from a schizophrenia because of the unbridgeable rift between their professionally acquired knowledge and their moral and political persuasions. In terms of the former, they are completely "liberal" and believe in market rationality; in terms of the latter, they are vehemently anti-establishment. They are in the good Anglo-American tradition of democracy, but not in the tradition of Marxism. None of them, surely not Steedman and Roemer, who have reduced Marxian economics to mere linear production models, has any further business to do with *Capital*. The Marxist economists of that kind tend to believe that there is nothing more to learn from *Capital*, which has become a museum piece, or a preserve of the more bookish and eccentric colleagues of our profession, known as historians of economic thought. Uno's approach differs radically from that kind in that he unambiguously opts to follow Marx's lead in the critique of liberal social science. Let us see what that involves.

Natural science and social science

The first claim that I wish to make is that "nature" and "society" are two altogether different things, and that we need different methods of studying them. This view is diametrically opposed to the widely held belief, sometimes called "reductionism", to the effect that there is only one scientific method, which is exemplified by physics, and that all sciences must imitate the practice of physics. We reject "reductionism" of that sort for the following reason.

Since we are not the creator of nature, we cannot know it totally. That is to say, we can never really lay bare the inner logic, or programme, that ultimately governs the motion of nature. Although we are part of nature, we are so only as natural objects. We are not for that reason any more privy to the working of natural laws. All we can do is to observe nature from the outside in various specific contexts, and find regularities of its motion. We thus gain partial knowledge of nature. Sometimes, our knowledge is good enough to enable us to make a reasonably accurate "prediction" of what nature might do next in the same or a similar context. It is this kind of knowledge that natural science seeks. We are, however, certain that the accumulation of this type of knowledge will not enable us to alter the laws of nature fundamentally, or to repudiate one nature and create another by a "revolution" to suit our need.

For instance, we may be able to predict, with a fair degree of accuracy, that an earthquake of a certain magnitude is about to occur in a given region. In the light of that knowledge, we may prepare evacuation plans and other appropriate measures with a view to minimising harm to ourselves. We cannot, however, stop the earthquake itself from occurring, or to let it happen at another time somewhere else. We must accept what nature has decided to do without consulting us, and do our best to circumvent the harm that will befall us in consequence. In other words, it is a matter of practical wisdom to "conform" to the order of nature, and to "piggyback" on its blind forces, if we can. Sometimes we talk of "taming", "controlling" or even "conquering" natural forces, but that is a matter of rhetoric. If we really believe that nature would adapt to us, rather than we adapting to it, we shall be soundly punished by ecological disasters and other serious calamities. We must approach nature, in which we are all embedded, with circumspection, respect and humility.

In summary, we can never know nature from inside out. We can only observe it from the outside to learn the regularity of its motion in various specific contexts, and conjecture what it might do next. Since we cannot get to the *Ding-an-sich* (thing-in-itself) of nature, we had better conform to its motion wisely and subtly, without becoming too arrogant. Conformism definitely is a matter of practical wisdom.

This wisdom, however, does not apply, as soon as we put "society" in place of "nature" in the above argument. Society is that which we ourselves make up. We are its creator, and we are (or ought to be) fully privy to its inner logic or its structural programme. No society is irrevocably given to us as a "natural order" to conform to. It is hypocritical to claim that it is something beyond us, whose regularities must be detected from the outside by repeated observation and experiment. Why do we need to hypothesise its laws which we know very well and pretend to test them empirically? That would amount to an unsound invitation to conformism, i.e., abdication of responsibility to improve upon our society. Instead of conjuring up such a fantasy, we should ask ourselves a much simpler and more straightforward question: what are we doing here? The method of inquiry into society, in other words, is altogether different from that into nature. Yet, our attention is deliberately diverted from this obvious truth. Why?

The reason is that it suits the ruling class of any society to make believe that the existing social order is either an extension of the natural order or ordained by divine wisdom. The doctrine of the divine right of kings is the best-known example of the ideology of the ruling class. If the existing social order is God-given, who can challenge it or criticise it? Similar tricks have been used in all class societies. Bourgeois society, too, is a class society, and it is in the interest of the capitalist class to pretend that its market-based economic order is natural, objective and inviolable. To say that economics is scientific, in the same sense as physics is, to make believe that capitalism, or bourgeois society, is as immutable as nature, which has an inner programme we can never know, and which we can never suspend. If you buy into this trick, it effectively forecloses all criticisms of bourgeois society. Yet many economists have been vain and pedantic; they would do anything to look like physicists and be called "scientific". Little do they know that, by the time they embrace the natural-scientific outlook of physics-like economics, they are already irrevocably enthralled and made slaves of capitalism, i.e., spokespersons of the bourgeois-liberal ideology. What they do then is no longer to lay bare how capitalist society is programmed to work, but to counsel how we most effectively conform to it and make the best use of it. That is why *the more we study economics, the more "capitalist" we tend to become.* Only Karl Marx knew this danger from the beginning, and thus undertook to criticise that "opium-like" science of bourgeois political economy.

Significance of economic theory

Classical political economy believes that all societies evolve to capitalist society, or that every society is at least implicitly a capitalist society. A society, according to the liberal dogma, consists of individuals whose behaviour is overwhelmingly governed by their "economic motives", i.e., tendencies to maximise gains and minimise losses to the extent that they are quantifiable. If, in pre-capitalist societies, people did not quite behave as their economic motives dictated, that is because, or so the story goes, they were underdeveloped and did not take the question of gains and losses seriously. Over many years, however, even the least intelligent would awaken to the calculus of gains and losses, so that the evolution of all societies to capitalist society will be inevitable. A capitalist society, it is asserted, is governed by the objective laws of the market, which harmonises diverse interests, and achieves the most rational economic organisation. This kind of outlook, or the liberal conception of history, is radically contradicted by empirical history, as Polanyi and others have shown. Human history did not so peacefully evolve into capitalism. The process of primitive accumulation which ushered capitalism in was, in fact, replete with violence, theft, swindles, expropriation and political repression. But the reminder of such empirical facts does not shake the liberal dogma at all, since it is by nature ahistorical.

Capital is not historical, though we, human beings, are. To explain why so we must understand what "capital" is. Since Marx, we have talked of it millions of times, but without clearly understanding what it really is. For hardly anyone has explained where capital comes from. This major omission has been a stumbling block to the sound development of Marxian economics. In my view, we obtain the concept of capital in exactly the same way as Feuerbach obtains his concept of God. According to Feuerbach, God did not create us in his image, rather it is we who create him in our image. Since we, humans, are finite, we are good, wise, and powerful to some extent, but never infinitely so. If, however, these wonderful attributes of ours, or human essences, as Feuerbach calls them, are made infinite and absolute, and extrapolated as attributes of an entity beyond us, we have created God. This is his celebrated thesis of *anthropomorphism*. Similarly, I would say that we, finite human beings, are all to some extent greedy and acquisitive, avoid waste and pursue efficiency, wish to accumulate material wealth, etc.; in short, we maximise gains and minimise losses. But we never do so infinitely. Let these "economic motives" be made infinite and absolute, and be extrapolated in an entity beyond ourselves. Then we have created "capital". In other words, capital is the god of our own "economic motives".

Many Marxists would react to this derivation of capital with suspicion because they have always believed that capital is something "material". They know that Marx meant by capital more than just capital goods; they also remember Marx's formula, $M - C - M'$. But that is about all. They can talk endlessly about capital going around circles, without ever being able to come to grips with it. They feel uncomfortable when I suddenly pinpoint the ontology of capital. It seems to them to lack something, and their first impression is that if capital is a product of our mind it cannot be "material". In this case, however, they need not worry about the thorny question of materialism versus idealism. It is true that the human mind tends to seek "idealisation", so that once we see various physical triangles we must conceptualise pure triangles in the mathematical sense. "Idealisation", however, occurs always in a specific material context, so that Euclidean geometry was just as much a product of ancient land surveying practice as a product of mathematical intellection. Indeed, previous to the age of capitalist commodity production, our minds could never fully develop the concept of capital. Even the word "capital" in the present sense dates only from the mid 16th century.

What is more important is that capital, like God, is an "idealisation" of ourselves rather than of an object outside us. It is a product of our human *self*-idealisation. Not only is capital a product of our mental "idealising" process, but it is also an infinitisation of *our own* attributes. That is why we know all about capital introspectively, i.e., capital has no "thing-in-itself" that exceeds our grasp. To understand the logic of capital, we only have to ask ourselves what we, as economic man, would do in this or that situation. Indeed, this is how we actually develop economic theory. Historians of economic thought know very well that we never acquired our classical economic theory by repeating empirical tests of our hypotheses. General equilibrium theory was discovered by introspection; it was not inferred by the experimental, trial-and-error method of the physicist. And that is as it should be, since the fundamental core of economic theory is, in effect, the definition of capitalism by capital itself.

This crucially important point has never been properly understood by bourgeois economics due to its self-complacent ideology. That is why micro and macro theories cannot be integrated. The neoclassical synthesis does not unify the micro price theory, which is deductive and *a priori* and the macro business cycle theory, which appears to depend on the inductive/empirical method. Only when we see the whole body of economic theory as the definition of capitalism by capital itself, i.e., as the logic of capital the unfolding of which constitutes capitalism, do we understand how the structural (or equilibrium) aspect of it and the dynamic (or cyclical) aspect of it can be brought together into a unified system. This we call the *dialectic of capital*. It is the signal accomplishment of Kôzô Uno (1897-1977) to have understood Marx's *Capital* as essentially a book of the dialectic of capital.

Thus, to summarise, in formulating economic theory, we do not observe the so-called "real world" out there, and construct in our mind an arbitrary set of hypotheses (i.e., a model or an ideal type), which we subjectively believe parallels reality, and whose validity we check by empirical testing. True economic theory is a definition of capitalism by capital itself. This definition or specification is objective because capital, being the infinitisation of our economic motives, transcends us. Yet we are privy to the operation of its logic because these economic motives are originally our own human attributes.

Theory and reality

The dialectic of capital, let me repeat, is the logic of capital the unfolding of which constitutes the ultimate reality of capitalism or purely capitalist society. If so, however, how does it relate with concrete-empirical facts of our own economic life in history? We must now address that problem. Since Uno's approach to economic theory is unique, its explanation of the relationship between theory and reality is also unconventional. I would begin by saying that *the inner logic of capital never operates in a vacuum, but always in a "use-value space"*, i.e., concrete-historical living conditions of human society involving a specific set of use-values. Only when the logic of capital "subsumes" a use-value space adequately does capitalism become a reality. Millions of use-values take part in our daily economic life, and the techniques of producing them are also extremely diverse. The use-values that were important in the economic life of 18th-century England are vastly different from those that are crucial to us today. In correspondence, different productive technologies evolved in different societies. In each of these cases, the extent to which the logic of capital subsumes and sways real economic life is different. Unless we assert some control over this matter, we cannot hope to understand economics.

The Uno school, therefore, advances the levels-of-analysis approach, which consists of distinguishing the three developmental stages of capitalism: mercantilism, liberalism and imperialism. Three typical use-value spaces characterise these stages of development of capitalism. Capitalism, at the mercantilist stage of development, crucially depended on wool; that, at the liberal stage, depended on cotton; and that at the imperialist stage, on iron and steel. The mode of accumulation of capital was also quite different in each of these stages, and that was also the reason why the economic policies of the bourgeois state differed from one stage to another. Thus, the use-value space is "typified" at the level of stages-theory. For pure economic theory, however, which describes a purely capitalist society, we need further control over use-values. In this context, use-values must be reduced to merely "different" objects for use or consumption x_1, x_2, ..., x_n. In other words, use-values must be sufficiently "emasculated" to enable a full subsumption of economic life under the logic of capital. Pure theory, therefore, presupposes a use-value space which is made deliberately abstract and unreal.

Even though economic theory has always done this, the bourgeois empiricist approach does not see the significance of it. Therefore, when it says "let x_1 be coal", we are never sure whether it is referring to purely theoretical "coal", which is merely an object different from steel, or stages-theoretic coal which was a key input of the turn-of-the-century steelworks, or real-historical coal, which my grandfather picked up and threw into the stove. In other words, the relation between economic theory and reality is left uncertain by that approach. And, indeed, that is expected of the natural-scientific approach of physics-like economics. For in natural science, in which we are interested only in the purity of the matter, there is no sophisticated problem of abstraction. Pure water is H_2O, but water in our living space is more or less "complicated" because of impure substances which are mixed with it. These impurities can be removed to the extent that is necessary under controlled experiments. In the same way, an ideal model of international trade usually removes transportation costs as impurities. That procedure is, however, different from specifying the degree of abstraction of the use-value space.

This point has significant bearing on what we expect from economics. The bourgeois approach, which adopts the natural-scientific method, expects economists to come up with policy recommendations. In other words, they are supposed to be like automobile mechanics, who can tell you exactly why your car does not run properly, and recommend which parts are to be repaired or replaced. Their knowledge can predict what will happen to the total mechanism, if this or that part fails to perform. It is, however, not his job to question the meaning of the total mechanism itself. In much the same way, economists are supposed to be versed in the total mechanism of the market, so that when it malfunctions because of untamed externalities, they can find various clever ways of "internalising" them so that these externalities no longer disrupt the smooth functioning of the market. If bourgeois economics insists on this kind of methodology, that is only to be expected of it. What is unbelievable and laughable, however, is that many Marxists whole-heartedly embrace this vulgar methodology, and shout revolution at the same time.

Uno's Marxism is not so naïve. Revolution or otherwise, what we want of economics is first and foremost an objective definition of capitalism, i.e., the knowledge of how a purely capitalist society is programmed to operate. We take that to be the "zero" of social science, for there is no other referent. This purely theoretical definition can be related with the historical reality of capitalism only by the mediation of a stages-theory. For example, the history of Japanese industrialisation at the turn of the century cannot be understood as an episode in capitalist history, except in light of the world-historic stage of imperialism, which then defined its surrounding conditions. What we pursue is the understanding of reality, including the present as history, and not as a mechanism. We do not, therefore, expect a technical application of our knowledge of capitalism. We do not offer policy recommendations, since we do not regard reality as a mechanism but as history. History does not predict; it "post-dicts", if there is such a word. This is what Hegel taught with his famed metaphor of the owl of Minerva. "The owl of Minerva spreads its wings with the falling of the dusk, when reality is cut and dried after its process of formation has been completed; it can no longer be rejuvenated but can only be understood".[1] Our theory, in other words, is "grey".

Now I wish to conclude quickly. What we learn from natural science is what "they" are or do, they being various things outside us. What we learn from history is what "we" are or do, in various contingent circumstances. These are essentially two different approaches. It is vitally important today for social scientists to understand which approach they follow. For history seems to be approaching a turning point. The 1990s may well be just as cataclysmic as the 1930s. What is the point of learning the mechanics of the existing institution, which is dying quickly, because it can no longer successfully "internalise" its unwieldy externalities? We live in the age of uncertainty. Surely, what is important for us is, above all, *to know ourselves, i.e., to know what we can and want to do.* Natural-scientific economics, which has systematically failed us, whether as Johnsonomics or as Reaganomics, is unlikely to guide us out of the impending economic crisis. At the deathbed of capitalism, we must fully comprehend what it was all about, if we are to make a successful leap forward.[2]

Notes and References

[1] Knox, T. M., *Hegel's Philosophy of Right* (Oxford University Press, 1973), p. 13.
[2] This lecture was first delivered on February 10, 1994 as part of "York Seminar in the History of Economic Thought" at York University, Canada.

The Dialectic, or Logic that Coincides with Economics

In the course of my training as an economist I have learned that true economic theory should take the form of *the dialectic of capital,* whose structure is a mirror image of Hegel's logic. My reason for writing this essay is to explain to you what all that means. With this preamble-caveat, I wish to begin with a personal episode relating me with Hegel.

Kôzô Uno (1897-1977) taught me economic theory when I was an undergraduate. But he never related his approach to economic theory with Hegel's logic. Nor did he, unlike Lenin, ever recommend to his students that they familiarize themselves first with Hegelian logic in order to correctly understand Marx's *Capital.* Much later, when I finished my doctoral dissertation in neoclassical economics at the London School of Economics (LSE), I had not the faintest idea of what "scientific method" was all about. I did not even know of Karl Popper, who was then still lecturing at LSE. But upon arriving at Simon Fraser University, I met Larry Boland, who introduced me to Popper. I read a few of his writings. Though I was not so terribly impressed by his ideas, I learned for the first time what "scientific method" involved, and took some interest in the subject. A few years later I had a sort of intellectual crisis in that I could no longer seriously live with, let alone enjoy, neoclassical economics. It was then that I met Uno again after many years of lapsed contact. I tentatively threw at him some logical positivist and Popperian ideas to see his reaction, only to find out that he was totally unperturbed. In fact, his aloofness to that sort of discussion impressed me greatly; for it was so complete and total. This made me suspect that Uno was hiding a scientific method of his own behind his economics, a kind that was not shared by any Western-trained scholar in social science around at that time. It took me a while before I worked out that it was indeed the Hegelian logic.

Uno claimed, on numerous occasions, that Marx's economics was a "science" and not a mere "ideology". By this he meant that it constituted an objective knowledge that should make sense to anyone regardless of class or ideology. This greatly angered some Marxists who stuck to the "partisan character" of Marxism, but pleased others who believed in its universal scientific validity. This "science-but-not-ideology" thesis of Uno's soon became a holy canon of all his followers. But few, even into the twenty-first century, have inquired seriously into what Uno in fact meant by "science" or "objective knowledge", despite his strenuous (but alas not so successful) efforts to insist on a (scientific) method peculiar to Marxian economics. The commonsensical view, promoted vigorously by the positivists, that only natural science constitutes a genuinely objective knowledge, is still quite widespread and persists even among Unoists. Perhaps to some extent Marx himself was responsible for this, as he never stinted praise of Newtonian mechanics as a model of science. Yet it is my belief that what Uno called the "[scientific] method" peculiar to Marxian economics" was nothing other than the Hegelian dialectic, which, I believe, does not apply to natural science. I regard this to be a matter of vital importance methodologically, epistemologically and onto-logically in our apprehension of the Marxian scientific tradition. First, I wish to explain why social science needs its own method distinct from that of natural science.

Natural science

Let me begin by reviewing the widely accepted idea that a knowledge of nature is *predictive, prescriptive* and *prospective.* This comes from the fact that nature exists out there (that is, outside of ourselves as human beings), so that we cannot know it totally. It, in other words, jealously guards its *thing-in-itself* and never reveals itself totally. In consequence, our knowledge of nature is bound to be *empirical* and *partial.*

All natural scientific propositions take the *predictive* form: $(a, b, c, ...) \rightarrow x$, meaning that, if the conditions $a, b, c, ...$ materialize, the event x will occur. Mathematical theorems too are always formulated in this way, except that the conditions and the event are axiomatic in mathematics, whereas they are factual in natural science. For example, "if water is heated to 100 degrees centigrade, it vaporizes" would be a natural-scientific statement. This kind of statement refers to a phenomenon per-taining to an aspect or a phase of nature, and gives us only a *partial* knowledge of nature. Because, if we ask how condition a did in fact ma-terialize, we must seek to establish another proposition such as $(a_1, a_2, a_3, ...) \rightarrow a$, and, if we further ask how a_1 did the same, we must again verify a conjecture such as $(a_{11}, a_{12}, a_{13}, ...) \rightarrow a_1$ and so on *ad infinitum.* Clearly, there can be no end to this type of inquiry. Furthermore, there is also the tricky issue (known as Hume's problem) that a factual verification of both the conditions and the event is never conclusive, so that the truth of a natural-scientific proposition is always tentative, being relative to the ex-isting state of knowledge. Even the widely accepted, factual proposition that water vaporizes at 100 degrees centigrade is only a so-far-so-good hypothesis, and is never established conclusively. For there is no assurance that it will not be overthrown in the next experiment. In other words, its truthfulness is never at par with that of an axiomatic proposition such as "the inner angles of a triangle add up to a straight line".

All this means that, no matter how much we accumulate this type of knowledge, we can never hope to know nature itself *in toto,* and, hence, that its inner logic, its integral programme or its ultimate software will for ever remain unknown to us. This is the case even though we benefit enormously from accomplishments in the natural sciences. The more we know of natural phenomena, the easier and the more convenient our lives can become. The reason is that the *predictive* form of knowledge lends itself easily to technical (that is, *prescriptive*) applications. So long as these applications are conceived correctly, they always benefit human beings. In this sense, our increasing knowledge of nature can be described as prospective. Unfortunately, however, in the present age of accelerated progress in "science and technology", we are frequently humbled by devastating misapplications of natural-scientific knowledge working ultimately against our own well-being. This, it seems to me, is a convincing proof that our knowledge of nature always remains *partial,* so that, as soon as we forget our limitations and arrogate to ourselves the power to reshape nature radically to suit our needs, our hubris will be punished. This being so, what we should learn from natural science is how we should conform to nature, and not how we should make it conform to us. It is a matter of practical wisdom on our part to comply with nature and to piggy-back on its forces to improve our living conditions as we protect ourselves from natural disasters.

Social science

Social science cannot share the same method with natural science. Its object of study, society, is wholly unlike nature. Society does not exist outside ourselves, the human beings who constitute it. Consciously or unconsciously, we ourselves make up our society. Therefore, we can, and must, know this object of study *totally,* by laying bare its inner logic, its programme and its ultimate software. Instead of conforming blindly to the existing order of society we must, if need be, seek to reshape and change it radically. Applying to the study of society the empirical method of natural science is tantamount to sanctifying it as absolute and immutable; that is, as something that dictates our conformity. Such a premise is from the beginning marred by an ideological bias and cannot possibly be regarded as objective. Society does not lie out there as a "real world" which allows us only to observe its disconnected features and lets us formulate hypothetical propositions in the predictive form to be tested empirically. If so, however, we clearly need to establish a scientific method fit for our needs, quite distinct from that used in the study of nature. What sort of scientific method will it be? My claim is that the dialectic is the method appropriate to social science. In particular, it applies to economics, which forms the core of social science, whence the title of this essay: "The Dialectic, or Logic that Coincides with Economics". Of course, I am here echoing Hegel's own dictum that "Logic coincides with Metaphysics".[1]

What characterizes dialectical knowledge is that it is *"post-dictive"* (or *grey*), *self-reflective* and *retrospective*. One should here remember Hegel's celebrated metaphor of the owl of Minerva, "which spread its wings with the falling of the dusk". "Philosophy comes on the scene too late to give instruction as to what the world ought to be", says Hegel. For "only when actuality is already there cut and dried, does the thought of the world appear"; "only when actuality is mature does the ideal apprehend this world in its substance, and build it up for itself into the shape of an intellectual realm".[2] In other words, we comprehend our own world only *retrospectively* as we get older (more mature) and capable of reflecting on what we have thus far done and therefore what we are. This kind of knowledge predicts nothing; it rather "post-dicts", if one may coin such a word. Nor does it lend itself to technical applications, for it prescribes nothing. Being *self-reflective,* it is only good for self-discovery and self-comprehension (that is, knowing oneself) of human beings. Instead of being prospective, it is retrospective; for, as Paul Valéry once said, aptly, "we enter the future by stepping backwards" *(nous entrons dans l'avenir à reculons).*

These are the properties essential to dialectical knowledge. Yet frequently they are half understood and, consciously or unconsciously, evaded because of the deeply entrenched popular notion that knowledge that does not lend itself to technical applications must be useless to humanity. As has already been explained, natural-scientific knowledge permits technical applications because it takes the predictive form. The virtue of its predictability is not always an unqualified boon. Because of its necessarily partial character, technical applications can be good or bad. Yet the spectacular achievement of "science and technology" in recent years has scarcely been doubted, giving them much credit. Under the circumstances, the fact that social-scientific knowledge permits no technical application appears to be rather disappointing. One therefore tends to resist this fact, conceding to the vulgar soul, to which it is nothing but a sign of the weakness and underdevelopment of social relative to natural science. Thus, Marx is often praised for having prophesied a future course of events accurately, just as he is depreciated for having failed to do so. Many Marxists claim themselves to be in possession of better "predictive" power than are bourgeois economists. These, to me, are indications of a gross misapprehension of the dialectic. Granted that bourgeois economists predict poorly, that does not make Marxists any better equipped with clairvoyance with regard to the future.

Materialist dialectics

Marxists' errors began with a wrong critique of Hegel based on the fancy that his dialectic could be grafted mechanically on to "materialism", that is, on to the highly doubtful materialism such as is often represented by the trite dictum "matter precedes idea", where "matter" is itself an abstract idea. The Engelsian invention that matter (or nature) could simply be substituted for Hegel's Absolute is a pure non-starter because matter is not a subject-object that can be induced to recount its own story. Elsewhere, I stated that a dialectic needs an autobiographical subject or a storyteller who can be induced to tell his story from within, and that such a subject should transcend us human beings.[3] The reason why Hegel could develop his dialectic successfully is that its subject, the Absolute, both originates in human beings and transcends them. My reasoning here is based on the Feuerbachian thesis of "anthropomorphism", which says that man creates God (the Absolute) in his own image rather than God creating man in His image. Man has many virtues but, being trapped in his finiteness, cannot pursue any one of them without limits, that is, unboundedly. But man, unlike animals, can undo his own bounds in his imagination and, thus, create God (the Absolute). Only a human quality, rendered absolute or infinite, in the sense of transcending human bounds, can be a dialectical subject. This is the point that orthodox Marxists have consistently failed to understand.

But if one reads *Capital* without pre-conceived ideas, be they political, ideological or revolutionary, one can see through its imperfections that it does indeed intend to be a dialectic of capital in the same sense as Hegel's *Logic* was a dialectic of the Absolute. This is how Uno read *Capital*. Just as Hegel's logic coincided with metaphysics, the dialectic of capital should coincide with economic theory – economic theory in the sense of the definition of capitalism by capital itself. Just as Hegel (according to Ludwig Feuerbach) reached his Absolute by undoing the boundedness (or finitude) of human virtues, we can reach capital by pushing human "economic motives" (the jargon I inherit from Karl Polanyi) to their limits. Indeed, capital is the god of "economic motives"; that is, the human propensity to maximize gains and minimize losses. All human beings are endowed with economic motives, which, however, they pursue only within limits. Scrooge and Eugénie Grandet, who seek abstract rather than concrete wealth, embody more of the capitalist spirit, but they are, to that extent, suspected of being "inhuman". Capital goes further, and wholly transcends human feelings and corporeity. The dialectic of capital, or economic theory, is the logical system in which capital synthesizes itself. Capital reveals itself completely by defining what capitalism in its pure form might be like.

From the above follows the meaning of "materialist" dialectic. What makes the dialectic of capital materialist and non-idealist is not that capital is "matter as opposed to idea", whatever that may mean. Capital is certainly a "software" and not a hardware, and, in that regard, it is no different from the Absolute. What makes the difference between them is the circumstances under which the software has developed. As Feuerbach pointed out aptly, human beings, unlike animals, tend to create religion presumably *under all material conditions,* though he did not say it in so many words. In contrast, human beings do not always create capitalism. Capitalism comes into being only when products can easily take the form of commodities, that is, *only when material conditions (pertaining to what to produce and how) are right.* We all know that such material conditions evolved first in seventeenth century England and not before. I use the phrase "use-value space" frequently for the material conditions on which the economic life of a society is built. Capitalism occurs when capital takes over (or subsumes under it) a "use-value space" suitable for organization under its logic. In other words, we need the right kind of hardware ("use-value space") to enable the software (the logic of capital) to fully work itself out.

Dialectics and social science

This way of understanding capitalism, which is inherent in Marx, is never more clearly expressed than by Uno, according to whom capitalism comes into being when the *form* of capital "grasps" or "seizes upon" the *substance* of use-value space. This, by the way, parallels closely Karl Polanyi's idea of capitalism.[4] In fact, the explanation of capitalism, as an *uncertain* union of the form of value and the substance of use-value space, constitutes the hallmark of all non-liberal (that is, non-bourgeois) approaches to economics, in sharp contrast to classical and neoclassical views, which presuppose a complete fusion of the form and the substance. Under this presupposition, "economic man" would be eternal, for "the propensity to truck, barter and exchange one thing for another" would be inherent in human nature, so that human society would always be a virtual capitalist society, the form of capital and the substance of economic life being in permanent and inseparable union. Yet many Marxists unwittingly allow themselves to be trapped into such bourgeois ideology, by believing that the substance determines its own appropriate form. By failing to understand capital correctly as a form or "software", one can easily be led astray.

Economics and the other social sciences, once bundled together and called political economy, are the products of the modern (capitalist) age, and are, therefore, inevitably laden with bourgeois-liberal preconceptions. This means that, even with a strongly motivated anti-capitalist ideology, one can easily be duped into embracing, rather than exorcizing, the presuppositions of bourgeois ideology. The most effective antidote to that, to my mind, is to grasp firmly the "materialist" dialectic as the method of social science. By pointing out that the circumstances under which capital developed as "software" differed from the case of the Absolute, I have contrasted the "materialist" dialectic with the old Hegelian dialectic. The same contrast carries into that between the two characteristic "contradictions" which set the dialectic into motion. The dialectic of capital synthesizes itself by solving the "contradiction between value and use-value", while Hegel's dialectic of the Absolute undergoes its spiral march by overcoming the "contradiction between being and naught". Here, "value" represents abstract-mercantile wealth, which capital seeks, and "use-value" the concrete-material side of society's economic life. Thus, capitalism, synthesized as value, prevails over the resistance put up by use-value restrictions. In the case of Hegel, "being" indicates the presence of the Absolute, and "naught" its absence. By prevailing over naught, being proceeds to establish the divine realm of reason. In this way, the structure of the dialectic is the same. But a fundamental difference seems to me to exist between "use-value" and "naught". Although, from the point of view of the materialist dialectic, value representing capital, its subject, prevails over use-value in order to synthesize capitalism, the real implication is that this can be done only in so far as the use-value side permits it. For capitalism is historically transient. This means that the real winner in the end is use-value (concrete wealth for human beings), which will remain even after the death of value (abstract wealth sought by capital). This is different from the implication of Hegel's dialectic of the Absolute. Once being succeeds in synthesizing fully the Absolute, naught (the absence of divine wisdom) is conquered and suppressed forever. In other words, Hegel's naught is strictly empty and passive; it is meant to be subdued forever by being. Since naught offers hardly any real resistance to the progress of being, the triumph of being over naught is a foregone conclusion in Hegel. This, it seems to me, renders his idealist dialectic somewhat lopsided, and explains why his reasoning validating the dialectical progress (from abstract-unspecified to concrete-synthetic) appears at times to be rather forced and unnatural. Needless to say, the materialist dialectic of value and use-value, as formulated by Uno, is more even-handed and free from such mental acrobatics. This, to my mind, is because use-value can exist outside the dialectic of capital as it does inside it.

Materialism and idealism

This point seems to me to give us a real clue in contrasting materialism to idealism in dialectics. To Hegel, the establishment of divine wisdom and the kingdom of reason was the ultimate aim of the dialectic. Once this was done, it only remained to see how that infinite reason of the Absolute manifested itself in nature, human beings (finite spirit) and history. There was clearly no question of abolishing the Absolute. That made Hegel's "dialectic of history" completely determinist, allowing no freedom to choose or even to err in the future course of humanity's evolution. In the materialist dialectic, in contrast, we let capital synthesize itself *in logic* precisely for the purpose of abolishing it later *in history*, and of thus emancipating ourselves, human beings, from the sway of its abstract universality. *Logic belongs to capital, but history is ours.* This we can say because use-value will never be completely assimilated to value; that is, because "use-value space", the material conditions on which the economic life of a society stands, maintains its own ontology.

In fact, even under capitalism, the subsumption of the use-value space under the logic of capital is never perfect; there are always remaining "externalities". Real capitalism exists when these externalities (that is, parts of the use-value space that do not submit to the logic of capital) can be "internalized" by economic policies of the bourgeois state. But the dialectic of capital, or economic theory in the sense of the definition of capitalism by capital itself, must presuppose an ideal use-value space. A use-value space is ideal when no part of it resists or exceeds subsumption under the logic of capital. Only by presupposing such an ideal use-value space, can we let capital synthesize pure capitalism, the theoretical definition of capitalism. The way in which this kind of economic theory is synthesized is, in fact, quite simple. In this ideal use-value space we need only specify a particular situation or context, before asking capital, "Now what do you want to do?" We always get the right answer from capital, and economic theory is no more than an ordered totality of such answers. But how do we know that capital's answer is always true? Because the truth is already in ourselves. Recall that capital originated in us before it transcended us. Since capital is our "economic motives" made infinite, we are in fact asking the question of ourselves and answering it. There is nothing inside ourselves that we do not know.

In other words, the truthfulness of the dialectic of capital has no epistemological ambiguity. Every dialectical proposition can, in fact, be confirmed *introspectively* and requires no further external verification (empirical test) to be validated, as would be the case with an axiomatic proposition. This, I believe, is an important conclusion pertaining to the nature of economic theory, which both bourgeois economics and orthodox Marxism fail to understand. Axiomatic propositions are derived logically from arbitrary axioms or postulates whose truthfulness remains open to doubt. Therefore, in principle, they cannot be accepted as being conclusively true before verification. Yet, as was also pointed out, no verification is conclusive in natural science, so that the latter cannot claim anything more than so-far-so-good truths, and not a conclusive truth of the kind that the dialectic of capital can claim. Economic theory, whether neoclassical or Marxist, which wants to be natural-scientific, will also be deprived of the self-assurance of the materialist dialectic.

The dialectic of capital and history

The fact that there are such things as "externalities", so that the logic of capital can never completely assimilate a use-value space even under capitalism, holds the key to the emancipation of humankind and socialism. For it means that capitalism can exist only to the extent that externalities are manageable by policies of the bourgeois state. If they are so rampant as to exceed the control of the bourgeois state, capital will no longer be able to function as the determining software of society. Capitalist society must then give way to its successor, which may or may not be socialism, depending on whether it is progressive or retrogressive in terms of the emancipation of humanity. But all this involves what Uno once called the "dialectic of history" and the "dialectic of revolution".

When the dialectic of capital synthesizes itself fully, defining capitalism, we must then see how capital asserts itself in real, that is, non-idealized use-value spaces. Here the theme is the "negotiation" between capital and the use-value space, which is quite unlike the unilateral self-imposition of divine reason on human contingencies as in Hegel's philosophy of history. In the Unoist doctrine, concrete-empirical use-values are reintroduced very carefully, first as types such as wool, cotton and steel, which were dominant in the three world-historic developmental stages of capitalism. For example, the liberal stage of capitalism is conceived as one in which all or most use-values are like cotton products, and produced with technology similar to that employed by the nineteenth-century English cotton industry. Thus, in the stages-theory, use-values remain controlled as "types" so as to bring out the mode of negotiation whereby capital manages to regulate a use-value space of a particular kind. Naked and multifarious use-values, as they exist in real history, are introduced at another level, the level of historical analysis. If we deal with a historical period of capitalism, the stage-theoretic determinations mediate between theory and reality. For the study of a non-capitalist period, such a mediation cannot be counted on. But, in either case, there is no place for historical determinism. Every episode in capitalist history is full of contingencies and freedom, and is informed by the logic of capital only in broad outlines and in part. The history of a non-capitalist era is even less subject to the logic of capital.

In explaining the three distinct levels of analysis, Uno referred to three kinds of necessity: the necessity of decennial crises, the necessity of an imperialist war, and the necessity of a revolution. The first of these is dictated by the logic of capital and is fully determinate. The second occurs at the stages-theoretic level. When the logic of capital asserts itself at the stage of development of capitalism typified by heavy industries such as steel and chemicals, bourgeois states are compelled to resort to imperialist economic policies, the consequence of which is a war between major powers for economic hegemony. This necessity is not explained completely by the logic of capital, but involves human factors reflected in the policies of bourgeois states. The third necessity refers only to the likely collective choice of human societies. Human beings must be protected from the brute force of the self-regulating capitalist market, as Polanyi says. This means that there comes a point where the capitalist pursuit of abstract-mercantile wealth becomes intolerable to the well-being of humankind, and, at or near that point, the latter will choose to terminate the rule of capital. It is, in other words, a prognosis of human behavior that is essentially free and contingent. In deference to the historicist tradition of Hegel and Marx, Uno talked of the dialectics of history and revolution. But clearly he did not subscribe to the eschatological biases of that tradition.

Conclusions

I would like to conclude this essay by drawing out the implication of this last statement. When the dialectic identifies a subject-object which spins its story (that is, the software that defines an operating system), the next step is to see how it actually works or manifests itself in reality. In Hegel's case, his logic, which coincided with metaphysics, defined the Absolute (the Christian *logos,* divine wisdom, reason, or whatever) as the subject-object. The Absolute then asserted its sway completely over nature and human beings in such a way that no contingency and freedom would remain after its establishment. It is this that made his dialectic "idealist". In contrast, the subject-object of the materialist dialectic, capital, is much less powerful in its actual working. For we can identify it as the software of capitalism only by imagining an idealized use-value space. In other words, real use-value spaces can never be subordinated completely to the logic of capital. There always remain "externalities" that escape the sway of capital. It is, therefore, "use-value" and not "value" that wins eventually. From our human point of view, we always need a use-value space, but we tolerate the dictates of capital only under certain circumstances. To me, it is this fact that makes the dialectic of capital "materialist" and not "idealist". The materialist dialectic synthesizes capital as software, in just the same way as the Hegelian dialectic does the Absolute. At this level, there is a complete parallel, almost a homomorphism. The distinction arises in what the software does. The Absolute insists on being omnipotent always, permitting no freedom for human beings to choose their own destiny, whereas capital wants to be omnipotent only when it can – that is, *only when material conditions are right* – thus assuring complete freedom for human beings to go beyond it.

Notes and References

[1] Hegel, G. W. F., *Logic,* trans. W. Wallace (New York: Oxford University Press, 1975), p. 24.

[2] Hegel, G. W. F., *Philosophy of Right,* trans. T. M. Knox (Oxford University Press, 1967), Preface.

[3] Sekine, T., *An Outline of the Dialectic of Capital,* vol. I (London: Macmillan, 1997), pp. 5-7. See also the next chapter in this volume.

[4] Polanyi, K., *The Great Transformation* (Boston, Mass.: Beacon Press, 1957), pp. 40-5.

The Dialectic of Capital:
An Unoist Interpretation

Marxian economic theory constitutes a dialectical, not an axiomatic, system. Although some important features of the dialectic have already been discussed elsewhere, a more systematic treatment of the subject, specifically of the Hegelian-Marxian version of the dialectic, may be in order. Of course, many explanations of this type of dialectic are available in Marxist literature, but unfortunately not all of them are dependable. In fact, some of them are more misleading than informative. Part of the difficulty stems from the fact that a dialectic cannot be explained generally, or in the abstract, since it is not a strictly formal (abstract-general) logic but rather a formal-substantive (concrete-synthetic) one. It, in other words, constitutes a teleological rather than a tautological system. In a dialectical exposition we often talk of proceeding from the abstract to the concrete. This means that we advance from an emptier and less specified concept to a more "enriched" and specified one. Here "concrete" does not mean "concrete-empirical" or "concrete-historical"; it means "concrete-synthetic" in the sense of "containing more logical specifications of the subject".

Perhaps it is useful to begin with the three fundamental characteristics of the Hegelian-Marxian dialectic: 1) it believes that "the truth is the whole"; 2) it claims the identity of the subject and the object; 3) it proceeds by synthesizing "contradictions" through the triad of thesis, antithesis and synthesis. The first two characteristics refer to the structure of the dialectic, and the third to its procedural aspect.

We know from our daily experience that a partial story is ultimately undependable. Only an unwise parent tries to settle a dispute between children on the basis of one party's tattle-taling. In order to be fair, he or she must listen to both parties concerned, and "synthesize" the whole story. A law court operates on the same principle. It does not pronounce its verdict until it believes it has been informed of "the whole truth" with regard to the case. Although human errors are unavoidable and the court oftentimes comes to a wrong decision on the basis of inconclusive evidence, it does not, in principle, accept tentative conjectures or refutable (falsifiable) hypotheses. The reason is simple. We know that for something to be really true, it must be absolutely or conclusively established to be true. A tentative hypothesis which we conventionally accept for the time being, "relative to the present state of our knowledge", does not qualify as the real truth.

The dialectic takes the same view in its logical synthesis of an entire story. It does not accept a conclusion based on tentative assumptions, hypotheses or conjectures. The result of a dialectical investigation must, in other words, stand on its own without depending on any axiom or postulate. The subject matter, or the object of study, must be made "self-explanatory" within the system in the sense that it leaves no unknowable or unexplainable "thing-in-itself". The logic of that system must, therefore, be inherent in it rather than imposed on it from the outside. That sort of self-explaining system is what Hegel called the "concrete logical idea". To bring out this character, I would say that the dialectic is "autobiographical". An autobiographical story can be told only *from within*, and not from without.

Since the dialectic is autobiographical, it must have *a story-teller or the subject*. It is important to identify who is telling us the story. In the case of Hegel, the Absolute (God or the Christian logos) is the subject of the dialectic; in the case of Marx, it is capital. This important point is often overlooked by Marxian materialists. In their eagerness to "abolish" Hegel's idealist concept of the Absolute, they do not stop to think what materialist subject they should put in its place. Engels, Lenin and the whole school of "dialectical materialists" put Nature (or matter) in place of the Absolute without much reflection. But their project, as it turned out, was a complete non-starter. It had to fail because Nature (or matter) does not come forward to tell us its own story. Since it is not "autobiographical", a dialectic of Nature (or of matter) is an impossibility. Nature passively sits out there and waits to be scrutinized, dissected, analyzed and described by us from the outside.

A dialectical subject must originate in human beings, yet it must also transcend us. Hegel's Absolute satisfies both conditions. For, as Feuerbach claimed, the Absolute is nothing but the "infinitization (or absolutization)" of human virtues. We human beings are good, wise, powerful, etc., only to some extent, and never infinitely or absolutely so. If, however, these desirable human characteristics are "infinitized" or "absolutized" in our mind, we can conceive of God, or the Absolute. Thus, instead of God creating us in his image, we, human beings, create God in our image. This is Feuerbach's well-known thesis of anthropomorphism. In this light, it is readily understandable why God privileges us, i.e., human beings, as his agents. He must reveal himself through us. We, human beings, for our part, understand the nature (logic) of the Absolute (i.e., the divine wisdom or Reason) because it is nothing but the extrapolation of our own "essence". The religious teaching that God always gives us his grace and allows us to comprehend his intentions and designs is expressed "philosophically", in the case of Hegel, by the thesis that the Absolute reveals itself completely to our finite reason.

We do not create Nature or matter by "self-idealization", i.e., by the process of infinitization of our own virtues. Nature, therefore, has no teleology to reveal to us. We can never know it completely. We can only gain partial knowledge of its behavior by constantly observing it from the outside. Nature does not privilege us by selecting us as its agent and letting us play out its logic. Although we belong to Nature, we have not created it. Consequently, we cannot see its logic from the inside, nor can we grasp it as a totality, i.e., as a "concrete logical idea". The "thing-in-itself" of Nature always remains beyond our reach. In other words, Nature or matter cannot be the subject of a materialist dialectic. If so, what else can the subject of a materialistic dialectic be? My answer is that it can be "capital".

Capital originates in our own "economic motives", even though it transcends us because in it these human traits are already "made infinite and absolute". Through the creation of capital our economic motives are "one-dimensionalized". Since, however, capital is obtained by our own "self-idealization", we comprehend it completely. All we have to do is to ask ourselves what we would do, if we pursued our own "economic" goals single-mindedly at the expense of all other considerations, i.e., if we behaved as mere "bearers of economic categories". In fact, that is how we learn the basics of economic theory. The present claim is equivalent to saying that capital, as the dialectical subject, reveals itself to us totally. Since capital is a product of our "self-idealization", it contains nothing that we cannot really comprehend.

The identity of the subject and the object is the immediate consequence of this fact. In the dialectic, capital tells us its own story. Having transcended us and our limitations, capital now possesses its own identity separate from us. It has become the object, in the sense that it has gone beyond our finite subjectivity. Yet we can fully understand how capital "thinks" because its "logic" is only an extended version of our own thought. In other words, we are privy to the subjectivity of capital. Our finite subjectivity and capital's infinite subjectivity are different, and yet they are connected by what Marx called the "force of abstraction".[1] By being "subsumed" under capital and becoming its agent, we can think like capital.

It is interesting to recall that "logic coincides with metaphysics" according to Hegel.[2] All metaphysical categories represent characteristics of the Absolute, i.e., purified human nature. The dialectic of the Absolute explains them in a logical order. We can similarly claim that "logic coincides with economics", meaning that all economic categories represent characteristics of capital, i.e., our economic motives "made infinite". In other words, the dialectic of capital is economic theory, and nothing else can be. Economic theory must, therefore, expose the logic of capital completely. The method of this complete exposition is the dialectic, which proceeds by the triadic steps of thesis, antithesis and synthesis.

A dialectical system is a self-definition in the sense that the subject of the dialectic defines (specifies) itself completely. The definition, however, cannot be completed at one fell swoop. Instead, the subject must be defined and redefined a great number of times, as we go through the many layers of its existence. As the level of discussion proceeds from abstract to concrete, the same concept returns many times, and each time it becomes more specified. The process ends only when it is fully synthesized or completely specified, all its layers being exposed.

The easiest way to understand the nature of this method is to think of how a painter works on a portrait. When he first begins with a few broad outlines, it is hard to recognize whose picture is being created. As he gradually adds details, however, the resemblance to the person who is sitting for him becomes increasingly clear. When the picture is completed, there is no longer any doubt as to whose portrait has been painted. Even in the first few of his bold brush strokes, however, the painter presupposes (has in his mind) the end result. He is aware that the spaces which he now leaves empty will be filled with elaborate detail in due course. In synthesizing something dialectically, we proceed in the same way. First, we begin with broad contours, which pre-assign the spaces into which further details (or specifications) will be introduced later.

Let us, at this point, consider the famous Hegelian triad of "being, naught and becoming". The following illustration may clarify the dialectical meaning of "contradiction" and its synthesis. Suppose that I ask a friend of mine the question: "Have you got a child?" If the answer is "Yes, I have one" (being) and "No, I have none" (non-being) at the same time, it is contradictory in the formal-logical sense. Either my friend is mentally confused or he does not seriously want to answer my question. Obviously such a contradiction cannot be synthesized, overcome or resolved. For it is *not* a dialectical contradiction. Yet many self-appointed exponents of the dialectic come forward with the false exegesis that precisely this elusiveness illustrates what Hegel calls "becoming". That most decidedly is *not* the case.

When the friend answers my query with "Yes, I have" (being), he has not yet specified his child at all. The child may, therefore, be a boy or a girl, a one-year old infant or an uncontrollable teenager, a whiz kid or mentally retarded, i.e., anything that a child can be. It is this absence of any specification that is called "nothing" or "naught". Indeed, without any further information other than merely that he exists, the child means absolutely "nothing" to me. If I were to open his file, it would remain totally blank, except for a hypothetical name that I may decide to give him for convenience. Yet I cannot ignore the fact that there is a child in my friend's family. This constitutes the dialectical contradiction.

"Becoming" means, in the present case, that I may ask more questions and begin to complete a meaningful file of the child, or I may simply forget about it. I am formally free to let the child "come to be" or "pass away". Since, from a formal point of view, there is no compelling reason for me to opt for either of the two alternatives, the state of "becoming" is said to be fluid and unstable. However, so long as my original question was not asked frivolously, and was motivated by genuine curiosity, I will seek more information about that child.

If my friend responds to my further questioning, his child will not remain a pure being, but will become a determinate (or specified) being. At the same time, my thought of the child moves from one level of abstraction to another, i.e., it progresses one step forward in its dialectical journey from abstract to concrete. Soon I shall obtain a more synthetic idea of the child, insofar as that is possible from an external description. Once his file is thus complete, I may now wish to meet the child personally for an in-depth study of his character or inner motivation, subjecting him to further, more probing questioning. At that point, I seek his "essence", having already confirmed his "being".

From the above example, it is apparent that dialectical "contradiction" is quite different from "contradiction" in the sense of formal logic. The dialectic clearly does not offend the so-called principle of non-contradiction in formal logic. A dialectical contradiction arises when a concept is posed without adequate specification. The concept itself demands more specification, which is not yet available. That constitutes a dialectical contradiction. To specify or determine something, however, is to relate it to something other than itself. For instance, a child can be a boy or a girl. To say that it is a boy means that it is not a girl. We thus determine the concept, in this case, by excluding its other possibility. This is in keeping with the well-known Spinozan contention that "all determination is a negation".

Unfortunately, an incorrect, and commonly encountered, explanation of the triad reverses this procedure and glorifies the mere truism that a boy (thesis) and a girl (antithesis) are both a child (synthesis). That, however, would be to move from the concrete (more specified) to the abstract (less specified). There is nothing dialectical in such a proposition. In the above illustration, by contrast, I first find out that there is a child. Next, I ask a question to determine whether it is a boy or a girl. Once told that it is a boy, I then ask a further question to determine, for instance, what sort of age bracket he belongs to. Having received this information, I next try to determine whether he is an extrovert or an introvert, etc. By proceeding in this fashion, I get to know what the child is like. I am in effect writing a "biography" of the child. If, however, there exists a systematic questionnaire, or method of exhaustive questioning, ready for use by everyone, my task will be simplified. If the "child" himself is mature enough, he can be his own interviewer and respondent with the help of this questionnaire. In other words, he can write his own "autobiography".

The greatness of Hegel lies in discovering such a systematic questionnaire for the first time. He was, according to Marx, "the first to present the general forms of working of the dialectic in a comprehensive and conscious manner".[3] By simply responding to the questionnaire that Hegel designed, a dialectical subject is made to reveal its full "autobiography". That questionnaire consists of the three doctrines of Being, Essence and the Notion.

The doctrine of Being is further divided into quality, quantity and measure. Roughly speaking, the dialectical subject (say, my friend's child) is specified externally in this doctrine, by the method of "becoming (transition)" or "passing over from one form to another". For instance, "the child" becomes "a boy", who becomes "a teenager", who becomes "an extrovert type", who becomes "a talented musician", etc. All items of information are put in the file of the child, which is in three parts. In the first part (quality), we find out what sort of a child he is *(Was für ein Kind ist es?)*, i.e., his being-for-self *(Fürsichsein)*. Suppose that he is musically talented. Then, in the second part (quantity) of the file, we find out how his immanent talent is recognized, tested and measured externally by society. Finally, the last part of his file (measure) explains how the inner talent and its external recognition combine to enable the child to grow into a full-fledged musician.

At this point we enter the doctrine of Essence, which consists of the ground, appearance and actuality. This doctrine corresponds to the phase of internal specification of the subject. The dialectical method at work here is often called "reflection (grounding)", which we may also call "internalization". In this case, the dialectical subject does not simply delimit itself by excluding or circumventing what is other than itself, but rather "internalizes" the opposing factors in a more positive and conciliatory fashion. For instance, the child may have inherited great musical talent from his forefathers, yet his family condition may not have been affluent enough to provide him with proper training in classical music. Under the circumstances he may have decided to adopt a simpler instrument and so developed into a popular musician. He thus preserves his talent (ground), but makes appropriate adaptations to the surrounding conditions (appearance) and establishes himself as a solid musician (actuality).

We then move to the last chapter of his autobiography, the doctrine of the Notion. We now look at the boy who has established himself as a popular musician. How does he fare and survive in this world? The doctrine is divided into the subjective notion, the object and the idea *(Idee)*, and the dialectical method at work here is that of "development or unfolding *(Entfaltung)*". For example, our musician must regulate his life according to his own principles or self-imposed discipline (the subjective notion). The principles must be systematic and consistent; they must also serve his purpose. His life, however, cannot be completely regulated by his principles alone. There are other facts of life which go beyond the purview of his subjective principles. Since they (the object) cannot be ignored, he must find ways to reconcile himself with their requirements. For example, in planning a concert trip, he cannot ignore business considerations nor can he forget about how his parents and siblings feel about it. He may have to make certain necessary concessions. Only when he has learned the wisdom of harmonizing his subjective principles with the objective conditions that constrain them, do we get the real "idea" of the person.

The present illustration is not meant to be a rigorous interpretation of Hegel's *Logic*. Far from that. However, what I wish above all to bring out with this exercise is that the Hegelian dialectic is not a mystical doctrine beyond the grasp of ordinary mortals. On the contrary, it is a very natural mode of thinking that we all practice in our daily life, whether we are conscious of it or not. For the dialectic is nothing but a system of our own "thought-forms or thought determinations". Our next task is to show how the same thought pattern is used to expose the concept of capital dialectically. In this case, we can afford to be a little more rigorous and precise in our interpretation of the dialectic.

The dialectic of capital too consists of the three doctrines of circulation, production and distribution. The dialectical methods used in those doctrines are respectively, becoming, internalization, and unfolding. The guiding force of the dialectic of capital is the contradiction between value and use-values. Capital, the dialectical subject, reveals itself step by step by letting "value", its most abstract specification, prevail over "use-values" which represent everything "other" than capital.

The doctrine of circulation. If you ask capital: "What are you first of all, prior to all further specifications?", it will answer: "I am abstract-general (i.e., commodity-economic or mercantile) wealth regardless of its concrete-specific or material property which satisfies you in one particular way or another." That abstract-general side of wealth is called "value", as opposed to the concrete-specific side, which is called "use-value". The simplest context in which the two "contradictory" terms appear, co-existing side by side, is the "commodity". That is why Marx says: "The wealth of bourgeois society, at first sight, presents itself as an immense accumulation of commodities, its unit being a single commodity."[4]

The value of a commodity cannot be seen. It is buried underneath the correlative use-value of the commodity. To overcome that restriction, value expresses itself in the form of a price, i.e., in a definite quantity of the use-value of another commodity. By adopting the use-value of *another* commodity, it frees itself, as it were, from its own correlative use-value with which it has to co-habit in the same commodity. Thus, it seeks a solution outside that commodity. This kind of procedure illustrates the method of transition or becoming.

The expression of value itself in terms of other commodities gives rise to money. Money is the commodity (such as gold) in the use-value of which all other commodities express their value. By virtue of this fact money purchases other commodities without qualitative restriction, and, in so doing, measures their value. It also takes the forms of active (transactions) money and idle money. The latter is money which stays outside the sphere of commodity circulation, awaiting the opportunity to become capital.

Capital is an operation that renders a sum of money into a greater sum of money by adopting one of these three forms. These are merchant, money-lending and industrial capital. The operation of the first is the most severely constrained by use-values, since the merchant is a middleman caught between producers and consumers. The last form can operate with the maximum of freedom from use-value restrictions, since an industrialist can, in principle, produce *any* use-value of his choice, provided that labor-power is available to him as a commodity.

The doctrine of production. Once the form of industrial capital is well established, a completely new type of "contradiction between value and use-values" arises. This one is between capital as a form of "chrematistic" (value augmentation) and supra-historic "real economic life"; that is to say, the production of use-values in general, which it subsumes. This time the contradiction is solved by a more adequate and secure subsumption of the real economy under the form of value augmentation. The real economic life common to all societies is "internalized" by the chrematistic form of capital.

Use-values must be produced in all societies. Under capitalism, however, they are produced only as the reflection (or *Schattenseite*) of the production of surplus value. Commodities are produced for the surplus value that they contain, and not directly for their use-values. The production of surplus value requires a development of the specifically capitalist method of production, which is most typically represented by factories equipped with machines. The use of machines entails the increasing perfection of labor-power as a commodity. The capitalist production of commodities, however, does not occur only inside the factory. What occurs inside it is controlled and regulated by what takes place outside it.

In this doctrine, the production of commodities as value, which contains surplus value, is studied in all its aspects, i.e., inside the factory (as the production-process of capital), outside the factory (as the circulation-process of capital), and as the continuing activity of the aggregate-social capital (the reproduction-process of capital). The purpose of this doctrine is to establish the capitalist mode of production as a self-dependent system of commodity production, consistent with the supra-historic norms of real economic life. In other words, it is to show that capitalism constitutes a real historical society, rather than a mere toy model which we arbitrarily invent.

The doctrine of distribution. Once the viability and reproducibility of surplus value production is demonstrated, capital then proceeds to develop its own market, the capitalist market. Although every commodity is always produced as value, i.e., indifferently to use-values, each commodity is, nonetheless, a distinct use-value, the production of which requires a specific technique. Sometimes, more than one technique is employed in the production of a particular use-value.

At this point, the "contradiction between value and use-values" arises in yet another form. This time it is a contradiction between the capitalist indifference to use-values and the unavoidability of technical variations in their production. Such a contradiction will be reconciled by the dialectic of unfolding or development, a method which is specific to the doctrine of distribution.

In the capitalist market, the surplus value that capital as a whole has produced is distributed to individual units of capital in proportion to the magnitude of its advance, and this involves the formation of the general rate of profit and production-prices (equilibrium prices) that deviate from values (the theory of profit). Industrial capital, however, is not the only partaker of surplus value. Although land does not directly participate in the production of value, it is, nevertheless, an indispensable factor in the production of use-values. Hence, capital must cede part of surplus value to landed property, which collects various forms of rent (the theory of rent). The ownership of land entitles one to a stream of periodic revenues as rent.

The experience of sharing surplus value with landed property in this manner enables capital to re-conceptualize itself as an asset or property. As a property, capital too is automatically entitled to a stream of interest revenues. Interest-bearing capital is the most synthetic and complete concept of capital (the theory of interest). This concept, however, can be reached only after industrial capital delegates its circulatory functions to loan-capital and commercial capital. These two forms of capital assist the surplus value production of industrial capital indirectly. By providing credit, loan-capital enables industrial capital to buy commodities which it would otherwise not be able to purchase. By taking over the difficult and time-consuming operation of selling commodities from industrial capital, commercial capital enables it to concentrate on the production of surplus value.

In all these cases, capital tries to distance itself from the production of use-values. The first principle of the distribution of surplus value as profit enables all units of industrial capital, regardless of the specific use-value they happen to be producing, to be equally rewarded in proportion to the magnitude of capital advanced. The second explains how surplus value may be shared between agriculture, which is land-intensive, and non-agriculture, which is not. The last principle of distribution shows how all capitalists, whether engaged productively in industry (production of use-values) or unproductively in commerce and finance, may equally partake of the existing pool of surplus value in the form of interest, rather than of profit, in proportion to the magnitude of the ownership of capital.

The above explains the structure of the dialectic of capital in a very condensed form. An uncanny homomorphism between Hegel's *Logic* and the dialectic of capital may be noticed. That, however, is not strange to me. For the dialectical subject is always part of ourselves, though magnified and extended. There must be only one way to let such a subject expose itself totally and systematically, and that is the dialectical way.

Notes and References

[1] Marx, K., *Capital*, vol. I (New York: International Publisher, 1967), p. 8.

[2] Wallace, W., *Hegel's Logic* (Oxford, England: Oxford University Press, 1975), p. 36.

[3] Marx, *Capital*, I, p. 20.

[4] Marx, *A Contribution to the Critique of Political Economy* (Moscow: Progress Publisher, 1970), p. 27.

An Essay on Uno's Dialectic of Capital

The compact book of Uno's, *Principles of Political Economy,* is a master-piece of *dialectic* although he does not even once mention this word dialectic in it. It will be difficult, I fear, for anyone to really appreciate the significance of Uno's *Principles of Political Economy* without an adequate conception of the method which characterises its exposition. In what follows I shall, therefore, try to clarify the nature of that method.[1] Uno's is certainly very different from what "materialistic dialectic" is made out to be in popular literature. I ought to stress immediately that the dialectic which underlies Uno's writing is a method of cognition, that is to say, that it is a method of "knowing" the subject-matter. It, in other words, has something to do with the theory of knowledge and nothing at all to do with social action, ideology, praxis, and the like. For this reason I begin by contrasting the dialectical method with another method of cognition, called analytical (or, perhaps better, empirico-analytical), which has come to dominate contemporary discussions on the scientific method (Section I). I shall next review Hegel's dialectic in order to establish what precisely is meant by "discovering the rational kernel within the mystical shell"[2] (Section II). Finally, I will show how Uno's dialectic boils down to the method of social science in contradistinction to the method of natural science (Section III).

I. The analytical method of natural science

At the beginning of the twentieth century physics was said to be in a state of crisis.[3] The realisation that the elegant system of classical mechanics approximated reality only in the case of low-velocity motions of bodies destroyed the faith in the Newtonian view of nature which had optimistically promoted the rationalism, determinism, and natural scientific materialism of the nineteenth century. To Mach, Duhem, Poincaré and others it suddenly appeared as though "matter has disappeared",[4] as the mystery of nature deepened calling for a drastic revision of the traditional view. The effect was acutely felt in philosophy and scientific methodology; it was, however, only after Einstein's discovery of the relativity "principle, which revolutionised physics that logical positivists began to propound their *analytical* theory of knowledge purporting to keep abreast with the new development of scientific practice.[5]

1. Meaning and truth

In an effort to reaffirm Newton's warning to "beware of Metaphysics", logical positivism demands a sharp dichotomy of theory and facts.[6] Thus all propositions or meaningful statements are, according to this school, either *a priori* analytic or empirically synthetic, other statements being residually defined as metaphysical, i.e., meaningless or nonsensical. *A priori* analytic statements are tautological in the sense that their denial involves a self-contradiction. Such statements are logically necessary, i.e., irrefutable from the standpoint of formal logic, although they are emphatically devoid of any factual connotation. They are nonetheless indispensable to scientific knowledge inasmuch as they stipulate the linguistic usage or convention of science. Synthetic-empirical propositions, on the other hand, refer to "matters of fact" and must be attested by human experience (i.e., by experiments or observations). Since science is concerned with matters of nature, it must, with the help of purely logical propositions, produce such statements as are empirically testable, and, hence, can be either validated or invalidated in fact.

The immediate difficulty that this methodological proposal faces, however, is the impossibility of conclusive "verification". For, as well known since Hume, it is impossible to guarantee that certain instances *will* be experienced because they have so far been repeatedly experienced, however great the number of repetitions may be. Thus, even such a self-evident proposition as "The sun rises once every twenty-four hours in the Mediterranean region" cannot be conclusively verified, there being always a possibility that the sun may not rise tomorrow as expected. Popper who rejects inductive logic, therefore, proposes to replace the verification principle with the falsification principle. With this replacement, it is possible to claim, although this is not Popper's intention, that a falsifiable statement is meaningful in the sense of non-metaphysical.[7]

To abandon the verifiability of scientific propositions and remain content with their falsifiability, however, has a far-reaching epistemological consequence. Since no testable hypothesis can be shown to be true or false once for all, science must renounce its claim to the knowledge of any definitive truth. Science can know for sure only what nature does not do but never what nature actually does.[8] If a scientific theory has not been falsified, it is only a so-far-so-good conjecture which may at any moment turn out to be an illusion in the light of new counter-evidence. No theory can, therefore, be conclusively pronounced to be true unless it is factually empty (i.e., merely tautologically or axiomatically true); it can be meaningful at most in the sense of being possibly true.

2. The problem of demarcation

Is it then possible to demarcate science from metaphysics or pseudo-science by this criterion of meaningfulness? This turns out to be impossible because no science can restrict itself to stating only meaningful sentences. A testable hypothesis cannot be proposed without simultaneously specifying how the test should be carried out. But the specification of the manner in which the test should be conducted can neither be tautological nor falsifiable. It is not tautological because its denial is not self-contradictory; it is not falsifiable because there is no way of empirically refuting it. Consequently, it has to be meaningless, i.e., willy-nilly metaphysical; yet it is obvious that no science can be free from such metaphysics. This difficulty can be easily illustrated by the following example.

Consider the well-known Euclidean theorem that the three inner angles of a triangle always add up to a straight line. This theorem is an immediate consequence of the axiom of parallel lines; it is tautologically true and factually empty. In order to translate this proposition into a testable hypothesis, however, one has to interpret some physical reality as an approximation to the theoretical triangle. Hence, if science wants to test this proposition, it must state an interpretative sentence, called a "bridge principle" by C. Hempel, which cannot on the basis of the above criterion be meaningful.[9] P. W. Bridgman's claim[10] that the theorem can be "operationally meaningful" if and only if it shows how a physical triangle may be constructed as an approximation to a pure triangle involves the same difficulty.[11] For short of an operational specification, which implies an interpretation, the theorem can never be "empirically refutable, [even] under ideal conditions",[12] i.e., the theorem can never be translated into a testable proposition.[13] If this translation, which no empirical science can avoid, is a metaphysical activity, the demarcation of science from metaphysics on the ground of meaningfulness becomes a crass joke, Newton's warning remaining completely ineffective.

This problem cannot be circumvented by merely declaring that an operational specification or a physical interpretation of theoretical concepts so far as it assists an experiment or observation shall, henceforward, be deemed "meaningful". In that case it becomes rather embarrassingly obvious that the definition of meaningfulness itself is and has always been metaphysical. It is, therefore, quite right for K. Popper to abandon logical positivism, together with its meaningfulness criterion. The alternative that he proposes, however, is the following:

> In contrast to these anti-metaphysical stratagems ... my business, as I see it, is not to bring about the overthrow of metaphysics. It is, rather, to formulate a suitable characterisation of empirical science, or to define the concepts "empirical science" and "metaphysics" in such a way that we shall be able to say of a given system of statements whether or not its closer study is the concern of empirical science.

> My criterion of demarcation will accordingly have to be regarded as a *proposal for an agreement or convention*. As to the suitability of any such convention opinions may differ; and a reasonable discussion of these questions is only possible between parties having some purpose in common. The choice of that purpose must, of course, be ultimately a matter of decision, going beyond rational argument.[14]

Popper here wishfully hopes that the scientific establishment can somehow agree on the meaning of the word "science" as a matter of convention, and that, once agreed upon, the adherence to such a convention should be deemed as a qualification for membership in the scientific community. He freely admits that "in aiming at my proposal I have been guided, in the last analysis, by value judgements and predilections".[15] These value judgements presumably include his unstinting praise of "the dignity of modern theoretical physics in which I and others see the most complete realisation to date of what I call 'empirical science'".[16] This view is tantamount to the practical definition that science is what scientists do, or more accurately that science is what good scientists like modern physicists appear to Popper to be doing. The question, therefore, boils down to what they in fact do. According to Popper good scientists offer falsifiable hypotheses or rather hypotheses that are most readily falsifiable. For example, scientists may predict that water vaporises when heated up to and beyond 100 °C. This proposition is readily falsifiable because anyone can test it as many times as he pleases and easily confirm the result unless his thermometer is inaccurate. To translate an abstract theory into an experimental "recipe" is part of the scientist's job even though it may involve metaphysics from the point of view of the logical positivists. To Popper only those theories from which one cannot generate a conclusively testable hypothesis are metaphysical or pseudo-scientific. The hypothesis must refer to "events that recur in accordance to rules and regularities" because only then can the result of the test be observed, in principle, by anyone and inter-subjectively (i.e., objectively) confirmed.[17]

Popper's "liberal" characterisation of science as opposed to pseudo-science would be adequate if, in fact, all scientists do what they are supposed to be doing. However, they may not be such paragons of methodological virtue, as Feyerabend has recently argued; so far as the method is concerned, they may indeed be ruthless opportunists in their hectic search for possible truth and quite oblivious of Popper's code of good behaviour.[18] At this point, it may be remarked that a disillusioned liberal often becomes an anarchist. When things work out automatically, one can afford to be a liberal, asserting complacently that the imposition of an organised discipline would always be futile. But if things do not work out nicely by themselves, the continued refusal to submit to any control leads to unprincipled permissiveness and the worship of chaos. Thus, when Feyerabend discovers that scientists are in fact not doing what, according to Popper, they should be doing, it is not surprising at all that methodological anarchism follows.[19] The liberal methodology of Popper has always lacked a self-confident philosophy, the philosopher not being supposed to think actively for himself but rather vicariously to record what scientists have already decided to do, right or wrong.

Thus, Popper himself may have sown the seed of methodological anarchism when he defined science by scientists' own practice. But the epistemological question: "How do modern physicists and chemists acquire valid knowledge of nature?" still stands. Feyerabend's "dadaist" answer that they resort to the anti-method of "anything goes" does not appear to be satisfactory because the philosophical problem of the validity of knowledge is not even faced by him, if instead surreptitiously replaced by the psychology of learning.[20] Again, Popper himself has prepared the ground for this abdication of philosophy by asserting that all knowledge is a conjecture which can never be absolutely validated. In this case, whoever possesses a falsifiable but not yet falsified hypothesis can claim a negative knowledge, i.e., the knowledge that the hypothesis has so far not been counter-evidenced. It is then very difficult to distinguish between an educated guess and a madman's fantasy,[21] if no authority can be trusted to rule on the distinction, anarchism cannot be avoided.

3. The dogma of reductionism

So far as physics and chemistry are concerned Popper's method, which intends to allow maximum freedom to scientific practitioners, may well be regarded as liberal, if verging on anarchism at the limit. But, so far as other (less dignified!) branches of science are concerned, his view develops in the diametrically opposite direction. The extreme intolerance and bigotry with which he misinterpreted and belittled Marxian political economy in some of his well-known books[22] shows how a liberal professor can overnight turn into a Spanish Inquisitor or a Stalinist bully, giving more credibility to the "broad-mindedness" of Feyerabend's anarchism. Reductionism, explicit or implicit, is a dogma (i.e., a metaphysical doctrine according to *any* criterion) most widely shared by the methodologists of the analytical school.[23] For this dogma, which requires all sciences, regardless of their purpose to model themselves after physics and chemistry, is a natural outcome of the analytical philosopher's fascination with early twentieth-century developments in the physical sciences. I do not need to quibble with the lexical definition of "science," a word so often used as a synonym for "natural science" in contemporary English; in the present methodological context, the word "science" is meaningful only in its original sense of objective knowledge, whether pertaining to nature or to society.

By denying social science its own method and by demanding its methodological compliance (or even subservience) to natural science, reductionism most unambiguously exhibits the limitation of analytical philosophy, including the critical rationalism of Popper. The limitation consists in prescribing arbitrary rules *in vacuo* and imposing them on science from the outside as constraints. This limitation is inherent in the analytical method of scientific cognition; for it does not (and cannot) arise from the nature of the subject-matter itself but is posed as a set of norms, artificially contrived by the philosophical observers of science, who are not even free from value-judgements. This difficulty stems from the fact that nature does not conclusively reveal its inner laws of motion.

If what Popper says is true, one can only be sure of the anti-knowledge of nature; that is to say, science can know only certain things that nature does not do. So long as natural science has to depend on empiricism, in other words, it is impossible to expose all of the jealously guarded secrets of nature; for empiricism knows no theory other than hypothetical or conjectural.

I personally do not wish to make any dogmatic assertion on the present state of knowledge concerning nature. There may be no such thing as "nature" cut and dried independent of our observation; there may be no pure empiricism, i.e., no presumption that experience is not already conditioned by theories. It may even be, as Bachelard is reported to have claimed, that no knowledge of nature need be philosophically sanctioned as objective for in the history of scientific practice truth imposes itself by itself.[24] What is obvious to me, however, is that the physical sciences cannot really be free from empiricism of some sort or other and, hence, not be free in the final analysis from Hume's problem. If therefore natural scientific truth is never absolute and natural scientific theories always conjectural and hypothetical, then nature (whatever it may be) cannot be totally known. Hence follows Popper's guarded statement: "If we wish to study a thing, we are bound to select certain aspects of it. It is not possible for us to observe or to describe a whole piece of the world, or a whole piece of nature."[25] This is another way of saying that the theory is not "grey" and hence that the world cannot be fully understood.[26]

If this is the case, it is certainly incorrect to apply the epistemological method of the natural sciences to the study of social phenomena; for any knowledge of society which is partial (and hence ideological) is strictly meaningless. For example a partial interpretation of an historical institution such as capitalism can make of it either a paradise of Pareto-optimality or a dismal world of alienation or anything that fits the fancy of the prevailing ideology. Neoclassical economics, which has most willingly followed the reductionists' advice,[27] has indeed created a travesty of celestial mechanics, dubbed general equilibrium theory, claiming it to be positive rather than normative. The impossibility of such a theory to produce readily falsifiable hypotheses, however, is surely not due to the economist's lack of enthusiasm but to the very nature of economic reality which in general does not permit sufficiently "repeatable" experiments or observations. The less rigorous and systematic the theory is, the more readily it is tested;[28] but the test is hardly ever refuted because econometric operations allow almost any amount of *ad hoc* justification. Contemporary economics, therefore, is not a good "empirical science" according to Popper's criterion.[29] This fact is becoming obvious to an increasing number of practitioners who frequently complain about the "emptiness of the theory". An economic theory, however, has never been abandoned because it is empty of empirical content; it has always been rejected on an ideological ground.[30] The analytical method of cognition is, thus, not fully satisfactory, even when it pertains to the physical sciences, though it may have to be tolerated in that context short of a better alternative. When, however, it is forcibly applied to the study of historically unique social phenomena, it does more harm than good. The purpose of social science is to overcome one-sided ideologies based on partial knowledge of society; social science can be objective because society, a complex of human relations, can be totally exposed.[31] If nature is a great mystery, it does not follow that society must also be. The dogma of reductionism, originating from the misconception of the nature and the purpose of social science, ties social reality to the Procrustean bed of a partisan ideology and constructs a pseudo-knowledge of society by disregarding (if not blatantly accusing) whatever fails to conform to the chosen prejudice as scientifically irrelevant. In order to be objective and rise beyond ideologies, social science must liberate itself from the tyranny of the analytical method; the only method of scientific cognition which fits the need of social science is the dialectical method. Let us, therefore, proceed to examine what this alternative method has to offer.

II. The dialectical method of Hegel

In 1817 Hegel wrote as follows:

> Newton gave physics an express warning to beware of metaphysics, it is true; but to his honour be it said, he did not by any means obey his own warning. The only mere physicists are the animals: they alone do not think: while man is a thinking being and a born metaphysician. The real question is not whether we shall apply metaphysics, but whether our metaphysics are of the right kind: in other words, whether we are not, instead of the concrete logical idea, adopting one-sided forms of thought, fixed by the understanding, and making these the basis of our theoretical as well as our practical work. [32]

According to Hegel, sensible things do not by themselves hang together in a coherent whole; only the super-sensible categories of thought can be logically interwoven in a total, self-contained system. The world of sensible objects is, therefore, irrational, illusory, and false; the world of pure thoughts or the metaphysical world is rational, real, and true. "Logic therefore coincides with Metaphysics, the science of things set and held in thoughts". [33] Man can know truth, or "the concrete logical idea", only because he "is a thinking being and a born metaphysician". To deprive man of metaphysics would therefore be to deprive him of his native intelligence, his faculty of thinking. Clearly metaphysics, as such, cannot be blamed. What Hegel criticises is the "one-sided forms of thought, fixed by the understanding", which characterised the method of "the Metaphysics of the past as it subsisted among us previous to the philosophy of Kant". [34]

By the "understanding" Hegel quite specifically means "the mode of mind which seeks precision above all things, and insists upon clear distinctions"; [35] it is the "stage of the development of mind at which it regards opposites as mutually exclusive and absolutely cut off from each other". [36] This understanding which tends to regard the categories of thought (or concepts roughly speaking) as "static, fixed, and lifeless" [37] and which therefore promotes dogmatic metaphysics is not an adequate mode of mind to deal with speculative issues. It is the power of "reason" that overcomes the one-sidedness, empty formality, and static lifelessness which the understanding imposes on cognition, thus making a comprehensible synthesis of the metaphysical world possible, the only aim of speculative philosophy. Reason's method of thinking is dialectic or the logic of synthesis.

1. The problem of idealism

Hegel does not deny that there is a world of sensible objects, i.e., a world of things external to thought. But this world, which provides mere sense-experience, cannot be objectively comprehended since the mental faculties of sensation and perception are individually subjective and, hence, not universal. Common sense and empirical sciences consequently proceed to the "picture-thinking or conception"[38] of the world consisting of isolated and finite concepts (or super-sensible objects) to which they apply certain forms of universality by drawing on the mental faculty of "understanding". Even here the knowledge is not fully objective; for, if its form is abstract and universal, its content is individually subjective.[39] "Philosophy may be said to do nothing but transform conceptions into thoughts".[40] Philosophy, in other words, uses the power of reason, the highest of the mental faculties, to construct the world of super-sensible objects which are logically related among themselves in an organic unity. It is this world of pure thoughts that constitutes the inner logic of the sensible world and that can be totally comprehended, i.e., comprehended without leaving Kant's thing-in-itself unknown. It is also this world of pure thoughts that can be objectively comprehended because pure thoughts, i.e., thoughts freed from sensuous qualities, are truly universal in that they are no longer interfered with by individual subjectivity either in form or in content.

	Existence-Reality	The Faculty of Mind	The State of Knowledge
I	Sensible world	Sensation-Perception	Sense-Experience
II	Super-sensible world (finite)	Understanding *(Verstand)*	Conception *(Vorstellung)*
III	Super-sensible world (infinite) $\equiv$	Reason *(Vernunft)* $\equiv$	Thought *(Begriff)*

Hegel characterises his own philosophy as absolute idealism, claiming that "every philosophy is essentially an idealism or at least has idealism for its principle".[41] "The idealism consists in nothing else than in recognising that the finite has no veritable being";[42] "a philosophy which ascribed veritable, ultimate absolute being to finite existence as such, would not deserve the name of philosophy".[43] This, however, does not mean that Hegel rejects the finite existence of material things prior to thought. Hence if Lenin asks "are we to proceed from things to sensation and thought?", the answer is "yes"; for Hegel does so in *Phenomenology*. But if Lenin further asks "Or are we to proceed from thought and sensation to things?"[44], the answer is also "yes"; for this is what Hegel does in *Encyclopaedia*. As Colletti has persuasively argued, it is quite incorrect to say that the first "yes" makes Hegel a materialist as the second "yes" makes him an idealist.[45] If Lenin's definition of materialism and idealism were to be believed, Marx himself would have to be split in the same way into a materialist and an idealist; for in his "descending method" or "method of inquiry" Marx proposes to move from the concrete to the abstract, and in his "ascending method" or "method of exposition" he does the reverse.[46]

Clearly, Hegel's idealism cannot be adequately represented only by such statements as "the real world is the copy of the Idea" or "the Absolute ≡ God creates the world", even though these statements do indeed dramatise some important aspects of Hegelian philosophy. What truly characterises Hegel's idealism, in my view, is the belief that "To think is in fact *ipso facto* to be free, for thought as the action of the universal is an abstract relating of self to self".[47] Hegel thus claims:

> In point of contents, thought is only true in proportion as it sinks itself in the facts; and in point of form *it is no private or particular state or act of the subject*, but rather that attitude of consciousness where the abstract self, freed from all the special limitations to which its ordinary states or qualities are liable, restricts itself to *that universal action in which it is identical with all individuals*. In these circumstances philosophy may be acquitted of the charge of pride. And when Aristotle summons the mind to rise to the dignity of that attitude, the dignity he seeks is won *by letting slip all our individual opinions and prejudices, and submitting to the sway of the fact.*[48]

In other words, thought is capable of self-abstraction or self-universalisation such that *pure* thought is no longer interfered with by subjective opinions, prejudices, etc., but becomes completely objective, having penetrated the inward truth of the object. Pure thought, divested of the individuality of the subject, the thinker, is objective because the subject has become universal so that thought itself has become inter-subjectively universal (the identity of Subject and Object in thought).[49] Having reached this state, however, thought can freely produce thought in the "abstract relating of self to self", and makes of itself a self-developing totality with increasingly concrete-logical, i.e., synthetic, specifications. This philosophical position is "idealist" because of its claim that thought can do all this *by itself*, i.e., *unassisted by any material motion.*[50] Even though Hegel does not deny the existence of matter, he would certainly deny the proposition that matter itself possesses the power of self-abstraction and self-synthesis automatically divesting itself of contingent irregularities and exhibiting itself as a rational system. *Hegel is an idealist for this reason.*[51]

Thus, if it is wanted to transform this idealism into a materialism, while preserving other properties of Hegel's philosophy, there is only one thing to do, namely, to assert that self-abstraction and the self-synthesis belong to the nature of the matter and that thought merely follows or copies the self-motion of material reality, instead of freely acting on its own. This is precisely what Marx did insofar as capitalism is the "matter". Engels, Lenin, and the whole school of dialectical materialism overlooked this crucial point completely. Even Colletti, whose devastating criticism of dialectical materialism is generally correct, does not see this point; with the belief that material reality by itself contains no contradiction, he is led to the inevitable conclusion that dialectic is inseparable from idealism.[52]

2. Dialectic or the logic of synthesis

Hegel begins with the phenomenology of the sensible world. But as consciousness, proceeding through the stages of sense, conception, and thought, "sinks into the facts" and reaches the inner truth of the world, it finds there the Christian Logos or "God as he is in his eternal essence before the creation of nature and a finite mind".[53] Logic, which "is to be understood as the system of pure reason, as the realm of pure thought"[54] is, therefore nothing but the wisdom of God, which underlies all the sensible things. In his encyclopedic system of philosophy, Hegel retraces his steps. Here, the divine wisdom or the inner logic of the world asserts itself in nature and finite mind so that the real world is shown to be fundamentally governed by the laws of God (or νοuσ). The manner in which these laws prevail upon ephemeral contingencies of the material world is sometimes described as "the cunning of reason". In the system of pure reason, however, no "cunning" is necessary, there being no contingencies to obstruct the self development of reason. The mode of this self-government of reason is dialectic.

Dialectic, in other words, is the logic of proceeding from the abstract to the concrete. But "the concrete" here does not mean a concretely sensible thing; it means instead a concretely specified, i.e., a synthetic idea. The purpose of dialectic is to totally comprehend its object of study X, i.e., to reproduce X in thought as the concrete universal or the true infinite X*. The procedure is as follows. First, X is viewed at its most general, i.e., the least specified, level of abstraction X^a. If, at this level of abstraction, X is predicated as A, this predication presupposes the opposite statement: X is non-A ($\equiv$A') such that X^a is completely described by being both A and A'. Then the relation between the two predicates A and A' must be studied. When this relation R_a (A, A') $\equiv$ A° is established, X is now viewed more concretely, i.e., at a more synthetic level of abstraction, as X^b; the same procedure repeats itself at this new level so that R_b (B, B') $\equiv$ B° gives rise to the third level of abstraction X^c. But the levels of abstraction too follows the dialectical sequence such that X^c is justified in consequence of the previously established relation R_x (X^a, X^b). The same procedure continues until no further elaboration is necessary or possible. The end-product of the dialectic X* is "the concrete logical idea" of X. Thus the form of dialectical reasoning is schematically shown as follows.

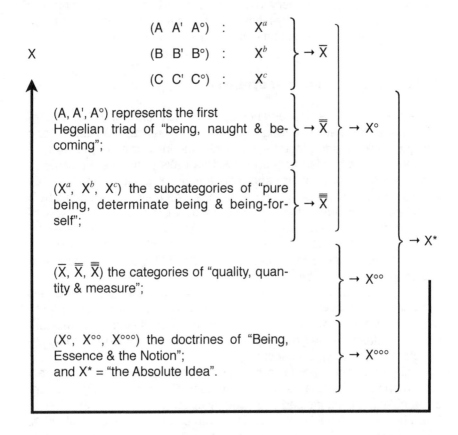

$$(A\ A'\ A°)\ :\quad X^a$$
$$X \qquad (B\ B'\ B°)\ :\quad X^b \quad \Big\} \to \overline{X}$$
$$(C\ C'\ C°)\ :\quad X^c$$

(A, A', A°) represents the first Hegelian triad of "being, naught & becoming"; $\to \overline{X}$ $\to X°$

(X^a, X^b, X^c) the subcategories of "pure being, determinate being & being-for-self"; $\to \overline{\overline{X}}$

($\overline{X}$, $\overline{\overline{X}}$, $\overline{\overline{\overline{X}}}$) the categories of "quality, quantity & measure"; $\to X°°$ $\to X*$

(X°, X°°, X°°°) the doctrines of "Being, Essence & the Notion"; and X* = "the Absolute Idea". $\to X°°°$

It is often wondered whether or not this method of dialectical reasoning contravenes the law of contradiction (in formal logic), since the mutual exclusiveness of A and A' is also called a dialectical contradiction. My belief is that dialectic does not offend the law of contradiction because the word "contradiction" in dialectic does not mean the same thing as in formal logic. For example, the law of contradiction prohibits such a statement as "Mr. Jones is a husband" to be both true and false. This is perfectly reasonable; for if he were simultaneously the husband of a woman (A) and not her husband ($\bar{A}'$), the predicate "being a husband" gives us no meaningful information at all. Dialectic, however, never claims that A and $\bar{A}'$ are simultaneously true. It merely says that if Mr. Jones is a husband, that does not prevent him from being a son, a father, an uncle, a brother, a cousin, etc., of someone other than his wife. It certainly does not offend the law of contradiction, therefore, to say that "Mr. Jones is a husband" (A) and, simultaneously that "he is something other than a husband" (A'). If this "something" includes all the properties of Mr. Jones other than, but at the same level of abstraction as (e.g., so far as his family relationships are concerned) being a husband, then the dialectic says that A and A' "contradict". But this contradiction in effect boils down to dividing the persons related to Mr. Jones into the two groups: his wife and the rest. The meaningfulness of such a partition depends on whether or not the wife (A) and the rest of Jones' family (A') are so related R (A, A') as to specify Mr. Jones more concretely and, hence, to let the idea of his person rise to a new level of abstraction (X^b). For example, if his wife and the rest of his family are on unfriendly terms, the first proposition at level X^b may become: "Mr. Jones is a worried husband" (B).

As we proceed in this way, the concept of "Mr. Jones as a husband" becomes more and more concretely informative even if we may never have an occasion to meet him in person. If, on the other hand, the dialectical procedure is not followed, the single statement that "he is a husband" (A) gives us only the trivial information that Mr. Jones is married like many other persons, and no more. Since there are millions of other married men, Mr. Jones very soon disappears from our memory into the archives of census data. Formal logic, or the method of the "understanding", with its law of contradiction, destroys the identity of Mr. Jones by merely letting him belong to the abstract-universal category of "being a husband" i.e., by merely classifying him as "married". Dialectic, or the method of reason, does precisely the opposite; it tells us everything we want to know about Mr. Jones by elaborating what he is step by step in an increasingly concrete-universal idea of his person. An important question, however, arises. How long should the dialectical process of reasoning continue before Mr. Jones is completely known? Where should the dialectic begin, and where should it end?

These questions cannot be answered formally without regard to the content of the subject-matter X. For example, if X is "Mr. Jones who divorced his wife", then the corresponding logical system X* must explain all circumstances that led up to his divorce. In the case of Hegel, X was the collection of all metaphysical ideas occurring in the history of philosophy up to his time,[55] and the corresponding X* was his *Logic*. Given that "philosophy advances nothing new", its business being "only to bring into explicit consciousness what the world in all ages has believed about thought",[56] Hegel had before him all the categories (at least the important ones) ready to be assembled together. His task was to arrange these categories from the simple to the synthetic, beginning with "pure being" and ending with "the absolute idea", in such a way that one idea leads to another in the dialectical sequence. What Hegel accomplished was, in other words, little more than a grand jig-saw puzzle of already known ideas. It should be remarked that these metaphysical ideas were strictly super-sensible objects even if they may have originated in the sensible world. Their synthesis therefore depended only on the "abstract relating of self to self" in thought and did not in any sense parallel the synthesis or genesis of materially sensible objects. If Hegel occasionally resorted to a pictorial illustration in terms of sensible things, he only violated his own principle in the heuristic vein. The problem would not have been so simple had X been other than the collection of metaphysical ideas sharply separated from the sensible objects. Had X been a collection of scientific categories the synthesis of ideas could not have been independent of the synthesis of different matters.

3. The theory is grey

If X is a collection of scientific categories with material objects or relations as their counterparts in the sensible world, the problem which Hegel's absolute idealism so tactfully circumvented can no longer be ignored. The abstraction and the synthesis must be confirmed "not only in theory but in reality",[57] where theory and reality respectively refer to thought and sensible things. This is the problem of facing the materialistic dialectic. The reason why the Engels-Lenin version of dialectical materialism has failed to solve this problem is this, that it places no restriction on the object of cognition, X. In their naïve enthusiasm dialectical materialists, indeed, want to outdo Hegel by claiming that the whole material world X is governed by some immutable laws (material νουσ) without realising that, in doing so, they only make themselves mystics, i.e., idealists worse than Hegel. Since the material world fundamentally consists of nature, man and society, as parts of natural history, dialectical materialists first undertake to build "the dialectic of nature" before specialised attention is given to historical materialism and political economy. But Engels' own unfinished work [58] shows that the dialectic of nature is an impossible proposition.

In 1873, when Engels began to work on the theoretical synthesis of nature, he may have vaguely felt that "science advances nothing new" apart from irrelevant details, and that at least the basic outline of the scientific view of nature had already been given by the path-breaking discoveries of the nineteenth century. Had this been the case, all the scientific categories of nature would have been available for Engels to assemble in a dialectical system. But in the early 1880s, when he ceased to work further on this theme, it must have become obvious to him that the contemporary scientific profession did not regard its knowledge of nature as nearly final. The so-called crisis of physics was already looming up on the horizon. All the scientific categories then available to Engels were quite plainly tentative, ready to be overthrown with the discovery of new evidence. How could nature be totally known if its knowledge was only "relative", i.e., dependent on so-far-so-good hypotheses and conjectures? The fundamental question that had to be settled before undertaking a dialectical synthesis of nature was why the knowledge of nature was incomplete and would always remain incomplete.

The answer to this important question is contained in Hegel's celebrated metaphor that "the owl of Minerva spreads its wings only with the falling of the dusk". These cryptic words are preceded by the following explanation:

> One word more about giving instruction as to what the world ought to be. Philosophy in any case always comes on the scene too late to give it. As the thought of the world, it appears only when actuality is already there cut and dried after its process of formation has been completed. The teaching of the concept, which is also history's inescapable lesson, is that it is only when actuality is mature that the ideal first appears over against the real and that the ideal apprehends this same real world in its substance and builds it up for itself into the shape of an intellectual realm. When philosophy paints its grey in grey, then has the shape of life grown old. By philosophy's grey in grey it cannot be rejuvenated but only understood. [59]

Precisely what Hegel means by the "world" or "the shape of life" here may not be clear, but there is little doubt that he vaguely refers to the object of cognition, X, by these terms. Thus, his message is as follows: Only when X "is grey", "has grown old", "has completed its process of formation", and "can no longer be rejuvenated", is it possible at all to obtain its concrete-logical synthesis, X*. The fact, as Hegel regarded it, that "philosophy advances nothing new" signifies that the metaphysical conception of the world *(Weltanschauung)* has reached a certain stage of maturity in the human mind, which is to say that God has by now revealed his wisdom to men almost completely. That is why Hegel was capable of constructing his system of metaphysical philosophy. But the scientific conception of nature is an altogether different thing from the metaphysical or religious conception of the world. The age of (empirical) sciences had just begun, when the age of theology and metaphysics was nearing its end.

It is therefore not surprising that the scientific conception, X, cannot so easily be systematised as the absolute knowledge X* of nature. The question is whether it ever will be. The scientific conception of nature cannot become "grey", unless nature itself becomes old, whatever this might mean. Even if nature is an evolutionary and historical process it is certainly not clear whether nature as a whole has any tendency at all to approximate its own ideal image. But if nature does not abstract itself, it does not logically synthesise itself either. A dialectical and, hence, total comprehension of nature is, in that case, impossible. This explains why Engels, or anyone else for that matter, has never succeeded in completing a dialectical system of nature, the "petrified intelligence", as Schelling called it. The impossibility of the dialectic of nature, however, does not imply the impossibility of materialistic dialectic itself. Whether the latter is possible or not depends on whether or not there exists a collection of material objects or relations, X, which actually possesses the powers of self-abstraction and self-synthesis. Marx identified at least one such X in the historical institution of capitalism.

Just as Hegel was a most accomplished historian of metaphysical thought, so was Marx of economic thought. When Marx wrote *Capital* in the 1860s not only had capitalism grown mature and grey, having "completed its process of formation", but political economy too had by that time generated most of the essential categories necessary to build a theoretical capitalist society. Not only in reality, but also in theory, the abstract synthesis of the capitalist mode of production was in the process of making. "Marx therefore worked at the right time", as Uno used to say, on the dialectic of capital. To Marx's mind, there was little doubt that the collection, X, of material relations that constitute capitalism could be dialectically synthesised "in their pure form",[60] as X*, since capitalist relations were becoming increasingly definite, divesting themselves of the remnants of pre-capitalist relations with the development of the capitalist method of production. Marx did not merely copy capitalism as it was; he also copied capitalism's own method of self-abstraction and synthesis. In this way Marx extracted "the rational kernel" of dialectic from "the mystical shell" of Hegelian metaphysics.

III. The dialectical method of social science

To say that only capitalism, an historically very particular society, possesses the powers of self-abstraction and self-synthesis and, hence, can be dialectically comprehended might appear to restrict the scope of materialistic dialectic much too narrowly. It may perhaps be disappointing that dialectic, which in Hegel's hand could explain every conceivable thing in the universe, should be reduced to as modest a rôle as the logic of theoretically describing capitalism, when "turned right side up". What is the use of materialistic dialectic, one may ask, if it cannot explain nature, history, and the whole material world? Marxist philosophers, who habitually talk of grand designs in an obscure language, may be exasperated by the suggestion that the only possible materialistic dialectic is the dialectic of capital, as the theory of a purely capitalist society. A closer examination, however, shows that the knowledge of society does not need any other "pure theory".

A purely capitalist society, as I shall presently explain, is a global commodity-economy in which all social relations appear necessarily as relations between commodities. In other words, social relations between men are completely reified and impersonalised in a purely capitalist society. But social relations which are not impersonalised cannot be deemed objective, or at least not "universal" in Hegel's sense of "identical with all individuals"; indeed, a "personal" social relation is a contradiction in terms. Hence capitalist society, which possesses the inherent and automatic tendency to reify basic human relations, is not just as any other society, from the point of view of the knowledge of society. Capitalist society, in which the relations between men tend to appear transparently in purer forms, i.e., increasingly divested of idiosyncrasies, arbitrary discretions, chance or habits, holds the mirror up to all other societies. That is to say, an objective knowledge of society would not be possible unless socio-economic relations were fully exposed for the first time in the context of a purely capitalist society. This important conclusion is indirectly borne out by the fact that a feudal society, though itself an historically unique institution, does not reify human relations and, hence, not develop social science in a systematic fashion. Feudal laws prescribe how human relations *ought to be* precisely because these relations do not evolve by themselves. If "the anatomy of man is a key to the anatomy of the ape"[61], so is, the comprehension of capitalist society to the comprehension of feudal and other societies.

1. The inner logic of capitalism

"Bourgeois society is the most advanced and complex historical organisation of production. The categories which express its relations, and an understanding of its structure, therefore, provide an insight into the structure and the relations of production of all formerly existing social formations".[62] This well-known thesis of Marx has never been seriously disputed. But Marx here makes an important error of omission. "Bourgeois economy provides a key to the economy of antiquity, etc.",[63] not simply because "bourgeois society is the most advanced and complex historical organisation of production" whatever "the most advanced and complex" is supposed to mean. Bourgeois or capitalist society organises its real economic life, with the principles of the commodity-economy; real economic life which is common to all societies, therefore, appears in reified and objectified forms only in commodity-economic bourgeois society. Marx was certainly not unaware of this fact (which he elsewhere referred to as the contradiction between use-value and value),[64] but his failure to constantly articulate its significance as exemplified in the above-quoted passage, has left some methodological ambiguities in his political economy. Uno's theoretical contribution lies fundamentally in removing such ambiguities from the system of *Capital* and restating the dialectic of capital as the theory of a purely capitalist society.

The theoretical concept of a purely capitalist society, i.e., a society in which real economic life is entirely governed by commodity-economic, and, hence, objective principles occupies in Uno's political economy, the same position as the *Logic* occupies in Hegel's philosophical system. In other words, a purely capitalist society is the theoretically synthesised concrete-universal, or the inner logic, of capitalism, X^*, to be set against the concrete-empirical totality of an historical capitalism, X. The significance of this parallel cannot be underestimated. According to Hegel, non-metaphysical thoughts, i.e., thoughts which are not yet "pure", retaining some sensuous connotations cannot be objective, and, hence, cannot form a dialectical system. In political economy, the "pureness" or the objectivity of social relations is proportional to the degree of reification in just the same way as the purity of thoughts in philosophy is proportional to the degree of non-sensuousness. Thus, for example, the direct exploitation of a serf by the lord is not a fully objective (i.e., pure) social relation because this form of master-servant relationship involves no tendency to be reified,[65] but the exploitation of wage-labour by the capitalist can be objective (or pure) because the rate of surplus value automatically tends to become uniform throughout the economy. The dialectic of capital is, therefore, possible on the ground of the reifying force that is inherent in the working of a commodity-economy.

Uno's *Principles of Political Economy* treats the theory of a purely capitalist society in the three doctrines of circulation, production and distribution in just the same way as Hegel expounds his *Logic* in the three doctrines of being, essence, and the notion. In both cases, the first doctrine studies the mode of existence (or operating principles) of the object of study without reference to its substantive content; the second doctrine shows the way in which the inner content of the object of study is subsumed by, and is consistently reflected in, its existential mode; the third doctrine exhibits that the object of study is capable of developing by itself once the consistency of its mode of existence and its substantive content is guaranteed. In the first doctrine, the logic of *transition* (or of passing-over from one form to another) determines or specifies the object of study externally; in the second doctrine, the logic of *reflection* (or of dependency) shows how the object of study can contain the ground or foundation of its existence within itself; and in the third doctrine the logic of *development* (or of self-fulfilment) lets the object of study unfold its working mechanism in an ideal environment. Thus, if the object of study is a purely capitalist society, as in Uno's dialectic of capital, the first doctrine of circulation studies the reifying properties of a commodity-economy as such without explicit reference to the general norms of economic life; the second doctrine of production examines how the real economic life, common to all societies, may be governed by commodity-economic principles so as to assure the self-dependency and self-containedness of the capitalist mode of production; the third doctrine of distribution shows how the capitalist mode of production develops and regulates its own market so as to produce all use-values that are socially needed in a manner that is most satisfactory to the self-adopted aim of capital.

This method of dialectical exposition conforms well to the nature of capitalism itself. Essentially, capitalism is a system of organising production as individual merchant activities. Commodity-trade never develops within a family or a self-subsistent tribal community; goods exchanged with aliens are the first to become commodities. Hence, commodities always imply external relations. The expansion of commodity exchanges not only increases contact with aliens but disintegrates the existing community into individual trading units. The distinction between external and internal trade becomes irrelevant so long as the same money is used to mediate commodity exchanges since any trade is external to trading units. Capitalists, who originally are merchant middlemen profiting from arbitrage, tend to unify a trading market, undermining the self-sufficiency of traditional economic communities. The historical evolution of commerce which generates commodities, money, and capital, agrees with the modal specifications of a fully developed capitalism 1) as the collection of commodities, 2) as a monetary exchange economy, and 3) as the unity of the chrematistic operations of capital, in the doctrine of circulation. The Hegelian triad of quality, quantity, and measure is here translated into the expressions of value by commodities, the functions of money as the value-reflecting object, and the operations of capital as value in motion. It is significant that, not only in theory, which here follows the logic of *transition*, but also in actual history the operating mode of capitalism (commodity exchanges) must precede capitalist production itself.

Although the development of commerce always undermines the integrity of the traditional mode of production, the latter never gives way to capitalism until labour-power itself is commoditised. The commoditisation of labour-power, which requires the extra-economic force of primitive accumulation, does not automatically follow the development of commodity exchanges and simple commodity production. Once labour-power is made available as a commodity, however, the chrematistic operation of capital can take possession of the labour-and-production process, which forms the material foundation or the inner substance of all societies. Only then does capitalism arise as a global commodity-economy in which all goods are produced as commodities by means of commodities. In the doctrine of production the consistency of the commodity-economic principles and the general norms of economic life is demonstrated by the logic of *reflection* which is timeless and, hence, does not, in general, reproduce the historical development of capitalism. The Hegelian triad of the ground, appearance, and actuality is now translated into the following propositions of the dialectic of capital: 1) capitalist production secures itself on the basis of the worker-versus-capitalist production relation; 2) industrial capital circulates indefinitely and without interruption while avoiding all unnecessary waste of resources; and 3) capitalist society reproduces itself on an expanding scale supplying basic and non-basic goods in an appropriate proportion, while alternating between the widening and the deepening phases of capital accumulation.

The ability of industrial capital to periodically innovate its productive technology so as to assure the availability of labour-power as a commodity makes capitalist society an historically viable society, i.e., a self-dependent system that Hegel calls "actuality". Capitalism, as the commodity-economy which completely engulfs within itself the substance of economic life, is thus securely established. It is on the basis of this knowledge that the dialectic of capital proceeds to the doctrine of distribution in which the capitalist-rational method of sharing already produced surplus value is explained. Here the logic of *development* only makes explicit what is already implicit in the nature of capital. The Hegelian triad of the subjective notion, the objective notion, and the Idea can now be translated into the following propositions of the dialectic of capital: 1) specialised units of industrial capital producing different use-values determine equilibrium prices in the capitalist market so as to divide surplus value among themselves in the form of average profits; 2) part of surplus value must be ceded as rent to private landed property, not only to guarantee the principle of equal opportunity to all units of capital, but also to ensure capital's access to land in general; and 3) in order to save unproductive costs of circulation, capitalist society develops banking and commerce as specialised capitalist operations, but the consequent division of average profit into interest and entrepreneurial profit "externalises the relations of capital" so that even capital itself can, in principle, be converted into a commodity.[66]

With its conversion into a commodity, capital returns to where it originated, completing its dialectical circle; a "commodity", in other words, is the simplest logical category (or the abstract-universal) which anticipates the genesis of capital and also the most synthetic logical category (or the concrete-universal) in which capital finds its ultimate expression.[67] A purely capitalist society, which constitutes the inner logic of capitalism, is thus completely exposed, without leaving a thing-in-itself unknown, as a self-generating and self-concluding totality, i.e., as the dialectic of capital. The dialectic of capital, therefore, means the self-explaining logic of capital, the latter being both the object and the subject. At this point the exact correspondence between the dialectic of capital and Hegel's *Logic* can scarcely be doubted; Hegel and Uno use exactly the same dialectical method of total comprehension except that the subject-object is different. If Hegel's subject-object was "reason", Uno's is "capital".

2. The cunning of capital

Uno did not arrive at this remarkable correspondence by studying Hegel's philosophy, in which he never claimed an expertise, but rather by developing what makes good economic sense in Marx's *Capital*. Since, however, Uno's logic coincided with economic theory in exactly the sense in which Hegel's logic coincided with metaphysics, Uno was able to complete the dialectic of capital more systematically than Marx, without, in the least, trying to "coquet the modes of expression peculiar to Hegel".[68]

The economic theory of capitalism does not permit arbitrary or mechanical abstractions but only such abstractions as the development of capitalism itself warrants. For example, the abstraction that the rate of surplus value is uniform throughout the capitalist economy is justifiable because, if it is not so at present, a further development of capitalism is expected to eliminate individual differences that still remain. But the abstraction that the value composition of capital should be equal over all industries is not, in general, permissible because no amount of capitalist development can conceivably eliminate technical differences in the production of different use-values.[69] Similarly, the abstraction that labour is simple and homogeneous is justifiable on the ground that the development of the capitalist method of production tends to mechanise the labour-process, enabling almost any commodity to be produced with simplified and unskilled labour. It is, however, not warranted to assert that the technique of producing a given use-value must always be unique because the development of capitalism does not, for example, remove differences in the natural conditions of production so that the same commodity may have to be produced with different combinations of productive elements.[70] If, by strictly following the self-abstracting process of capitalism itself, economic theory constructs the system of a purely capitalist society, this system cannot be a mere figment of the imagination but must be "a product of the thinking intellect which assimilates the world in the only way open to it".[71]

The self-contained theoretical system of a purely capitalist society, in other words, is the product of copying the factual tendency of capitalism to increasingly purify itself. Without this tendency there would be no such theoretical construct; for economic theory cannot be constructed without presupposing the limit of this tendency as a self-contained, and, hence, a permanently self-repeating, system. The classical economists justified this methodological presupposition by claiming that the perfection of capitalism was the ultimate goal of human civilisation. Marx instead viewed capitalism to be a historically transient institution but believed that a purely capitalist society, which works as if it were a self-perpetuating system, would in fact materialise in history before breaking up. Of course, Marx made significant scientific progress by regarding capitalism as an historical entity, but his conviction that a purely capitalist society would be factually realised was contradicted by the subsequent development of capitalism.

Although economic theory must always "extrapolate" the tendency for capitalism by itself to become purer (which was real enough) and envisage a purely capitalist society, it is not correct to believe that such a theoretical society should in fact come into existence at any moment in history. Marx, who did not have a chance to observe the full evolution of capitalism in its imperialist stage, did not clearly realise this problem and treated in *Capital* the following three things as if they needed no differentiation at all. These three things are: the theory of a purely capitalist society, capitalism in its liberal stage of world-historic development, and the economic history of England up to the middle of the nineteenth century. Marx's failure to differentiate these three levels of economic study left his dialectic of capital incomplete; the relation between the inner laws of capitalism and their external manifestation was never explicitly shown. As Uno states in the introduction to *Principles of Political Economy*, however, the problem of Revisionism cannot be overcome unless this crucial relation is satisfactorily established.

The theoretical construct of a purely capitalist society presupposes that real economic life is *wholly* organised by the principles of a commodity-economy. But real economic life capable of being completely engulfed and governed by the reifying force of a commodity-economy is a theoretical abstraction which can only be approximated in reality.[72] Even in mid-nineteenth-century England, in which capitalism most closely approximated its theoretical image, a considerable part of real economic life remained outside the commodity-economic management and thus incapable of being fully reified. If capitalism tended to eliminate such non-commodity-economic elements during the period 1848-1870, it was because the development of productive technology historically supported that tendency in that period. But the autonomous development of technology does not always play into the hands of the commodity-economy. If the first industrial revolution of the late eighteenth to the early nineteenth century produced such technology as most fitted commodity-economic exploitation, the second industrial revolution in the 1870s and 1880s, highlighted by the adoption of new steel-making techniques, did not so easily conform to the commodity-economic design.[73]

Generally speaking, an industrial economy whose output is standardised and is not directly affected by changes in natural conditions can be more easily managed capitalistically than an agricultural economy. But even a predominantly industrial economy can be at different stages of technological development and be more or less difficult to operate as a commodity-economy. The light industries of mid-nineteenth-century England centering around the mechanised production of cotton goods provided an almost ideal technological base for industrial capitalism. The handicraft manufactures prior to the Industrial Revolution, however, required the ascendancy of merchant capitalism over industrial capitalism, as the steel-based heavy industries in late nineteenth-century Europe needed the corporate system or the financial control of production to be capitalistically operated. Capitalism in history approximates its theoretical image of a purely capitalist society only to the extent that the technological characteristics of real economic life conform to the reifying force of a commodity-economy. Thus, it is warranted to distinguish the three typical stages of capitalist development (the mercantilist, the liberal, and the imperialist stages) on the ground of the distinct technological peculiarities of real economic life to be subsumed under the commodity-economic principles in each of these stages.[74]

After referring to "the infinite wealth and variety of forms and, what is most irrational, the contingency which enters into the external arrangement of natural things", Hegel declares that "this impotence of Nature (to strictly adhere to the Notion) sets limits to philosophy" and that "it is improper to expect the Notion to comprehend these contingent products of Nature".[75] In other words, Nature is not wholly, i.e., in every detail, governed by the Notion since there are contingent factors that escape from the dictate of reason. Hegel further continues:

> Nature everywhere blurs the essential limits of species and genera by intermediate and defective forms, which continually furnish counter examples to every fixed distinction. [Even within the genus of man, for example, monstrous births occur.] In order to consider such forms as defective, imperfect and deformed, one must presuppose a fixed, invariable type. This type, however, cannot be furnished by experience, for it is experience which also presents these so-called monstrosities, deformities, intermediate products, etc. The fixed type rather presupposes the self-subsistence and dignity of the determination stemming from the Notion.[76]

In other words, "man" in nature is not a logical category; it is a "fixed type".[77] This type cannot be obtained from empirical observations, which always include exceptions and degenerate cases; it can only be justified as a specific mode of the external manifestation of the Notion.

One merely has to substitute "the world-historic stages of capitalist development" for "Nature" and "the logic of a purely capitalist society" for "the Notion" in order to translate Hegel's philosophical language into the language of political economy. It is indeed improper to expect economic theory to comprehend the "contingent products" of historical capitalism; the stages of capitalist development, as "the external arrangements of historical things", cannot be fully explained by the dialectic of capital alone because the reifying force of a commodity-economy cannot by itself determine the technological peculiarities of real economic life which shape the stages of capitalism in history. Its "impotence" to strictly adhere to the logic of a purely capitalist society sets limits to economic theory. The stage-characteristics of capitalist development, in other words, must not be directly inferred from the logical categories of economic theory; these characteristics form a "type" which mediates economic theory and historical contingencies of capitalism. Thus, according to Uno, the three stages of capitalist development (mercantilist, liberal, and imperialist) are typified by the mode of accumulation of the three dominant forms of capital (respectively merchant capital, industrial capital, and finance-capital).

In one of the so-called "plans" Marx sketched the proposed scope of political economy as follows:

> The disposition of material has evidently to be made in this way: (1) General abstract definitions, which ... appertain in some measure to all social formations ... (2) The categories which constitute the internal structure of bourgeois society and on which the principal classes are based. Capital, wage-labour, landed property and their relation to one another. Town and country. The three social classes; exchange between them. Circulation. The (private) credit system. (3) The State as the epitome of bourgeois society. Analysis of its relation to itself. The "unproductive" classes. Taxes. National debts. Public credit. Population. Colonies. Emigration. (4) International conditions of production. International division of labour. International exchange. Export and import. Rate of exchange. (5) World markets and crises.[78]

It is not clear what exactly Marx meant by (1) and (5). But something like a formulation of historical materialism may have been meant for (1), and economic history of capitalism with particular attention to "world markets and crises" for (5). Then the remainder consists of: (2) the inner logic of bourgeois society, (3) public finance and national economic policies, and (4) international economic relations. But the content of *Capital* corresponds roughly to (2) only, and omits any systematic discussion of (3) and (4). Thus, the question is asked whether or not a self-contained dialectic of capital is possible without incorporating the materials of (3) and (4). Some Marxists insist that the three volumes of *Capital* do not conclude Marx's economic theory in view of the omission of (3) and (4).

It is, however, an easy matter to show that the pure dialectic of capital cannot contain the materials of (3) and (4) without negating its own significance. If indeed capitalism is a system which "internalises" the commodity-exchange relations, the relations that originally arose outside of a self-sufficient economic community,[79] a fully developed capitalist society cannot distinguish between external (foreign) and internal (domestic) trade. Otherwise, a fully developed capitalist society would have to consist of at least two economic communities of which external trade relations are not yet completely assimilated to each of the two constituent communities. If that were the case, neither of these communities, nor their union, could be properly described as a "fully developed" capitalist society. Hence, it involves a contradiction to say, on the one hand, that a purely capitalist society is capitalistically fully developed, and, on the other hand, that foreign trade and domestic trade must be distinguished in a purely capitalist society. But, if there is no national boundary in a purely capitalist society, there cannot be a state and its public finance either. The state, clearly, is an institution alien to capital. The whole purpose of the dialectic of capital is precisely to show that capital can by itself constitute historical society without depending on alien principles. Hence follows the conclusion that the dialectic of capital cannot achieve a self-contained logical synthesis without leaving aside public finance and economic policies (3) as well as foreign trade distinct from domestic trade (4).

This, of course, does not mean that a capitalist nation has ever actually existed without foreign trade and public finance. Their obvious presence simply confirms our proposition that a purely capitalist society *per se* is never, in fact, realised in history and that capitalism in history always leaves part of real economic life uncommoditised. When that part is minimal, the policies of laissez-faire and cheap government render the state and its national boundary almost negligible.[80] But, if that part is substantial, more active economic policies are called for to clear the ground and to consolidate the external conditions for the self-propelled motion of the commodity-economy; a nation-state is clearly needed to carry out these policies. It is, therefore, not at all surprising that the three distinct types of economic policies of the leading capitalist state in the mercantilist, the liberal, and the imperialist era most obviously characterise the three stages of capitalism in its world-historic development. Thus, if for technological reasons, real economic life cannot be wholly contained in the commodity-economy, capitalism requires national states to pursue economic policies such as to ensure the maximum efficiency of society's commodity-economic management. The way in which capitalism makes use of the bourgeois state, an institution alien to capital,[81] and consolidates the external conditions for the best working of the commodity-economy may be referred to as "the cunning of capital" in imitation of the well known expression "the cunning of reason" in Hegel's philosophy of history.

3. The knowledge of society

If, in each stage of capitalist development, part of economic life always remains uncommoditised, that certainly does not diminish the supremacy of capital, so long as labour-power is still available as a commodity. The dominant form of capital in each stage controls the core of society's real economy, historically characterised by a particular technology, and shapes economic policies of the state such as to ensure a maximum efficiency for capitalist commodity-production. The national state in which these policies are practised in the most typical manner and in which the capitalist organisation of production is therefore most successful constitutes the centre of capitalism in its world-historic development. The concept of the stage, roughly speaking, corresponds to the economic aspect of the centre-state which would be unchanged if transplanted to other countries. The centre-state and the international economic relations surrounding it form a type specific to the stage of capitalist development.

In the periphery of the capitalist orbit, however, there may exist countries or regions in which the commoditisation of labour-power is not secured. These areas cannot be described as capitalist even though they, in fact, maintain active trade relations with the centre of capitalism. Economic development generally tends to establish capitalism even in these areas, unless obstructed by extra-economic forces, working either inside or outside of them.[82] From this, it is sometimes adduced that the existence of capitalism depends on non-capitalist regions in its periphery.[83] This questionable thesis, originally propounded by Rosa Luxemburg, puts the cart before the horse. Capitalism, though logically self-dependent once labour-power is commoditised, always tolerates alien elements, tending however to assimilate them if necessary. Capital creates for itself the required form of landed property, the state, peripheral regions, etc., so as to make them "suit" the capitalist mode of production.[84]

If the non-capitalist part of economic life remains, whether in the centre-state or on a more extended scale in the periphery, that part of economic life does not reify itself of its own accord. Economic history, therefore, cannot objectively describe the socio-economic relations subsisting in that part unless they are studied in the light of the corresponding relations in the reified part of the world economy. For example, in the post-liberal era pre-capitalist peasant agriculture does not necessarily disintegrate, even with the development of capitalism, so that peasants constitute an important social class, whose economic position cannot be directly accounted for by the laws of capitalism. If economic history merely collected concrete-empirical data concerning the living conditions of the peasants and imposed some conclusions based on arbitrary value judgements, it would hardly be a scientific enterprise. Economic history, in order to be objective, must show how peasant agriculture differs from capitalist agriculture[85] and explain to what extent that difference may be due to the *modus operandi* of the dominant form of capital that characterises the stage of capitalist development, and to what extent it is attributable to purely geographical, traditional, and other contingent factors. Similarly, the question of colonies during the imperialist era cannot be objectively studied except in their relation to the mother country, the world market, and the mode of accumulation of finance-capital, which characterise the world-historic development of capitalism in its imperialist stage.

The same considerations apply to the study of pre-capitalist economic life, which fails to exhibit itself objectively in a reified form. Economic historians, however, can probe into the production-relations of pre-capitalist societies, if enlightened by the knowledge of reified production-relations that form themselves under capitalism. Hence follows Uno's conclusion that historical materialism cannot be directly confirmed *in toto*. It is, for instance, impossible to claim that the economic substructure determines the ideological superstructure of any society unless there is such thing as the substructure separable from the superstructure as in capitalist society. It is not reasonable to conjecture that production-relations always depend on the level of development of productive powers except after the conversion of labour-power into a commodity (upon which capitalism hinges) is shown to require a certain range of productive technology. Nor is it meaningful to claim that a class society should be characterised by the specific manner in which surplus labour is appropriated, unless the capitalist method of appropriating surplus labour in the form of surplus value is first explicitly shown.

Historical materialism, in other words, is a fundamental hypothesis in the study of precapitalist societies in view of the objective social relations which are exposed for the first time in capitalist society. Historical materialism, a hypothesis, is grounded on the science of political economy; not the other way around. Another way of saying the same thing is that social science is impossible prior to the historical experience of capitalism. But, even under capitalism, the objective social relations that constitute it do not appear directly; they appear always as an historical type, mediated by the state, which, as the agent of economic policies, forms the vital link between the substructure and the superstructure of capitalist society. The relations between political economy and the other social sciences must be understood against this background. Through political processes the state legislates and enforces laws that organise the socio-cultural life of men; but the capitalist state is an institution that brings the inner laws of capitalism into observable action.[86] Political science, jurisprudence, and sociology accordingly develop as studies of the different aspects of the capitalist state, the foundation of which is given by political economy. All social sciences can, therefore, be integrated in the study of capitalist society. Other societies, even in their non-economic aspects, can be scientifically accounted for only in the light of an integrated knowledge of capitalist society.[87]

With respect to capitalist society, in which human relations reify themselves, social science can form an integrated system rather than a collection of fragmentary and practical lessons, because the political economy of capitalism possesses objective laws. The study of capitalist society requires political economy to adopt the three-level approach consisting of i) the theory of a purely capitalist society, ii) the characterisation of the three developmental stages as types, and iii) the empirical investigations of economic history. In this approach "theory", "policy", and "history", into which political economy is ordinarily trichotomised, are systematically related rather than merely paralleled. Political economy, however, is on its own only in pure theory; stage-characteristic economic policies cannot be studied without regard for such concrete economic institutions as the financial system, foreign trade, public finance, etc., which directly involve political, juridical, and sociological considerations. The fact that these concrete economic institutions form different types in the three stages of capitalist development suggests that the political, juridical, and sociological processes reflecting themselves in those economic institutions are also stage-typical. It follows that the political science, jurisprudence, and sociology of capitalism, which ignore the three stages of capitalist development, lose contact with political economy and soon degenerate into an ideological doctrines built on empty generalisations, or into sets of practical rules-of-thumb applicable only to certain clinical cases under capitalism.

The systematic knowledge of capitalist society, which also throws light on the understanding of other societies, does not, however, make predictions.[88] The knowledge is systematic because it is "grey"; social science claims objective knowledge because "the prehistory of human society" ends with capitalism.[89] Social science, therefore, cannot be said to be an empirical science in the same sense as natural science is an empirical science; social science does not offer testable hypotheses. Social science should rather be called historico-empirical because its "empiricism" consists only in its unquestioned acceptance of the experience of history (no one denies capitalism, for instance, as historical experience). Hence, the method of social science necessarily differs from the method of natural science, which does not expose the inner laws of nature *in toto*. Since nature cannot be totally known, natural science only teaches how to predict, and how to conform to, the blind forces of nature on the basis of its partial knowledge. A question such as reforming nature or creating a new natural order has never even been posed. But, if conformity to nature is ideologically neutral, conformity to the existing social order cannot be.[90] Popper's call for "piecemeal social engineering"[91], rather than a wholesale social reform, merely amounts to an indirect admission of reactionary conformism, which Popper rationalises by the questionable dogma of reductionism. It is, therefore, strange that even a philosopher as clear-headed as Colletti, unable to overcome the reductionist aberration, has felt compelled to opt for Popperian "neo-positivism" rather than the "spiritual idealism" that dominates today's Continental European philosophy. Colletti clearly does not know the third alternative offered by Uno.[92]

Without this third alternative, however, which grounds historical materialism on the science of political economy, the significance of socialism would not be understood. According to Engels, socialism is "the ascent of man from the kingdom of necessity to the kingdom of freedom". His explanation is as follows:

> Man's own social organisation, hitherto confronting him as a necessity imposed by nature and history, now becomes the result of his own free action. The extraneous objective forces that have hitherto governed history pass under the control of man himself. Only from that time will man himself, with full consciousness, make his own history - only from that time will the social causes set in movement by him have, in the main and in a constantly growing measure, the results intended by him.[93]

Although the broad outlines are correctly drawn, this explanation contains a few ambiguities. For example, it is not obvious what Engels means by "the extraneous objective forces that have hitherto governed history"; it is much too vague to talk, for example, of capitalism merely "as a necessity imposed by nature and history". Hence, the significance of "man himself making his own history" remains quite obscure. It would be a mistake not to recognise that capitalism too accomplished an important freedom; capitalism freed real economic life from extra-economic coercions. In fact, the only fundamental non-freedom that capitalism still retains is the necessity or compulsion of managing society's real economic life under the commodity-economic principles.[94] It is for this reason that every "piecemeal social engineering" or "policy prescription" under capitalism works only as a catalyst of the cunning of capital. Man is not free under capitalism because he cannot act against its inner laws of motion; he is forced to conform and comply to the sway of capital so long as he inhabits the capitalist "kingdom of necessity".

With this irrevocable conclusion political economy points to the unspoken alternative: the socialist "kingdom of freedom", in which man is free to manage his real economic life unconstrained by commodity-economic necessity. Political economy, however, only poses the question of socialism without offering to solve it.[95] Although capitalism can be abolished by reconverting labour-power into a non-commodity, that does not *ipso facto* guarantee socialism in the true sense of the word, since uncommoditised labour-power can still be subjected to extra-economic coercion. In order to enable man to freely manage his economic life a political organisation which can stipulate the aim of society as the "volonté générale", rather than the "volonté de tous", of the public must be formed.[96] It is this that requires the true wisdom of man. Even in socialism, the economic life that constitutes the material foundation or substructure of society does not disappear; but it is the superstructure that must now dictate the management of the substructure. The economic life under socialism must be so planned and executed as to maintain and develop a particular superstructure of man's free choice. This implies an "overturning" of historical materialism; for "man himself will make his own history" if and only if the substructure is under his control. Thus, in the construction of socialism, economic planning will have to be reduced to a technical handmaiden in service of the (democratically appointed) political and administrative authorities, whose function is to directly promote creative social life and to ensure the management of the economy consistent with that goal.

Notes and References

[1] In *Principles of Political Economy* Professor Uno does not utter mere opinions of a Japanese Marxist; he makes a positive contribution to the objective knowledge of society. The purpose of this essay is to specify what precisely is meant by the objective knowledge of society and to show how Uno actually achieves it.

[2] "The mystification which dialectic suffers in Hegel's hands, by no means prevents him from being the first to present its general form of working in a comprehensive and conscious manner. With him it is standing on its head. It must be turned right side up again, if you would discover the rational kernel within the mystical shell." Afterword to the Second German Edition of *Capital*, I. (Marx, *Capital, A Critical Analysis of Capitalist Production,* Vol. I., Moscow: Progress Publishers, 1963, p. 20).

3 Bocheński, I. M., *Contemporary European Philosophy*, translated from the German by D. Nicholl and K. Aschenbrenner (University of California Press, 1956), pp. 12-14.

4 Lenin, V. I., *Materialism and Empirio-Criticism* (Moscow: Progress Publishers, 1964), p. 240.

5 Ayer, A. J. (ed.), *Logical Positivism* (New York: The Free Press, 1959).

6 Ayer, A. J., *Language, Truth and Logic* (Harmondsworth: Pelican Books, Penguin Books Ltd., 1971).

7 Popper, of course, rejects the whole question of "meaningfulness"; hence, it is quite contrary to his intention to use falsifiability as the criterion of meaningfulness. However, Popper himself complains that "my position has repeatedly been described as a proposal to take falsifiability or refutability as the criterion of *meaning* (rather than of demarcation) ... Even Carnap ... feels himself compelled to interpret [my position] as a proposal to exclude metaphysical statements from some language or other" (Popper, K. R., *Conjectures and Refutations, The Growth of Scientific Knowledge*, sec. ed., New York and Evanston: Harper Torchbooks, Harper & Row, Publishers, Inc., 1968, p. 253).This suggests that some logical positivists believed it possible to appropriate Popper's innovation to their advantage.

8 Science, for example, knows for sure that water does not boil at 95°C because a statement to that effect has been conclusively falsified. However, the fact that water in fact vaporises at 100 °C is not definite or conclusive because it may still be falsified in future.

9 Hempel, C. G., *Philosophy of Natural Science* (Englewood-Cliffs, N. J.: Prentice-Hall, Inc., 1966), pp. 72-5.

10 Bridgman, P. W., *The Logic of Modern Physics* (New York: The Macmillan Company, 1961).

11 Hempel, C. G., *Philosophy of Natural Science,* pp. 88 ff. and Hempel, C. G., *Fundamentals of Concept Formation in Empirical Science* (The University of Chicago Press, 1952), p. 34.

12 Samuelson, P. A., *Foundations of Economic Analysis*, with a new Introduction (New York: Atheneum, 1965), p. 4.

13 According to Milton Friedman *(Essays in Positive Economics,* The University of Chicago Press, 1953), economic theory is on the one hand "systematic and organised methods of reasoning" and, on the other hand "a body of substantive hypotheses designed to abstract essential features of complex reality" (p. 7; p. 91). In Hempel's language, these correspond to "internal principles" and "bridge principles" of the theory, respectively. For example, the concept of a "commodity" is to Friedman an "analytical filing box" or a "label," but "not a word for a physical or technical entity to be defined once and for all independently of the problem at hand" (p. 57). As Marshall wrote, "the question where the lines of division between different commodities should be drawn must be settled by convenience of the particular discussion" (ibid.). Thus, black tea and green tea may be viewed either as two distinct commodities or may be combined into a single commodity "tea", depending on the purpose of the analysis. The statement of the purpose cannot, of course, be either tautological or empirically testable.

[14] Popper, K. R., *The Logic of Scientific Discovery*, the translation of *Logik der Forschung* (New York and Evanston: Harper Torchbooks, Harper & Row, Publishers, Inc., 1968), p. 37, italics original.

[15] Popper, K. R., *The Logic of Scientific Discovery*, p. 38.

[16] Ibid.

[17] Popper, K. R., *The Logic of Scientific Discovery*, p. 44-5.

[18] Feyerabend, P., *Against Method, Outline of an Anarchistic Theory of Knowledge* (London: NLB, 1976).

[19] "Wherever we look, whatever examples we consider, we see that the principles of critical rationalism and, *a fortiori*, the principles of logical empiricism give an inadequate account of the past development of science and are liable to hinder science in future. They give an inadequate account of science because science is much more 'sloppy' and 'irrational' than its methodological image. And, they are liable to hinder it, because the attempt to make science more 'rational' and precise is bound to wipe it out ... The difference between science and methodology which is such an obvious fact of history, therefore, indicates a weakness of the latter, and perhaps of the 'laws of reason' as well. For what appears as 'sloppiness', 'chaos' or 'opportunism' when compared with such laws has a most important function in the development of those very theories which we today regard as essential parts of our knowledge of nature. *These 'deviations', these 'errors', are preconditions of progress.* They permit knowledge to survive in the complex and difficult world which we inhabit, they permit *us* to remain free and happy agents. Without 'chaos', no 'knowledge'" (Feyerabend, *Against Method, Outline of an Anarchistic Theory of Knowledge*, p. 179). "Like the Dadaist, whom he [the epistemological anarchist] resembles much more than he resembles the political anarchist, he not only has no programme, he is against all programmes ..." (p. 189).

[20] In chapter 17 of his book Feyerabend considers "incommensurability" (between theories) which "depends on covert classification". This "phenomenon" to which "the reader must be led up by being confronted with a great variety of instances" (p. 225) does not permit "an explicit definition". Since this kind of question "must be attacked by *research*, and cannot be settled by methodological fiat" (p. 229), Feyerabend examines a large number of psychological findings. Having abandoned all epistemological programmes, Feyerabend has nothing left but psychological research to bear upon the problem of cognition. It is noteworthy that Popper *(Objective Knowledge, An Evolutionary Approach,* Oxford: The Clarendon Press, 1975, pp. 3-4), has reduced Hume's problem of induction to "a logical problem (H_L) and a psychological problem (H_P)." Since Feyerabend dismisses the logical side of the Humean method, there is only the psychological side left to consider.

[21] See Russell, B. *(History of Western Philosophy*, George Allen & Unwin Ltd., Unwin University Books, 1971, pp. 645-47), the relevant part of which is quoted by Popper *(Objective Knowledge, An Evolutionary Approach,* Oxford: The Clarendon Press, 1975, p. 5). Russell talks of a clash between empiricism and rationalism when beliefs based on repeated observations cannot be logically verified. Popper, on the other hand, claims that conjectural knowledge and the trial-

and-error approximation to truth that it implies are critically rational. But clearly the issue is not solved by Popper's restatement of Hume's logical problem and its "heuristic transference" to the psychological problem of beliefs. The "intellectual difference between sanity and insanity" is merely reduced to the matter of "pragmatic preference" (Popper, *Objective Knowledge, An Evolutionary Approach*, pp.21-2). Scientists are said to be more sensible than madmen by definition, i.e., by logicians' fiat.

[22] Popper, K. R., *The Open Society and its Enemies* (London: Routledge & Kegan Paul, 1973) and Popper, K. R., *The Poverty of Historicism* (London: Routledge & Kegan Paul, 1972).

[23] Typically inconclusive discourses on reductionism are found in Hempel (*Philosophy of Natural Science*, pp. 101 ff.; Hempel, C. G. (*Aspects of Scientific Explanation and Other Essays in the Philosophy of Science,* New York: The Free Press,, 1965, pp. 439 ff.); Nagel, E. (*The Structure of Science, Problems in the Logic of Scientific Explanation,* New York and Burlingame: Harcourt, Brace & World, Inc., 1961, pp. 336 ff.). It is, however, a great mistake to believe that Marxists are generally exempt from this dogma. On the contrary, leading Marxist writers including Engels, Lenin, Mao, etc., and even in some cases Marx himself appear to take an implicit reductionism for granted.

Thus, according to Lucio Colletti: "There is a second position which insists on the heterogeneity of the social and natural sciences. The danger of this alternative is that the social sciences then tend to become a qualitatively distinct form of knowledge from the natural sciences, and to occupy the same relationships towards them, as philosophy used to occupy towards science as such. It is no accident that this was the solution of the "German historicists – Dilthey, Windelband and Rickert. It was then inherited by Croce, Bergson, Lukács and the Frankfurt School. The invariable conclusion of this tradition is that true knowledge is social science, which because it cannot be assimilated to natural science, is not science at all but philosophy. Thus either there is a single form of knowledge, which is science (the position I would still like to defend) – but then it should be possible to construct the social sciences on the bases analogous to the natural sciences; or the social sciences really are different from the natural sciences, and there are two sorts of knowledge – but since two forms of knowledge are not possible, the natural sciences become a pseudo knowledge. The latter is the ideologically dominant alternative. Continental European philosophy in this century has been virtually united in its attack on the natural sciences – from Husserl to Heidegger, Croce to Gentile, Bergson to Sartre. Against the dangers of this spiritualist idealism, I personally would prefer to incur the opposite risks of neo-positivism. But I am divided on the issue, and have no ready solution to the problem" (Colletti, "A Political and Philosophical Interview", in *New Left Review,* 86, 1974, p. 20).

Clearly Colletti's problem lies in the "either reductionism or social sciences ≡ philosophy" alternative. In view of the last quoted sentence, I hope that he will reach a more satisfactory solution once Uno's third alternative is explained to him. See part III of this essay.

[24] Lecourt, D., *Marxism and Epistemology* (London: NLB, 1975), p. 12.

[25] Popper, K. R., *Objective Knowledge, An Evolutionary Approach* (Oxford: The Clarendon Press, 1975), p. 17.

[26] The significance of this statement will become apparent in the following section. See part II of this essay.

[27] "There are no separate methodological problems that face the social scientist different in kind from those that face any other scientist. It is true that the social scientist is part of the reality he describes. The same is true of the physical scientist. It is true that the social scientist in observing a phenomenon may change it. The theory of quantum mechanics, with its Heisenberg uncertainty principle, shows that the same is true of the physical scientist making small scale observations. Similarly, if we enumerate one by one the alleged differences between the social sciences and other sciences, we find no differences in kind" (Samuelson, P. A., "Economic Theory and Mathematics: An Appraisal", in *The American Economic Review*, XLII, 1952, pp. 61-2).

[28] For example, the so-called Philip's curve, the quantity theory of money, etc., are most readily testable so long as they remain broad empirical assertions free from sophisticated theoretical reservations.

[29] "Some genuine testable theories, when found to be false, are still upheld by their admirers - for example by introducing *ad hoc* some auxiliary assumption, or by reinterpreting the theory *ad hoc* in such a way that it escapes refutation" (Popper, *Conjectures and Refutations, The Growth of Scientific Knowledge*, p. 37).

[30] The so-called theory of comparative advantage, whether in its original Ricardian form or in its neo-classical Heckscher-Ohlin version, has never been empirically established, but continues to occupy the core of international economics. In the "development" context, however, few believe in the relevance of the static specialisation theory.

[31] This thesis, which is most clearly articulated by Uno in *Principles of Political Economy* has never been appreciated by dialectical materialists who follow Lenin, Mao, etc., and, thus, demand a "partisan" outlook on social science. Since they are reductionists (see note 23), natural science too must be partisan (see below II.3. of this essay) By an "ideology" I mean any set of value judgements, more or less clearly stated, leading to a definite social action or practice. It may also be called a vision or an *Anschauung* provided that it implies a definite action (including conscious acceptance of the status quo). In its widest sense "ideology" may include Popper's "pragmatic belief in the results of science" (Popper, *Objective* Knowledge, An Evolutionary Approach, p. 27). Thus, in general, any partial or incomplete knowledge, unless it is irrelevant to human practice, entails an ideology. But, as Popper claims, it is not necessarily irrational to pragmatically assume that the sun will rise tomorrow. Nor is it irrational or reactionary to tentatively believe in certain regularities of nature and to try to conform to them. Such an ideology or practical wisdom merely defines the relationship of men in general to nature and may be described as neutral. On the other hand, an ideology which accompanies a one-sided interpretation of social reality cannot be neutral; it divides people into factions and sets them antagonistically against each other.

The purpose of social science is to expose the partiality and one-sidedness of the pseudo-knowledge that breeds such an ideology.

32 Wallace, W. (trans.), *Hegel's Logic* with Foreword by J. N. Findlay (Oxford: The Clarendon Press, 1975), p. 144.

33 Wallace, W., *Hegel's Logic*, p. 36.

34 Ibid., p. 47.

35 Stace, W. R., *The Philosophy of Hegel - A Systematic Exposition* (New York: Dover Publications, Inc., 1955), p. 101.

36 Ibid.

37 Ibid.

38 Wallace, W., *Hegel's Logic*, p. 30.

39 For example, the concept of "speed" is not free from sensuous connotation. Thus, the same speed at which a motor-car runs may be felt too fast by the cautious driver and too slow by the reckless one. But the speed can be given a universal form of a number (e.g., 70 mph). In this case, the sensuous content of the speed and the individually subjective sensation of it drop out completely. It is often said that the concept of "force", axiomatically defined in mechanics must not be taken to imply the exertion of muscles or energy. The sensuous content with which the primitive notions of speed, force, etc., are still associated is artificially suppressed in the formal definitions, which the "understanding" imposes. The objectivity of these concepts are, in Hegel's view, imposed from the outside and do not emanate from the inside of the concepts themselves. This incongruity of the form and the content does not exist in the truly abstract categories such as being, naught, essence, etc. These sensuousness-free categories are called pure thoughts.

40 Wallace, W., *Hegel's Logic*, p. 31.

41 Miller, A. V. (trans.), *Hegel's Science of Logic* (London: George Allen & Unwin Ltd., 1969), p. 154-5.

42 Ibid., p. 154.

43 Ibid., p. 155.

44 Ibid.

45 Colletti, L., *Marxism and Hegel*, translated from the Italian by Lawrence Garner (London: NLB, 1973).

46 The expression, "the ascending method" is suggested by Marx's phrase: "die Methode vom Abstrakten zum Konkreten aufzusteigen". Marx does not, I believe, use the expression "the descending method". Marx, however, distinguishes between "the method of enquiry" and "the method of exposition" in the Afterword to the Second German Edition of *Capital*, I (Marx, *Capital, A Critical Analysis of Capitalist Production*, p. 19).

47 Wallace, W., *Hegel's Logic*, p. 36.

48 Ibid. Italics in the quotation are mine.

49 Because of the identity of the subject and the object, epistemology and ontology need not be distinguished in Hegel's idealism.

50 By "material motion", I mean any dynamics of the existents outside of thought.

51 This statement might be surprising to some. But if Lenin's definition of idealism and materialism is seen to be inadequate, and if it is still desired to characterise Hegel as an idealist in contrast to materialist Marx, this is the only possible way I can think of.

52 Colletti, L., "Marxism and the Dialectic", in *New Left Review*, 93 (1975) pp. 3-29.

53 Miller, A. V., *Hegel's Science of Logic*, p. 50.

54 Ibid.

55 Or perhaps, more accurately, in the history of man's metaphysical conscious-ness of which the history of philosophy up to Hegel's time is the record.

56 Wallace, W., *Hegel's Logic*, p. 35.

57 This, or a similar phrase, recurs from time to time in Marx's writing. For exam-ple, in an unfinished rough draft originally intended for the introduction to *A Con-tribution to the Critique of Political Economy* but not published in Marx's lifetime: "Labour, not only as a category but in reality, has become a means to create wealth in general, and has ceased to be tied as an attribute to a particular indi-vidual" (Marx, *A Contribution to the Critique of Political Economy,* Moscow: Pro-gress Publishers, 1970, p. 210).

58 Engels' *Dialectics of Nature* was published posthumously by the MEL Institute in Moscow in 1925 based on his notes written between 1875 and 1882 (Engels, F., *Dialectics of Nature,* Moscow: Foreign Language Publishing House, 1954).

59 Knox, T. M. (trans.), *Hegel's Philosophy of Right* (Oxford University Press, 1967), pp. 12-3.

60 "But in theory it is assumed that the laws of capitalist production operate in their pure form" (Marx, 1894, p. 175).

61 Marx, K., *A Contribution to the Critique of Political Economy* (Moscow: Pro-gress Publishers, 1970), p. 211.

62 Marx, K., *A Contribution to the Critique of Political Economy,* pp. 210-11.

63 Marx, K., *A Contribution to the Critique of Political Economy,* p. 211.

64 The contradiction between value and use-value is the fundamental contradic-tion that characterises capitalist society. The simplest expression of this contra-diction is already seen in the fact that a commodity is made up of the two mutu-ally exclusive properties of value and use-value. But the contradiction recurs throughout the dialectic of capital in many other forms. For example: no use-value can be produced except as a value; surplus labour (or surplus product) cannot be appropriated except as surplus value; capital must circulate as well as produce; the depreciation of fixed capital does not exactly correspond with the diminution of its use-value; the accumulation of wealth occurs only in the form of the accumulation of capital; the reproduction of the capitalist social relation can-not be independent of the reproduction of the means of production and the arti-cles of consumption as use-values in an appropriate proportion; the accumula-tion-process of capital alternates between the widening phase in which the or-ganic composition is constant and the deepening phase in which it is raised. All

these and more are manifestations of the contradiction between value and use-value in different contexts. The general sense of this fundamental contradiction, therefore, is that capitalist society has to manage its real economic life by the commodity-economic principles. Since capitalism is a synthesis of the commodity-economic management (the value aspect) and real economic life (the use-value aspect), the two aspects are viewed as "contradictory" to each other. The contradiction, however, does not mean absolute incompatibility; it means that the synthesis of the two aspects can be achieved only in an historically particular period and not always.

65 This does not mean that the exploitation of a serf by the lord is only imagined or non-existent; it is factual. But the purely social relation that underlies this fact cannot be objectively identified because of the many contingent factors which pervert and obscure that relation. Thus, exploitation may be harsh or lenient, depending upon the greed of the lord, the geographic and climatic condition of agriculture, the religious and cultural traditions of the fief, etc. There is no inherent force in the feudal master-servant relation to automatically establish a socially uniform pattern. Medieval historians are, therefore, obliged to subjectively construct a pattern or an ideal type and impose it on the fact, so to speak, from the outside in order to generalise it. This is the method of the "understanding" not of "reason" in Hegel's language.

66 By the "Externalisation of the relations of capital in the form of interest-bearing capital" (the title of chapter XXIV, *Capital* III) Marx means roughly the following. Capital is a chrematistic operation which produces and distributes surplus value; capitalist society is organised by the social relations that capital establishes with other parties in the course of the production and the distribution of surplus value. But, on the reified surface of the market, those social relations, internal to capitalist society, are not visible. The exterior of the activity of capital, thus, appears only as the mysteriously interest-bearing force of an asset. As this asset acquires the form of a tradable item, it is converted into a commodity.

67 After explaining the nature of the dialectical logic in some detail, Hegel writes as follows: "Each step of the *advance* in the process of further determination, while getting further away from the indeterminate beginning, is also *getting back nearer* to it, [so that] what at first sight may appear to be different, the retrogressive grounding of the beginning and the *progressive further determining* of it, coincide and arc the same. The method ... thus winds itself into a circle" (Miller, p. 841). "By virtue of the nature of the method just indicated, the science [of metaphysics or speculative philosophy] exhibits itself as a *circle* returning upon itself, the end being wound back into the beginning, the simple ground, by mediation" (p. 842).

68 "I therefore openly avowed myself the pupil of that mighty thinker [Hegel], and even here and there, in the chapter on the theory of value, coquetted with the modes of expression peculiar to him". Afterword to the Second Edition of *Capital*, I (Marx, *Capital, A Critical Analysis of Capitalist Production*, pp. 19-20). In public,

Uno always disclaimed any expert knowledge of Hegel's *Logic*. He never suggested a Hegelian interpretation of *Capital* or a Marxian interpretation of the *Logic*. He even took exception to Lenin's well known advice that the *Logic* must be fully studied in order to understand Marx's *Capital*. Although it is likely that Uno carefully studied the *Logic* at least once, he certainly did not allow Hegel to dictate economic theory. For example Uno's theory of the circulation of surplus value cannot possibly be deduced from Hegel's doctrine of Correlation (Verhältnis). Uno believed that the dialectic of capital can throw light on the meaning of the *Logic*, not the other way around.

[69] In the doctrine of production, however, inter-industrial differences in the value composition of capital may be abstracted from because capitalists' specialisation in the production of different use-values is as yet irrelevant in that context. Only in the doctrine of distribution must differences in the value composition of capital be explicitly questioned. Hence, the appearance of parenthetic phrase "in general" in this sentence.

[70] Uno's treatment of "skilled labour" in *Principles of Political Economy* is a good illustration. The development of the capitalist method of production increasingly simplifies the labour-process by mechanisation. Labour is "simplified" if it can be shifted from one concrete-useful form to another without significant cost. Thus, even if a skilled craft still subsists in capitalist society, the same product can be supplied more flexibly in the mechanised process with simple labour. In view of the principle of market value, it is warranted to neglect skilled labour. But the principle of market value cannot be explained, if the technique of producing a use-value is from the beginning supposed to be unique.

[71] Marx, K., *A Contribution to the Critique of Political Economy*, p. 207.

[72] Perhaps it may be said that "purely capitalist society" is as unreal as the miracle of levitation. Even a most saintly person cannot levitate because his body weight is heavier than the weight of the air. When, however, this earthly fact becomes irrelevant, relative to his saintliness, he may be imagined to actually lift himself in the air. Similarly, even the most liberal capitalism does not in fact reify all human relations. But, when the unreified part of real economic life tends to become negligible relative to the commodity-economic organisation of society, it is possible to conceive a purely capitalist society.

[73] A commodity-economy is always an important catalyst of the transmission of technology. Thus, even in ancient times, the techniques of making pottery, weaving cloth, and working various metals quickly spread from China to Europe through Persia. It is, however, a grave mistake to suppose that technology does not develop without commerce, or always develops in such a way as to consolidate a commodity-economy. In general, only the techniques of manufacturing small, i.e., readily commoditisable, objects with relatively "light" means of labour agree with the working of a commodity-economy. The development of industrial technology from the first industrial revolution up to the 1860s was largely of this kind.

[74] It is often wrongly believed that "free competition gives rise to the concentration and centralisation of production, which, in turn, leads to monopoly". Free competition implies a large number of firms in each industry. If they all accumu-

late capital and concentrate production, more or less uniformly, the number of firms does not decline; it may even increase with "the division of property within capitalist families" (Marx, *Capital, A Critical Analysis of Capitalist Production*, p. 625). Hence, the concentration or accumulation of capital, as such, does not automatically "lead to monopoly". But, if in consequence of technological advances the production of many use-values requires heavy investment, small partnerships will be displaced by joint-stock companies. Large monopoly firms then tend to dominate industry, abolishing the regime of free competition. If even products become "heavy" or "large", a commodity production becomes still less viable. For example, steamships cannot be "anarchically" produced in large quantities and marketed for whatever price they can fetch. They must be produced under some sort of contract, but contractual production is not a genuine commodity production.

75 Weiss, F. G. (ed.), *Hegel, The Essential Writings* (New York, Evanston, San Francisco, London: Harper & Row, Publishers, Inc., 1974), pp. 220-1.

76 Ibid., p. 221.

77 In other words, the "logic which coincides with metaphysics" does not produce "man" as a metaphysical category. Man belongs to nature. But man, as he ought to be (or *comme il faut*) in the light of reason, constitutes the "type" of man. A man of subnormal intelligence or excessive violence would then be an empirical "counter example" or "deformity", in the sense of Hegel, and must be evaluated as a deviation from the standard type. In other words, "man" as a type mediates reason and an empirically observable man.

78 Marx, K., *A Contribution to the Critique of Political Economy*, p. 214.

79 "In fact, the exchange value of commodities evolves originally not within primitive communities, but on their margins, on their borders, the few points where they come into contact with other communities. This is where barter begins and moves thence to the interior of the community, exerting a disintegrating influence upon it" (*A Contribution to the Critique of Political Economy*, p. 50). "The exchange of commodities, therefore, first begins on the boundaries of such communities [a patriarchal family, an ancient Indian community, a Peruvian Inca State, etc.], or their points of contact with other similar communities, or with members of the latter. So soon, however, as products once become commodities in the external relations of a community, they also, by reaction, become so in its internal intercourse" (Marx, *Capital, A Critical Analysis of Capitalist Production*, p. 87).

80 Political anarchism is probably a mental reflection of this tendency. But, even in the liberal stage, capitalism, in fact, needed the apparatus of a national state to maintain the law and order of the home market and to oversee the reproduction of labour-power as a commodity. It is interesting that the bourgeois state in this period was still largely dependent on the representatives of the land-owning class, who alone had resources to invest in social capital and time to spare for politics.

81 The bourgeois state is an institution alien to capital because a purely capitalist society is logically self-sufficient without making the state explicit.

[82] For example, the pre-1868 feudal system in Japan strictly tied peasants to land and restricted the activities of merchant capital in various manners so as to make the conversion of labour-power into a commodity virtually impossible. In this respect, extra-economic forces worked inside Japan against the introduction of capitalism. On the other hand, the collapse of the Japanese feudal system under external pressure could have occurred earlier than 1868, if European powers had taken less time to commercially stabilise the Chinese Empire. In this respect, the modernisation of Japan was postponed by extra-economic forces working outside her.

[83] Luxemburg, R., *The Accumulation of Capital*, translated from the German by Agnes Schwartzchild (London: Routledge and Kegan Paul, 1951), pp. 351-52.

[84] "But the form of landed property with which the incipient capitalist mode of production is confronted does not suit it. It first creates for itself the form required by subordinating agriculture to capital. It thus transforms feudal landed property, clan property, small peasant property in mark communes – no matter how divergent their juristic forms may be – into the economic form corresponding to the requirements of this mode of production" (Marx, *Capital, A Critique of Political Economy*, Vol. III, Moscow: Progress Publishers, 1966, p. 617). Capitalism does not create landed property; it inherits the existing form of landed property, which it adapts to its own need. The same thing can be said of the state and peripheral regions. It is not always necessary to transform the existing state into a strictly bourgeois state or to fully capitalise the existing non-capitalist regions so long as capital can subordinate para-feudal states and underdeveloped regions to its advantage.

[85] The "subordination of agriculture to capital", however, is a particularly difficult operation. Although the theory of a purely capitalist society must presuppose a fully capitalist management of agriculture, the tendency towards it could be observed only to a limited extent even in mid-nineteenth-century England. Agriculture which is so unpredictably dependent on the variability and vagaries of nature is not an industry congenial to commodity-economic management. Since, however, agriculture forms the foundation of real economic life, the bourgeois state is never without a ministry of agriculture, commissions on agrarian affairs and a series of agricultural policies.

[86] This point is often overlooked by the so-called Marxist theory of the state according to which the state is always an instrument of the oppression of the productive class. Such a theory is as empty and "hypothetical" as the propositions of historical materialism. Only in the light of a more specific theory of the bourgeois state can the function of the state in general be evaluated.

[87] For instance, such a currently fashionable topic as the rôle of women in society could not be objectively studied if the rôle that capitalism assigns to women in its superstructure is not clearly grasped. Unless the reason why the bourgeois state in its juridical and sociological process constrains the freedom of women is properly understood, it is not clear what women should be emancipated from. So-called "male chauvinism" would be much too general a concept to be helpful at all to scientific women. See note 94 below.

[88] "The only relevant test of the *validity* of a hypothesis is comparison of its predictions with experience. The hypothesis is rejected if its predictions are contradicted; it is accepted if its predictions are not contradicted" (Friedman, M., *Essays in Positive Economics,* The University of Chicago Press, 1953. pp. 8-9). Thus empirico-analytical science always "predicts". Popper (in his *The Poverty of Historicism, passim)* argues that empiricists' predictions are of different kind from historicists' prophesy. Dialectical knowledge makes neither prediction nor prophesy, empirical or historical.

[89] Marx, K., *A Contribution to the Critique of Political Economy,* p. 22.

[90] See note 23 above.

[91] Popper, K. R., *The Poverty of Historicism* (London: Routledge & Kegan Paul, 1972), pp. 64 ff.

[92] See note 23 above.

[93] Engels, F., *Anti-Dühring; Herr Eugen Dühring's Revolution in Science* (Moscow: Progress Publishers, 1969), p. 336.

[94] This point should be relevant to my comments in note 87 above.

[95] In this sentence "political economy", of course, means the political economy of capitalism or Engels' political economy in the narrower sense.

[96] "The distinction ... between what is merely in common, and what is truly universal, is strikingly expressed by Rousseau in his famous *Contrat social,* when he says that the laws of a state must spring from the universal will *(volonté générale),* but need not on that account be the will of all *(volonté de tous).* Rousseau would have made a sounder contribution towards a theory of the state, if he had always kept this distinction in sight. The general will is the notion of the will: and the laws are the special clauses of this will and based upon the notion of it" (Wallace, *Hegel's Logic,* p. 228).

II. Theoretical Essays

Uno School Seminar on the Theory of Value

In the following ten sets of questions and answers, I intend to give a concise account of the theory of value as it is conceived in the dialectic of capital, i.e., the Marxian economic theory which the late Professor Kôzô Uno (1897-1977) developed as a dialectical system. Members of the Uno School, may not be unanimous in what they consider to be the gist of Uno's value theory. What follows should, therefore, be understood to represent my own interpretation of it.

1. Are "value" and "exchange value" the same thing?

No. The synonym for "exchange value" is price or value-form, and not "value". Exchange value is an expression of value, but it is not itself value. The latter refers to that property of the commodity which makes it qualitatively the same as, and only quantitatively different from, another commodity. In other words, value refers to the commodity as representing a part (fraction) of the abstract-general (i.e., mercantile or commodity-economic) wealth of society.

Although at the beginning of *Capital*, Marx follows the classical practice in stating that "value-in-use" and "exchange value" are the two elements of a commodity, he admits the inappropriateness of that usage only a few pages later and recommends the substitution of the word "value" for "exchange value" there.[1] Yet the importance of this correction has been frequently overlooked.

The confusion between value and price is reinforced by the ambiguous orthodox (neoclassical) usage according to which, for example, the phrase "value and distribution" is just another way of saying "the pricing of outputs and the pricing of inputs". Debreu's *Theory of Value* (1959) merely discusses how general equilibrium "prices" are formed. Nowhere is value defined as distinct from price.

Thus, most would-be critics of the *labour theory of value* (which states that "socially necessary labour" forms the substance of commodity-values) are, in fact, unknowingly criticising a *labour theory of prices* (which presumably claims that the equilibrium relative prices of commodities should be proportional to the quantities of labour embodied in them); an incorrect theory for which the dialectic of capital is *not* responsible.[2]

What is vital to the make-up of capitalism is that commodities are produced as value, rather than as use-values. That is to say, they are produced as instruments of trade indifferently to their use-values. Indeed the primary sense of the word "value" is simply "indifference to use-value". Whereas commodities are materially heterogeneous as use-values, they are socially homogeneous as value. It is, moreover, not necessary to know what the substance of this qualitative uniformity is, in the first instance, in order to demonstrate that it gives rise to economically meaningful prices.

All one needs to know is the following. No commodity can express its value except by means of a given quantity of the use-value of another commodity, i.e., by a price. The fact that all capitalistically produced commodities should have an economically meaningful price stems from the fact that they are value-objects.[3]

It is true, of course, that the commodity-form can occasionally (i.e., by chance) attach to such things as works of art, personal services, and even a person's honour and pride, giving them "prices" which express no (economic) value. Such prices are, however, arbitrary, since they do not reflect the underlying allocation of society's resources, which equilibrium prices of genuine commodities do.

Value is thus a property of the genuine commodity produced indifferently to its use-value, and reflects the degree to which its provision costs society in real terms. Only at a later stage of analysis can we explain "in which real terms", however. For the mere observation of commodity exchanges does not enable us to specify the substance of value as labour, or as anything else for that matter.

Marx convinced no one with his immediate deduction from "1 quarter corn = x cwt. iron" that both sides of the exchange equation must contain an equal amount of productive labour.[4] What the equation shows is merely that both sides are equally priced in trade, without any necessary implication that they are of equal magnitude in value. The equation rather implies that the two totally distinct use-values carry a socially uniform quality, a "third" factor, which may be called either value or "moneyness" (convertibility into money), and it is this latter factor that gives rise to economically meaningful prices for all commodities.

2. What does the value-form theory do?

Let me repeat that a commodity can express its value or "moneyness" only in terms of a definite quantity of the use-value of another commodity, which is called an "equivalent". By virtue of the prior expression of value by the first commodity, the equivalent acquires the immediate purchasing-power over it within the terms of the proposed exchange. Indeed, the value expression amounts to nothing other than a trade proposal.

For example, in the simple value-form: "20 yards of linen (→) 1 quarter corn", the value of linen is expressed in corn, the *equivalent commodity*. The sign (→) here should be read "are yours for". This indicates the willingness of the owner of linen to part with its 20 yards, so long as 1 quarter of corn is obtainable. Hence 1 quarter corn is already a "little money" which can buy 20 yards of linen from its owner at a moment's notice. The "moneyness" of linen is thus revealed "accidentally", when its owner renders corn a "little money" with the qualitative and quantitative restrictions, attendant on his trade proposal.

What the value-form theory does may be said to remove such qualitative and quantitative restrictions from the "little money" chosen by the linen-owner, and to show that one particular commodity always emerges in the end as the general equivalent or money, in terms of which all other commodities may express their values. With the exclusion of one particular commodity as money (which no longer expresses its own value in terms of another commodity), and with the consequent pricing of all other commodities in its terms, the value expression is completed as: "all the available stock of my commodity (→) whatever it is worth in money", i.e., as the money form of value.[5]

What this statement means is that the necessity of commodities to express their "immanent" value calls money into being. Money here is the universal value-reflecting object, an "external" form of value, i.e., an external object which directly represents value.

We can, therefore, say at this stage what the value of a commodity is like (at least, in the mind of its owner). It is like a given quantity of gold, if gold is the commodity universally adopted as money. Concretely, if I have 1,000 pencils for sale and I price them at 50¢ (in gold) apiece, this means that the value of my merchandise has, in my mind, transformed itself into a $500 worth of gold. Thus, the value-form theory makes value, an intangible property of the commodity, tangible, as a given amount of the monetary commodity such as gold. In the present context, however, money is still imaginary (in the mind of the seller) rather than real (in the hands of the purchaser). No physical money need exist merely to price commodities in its terms, that is to say, to put a price-tag on them.

3. What does the "measure-of-value function of money" mean? Does one "determine" value while "measuring" it?

All commodities appear in the market with supply prices, which their sellers (owners) quote tentatively in expressing their values. Since these are money prices, owners of physical money (which is the means of purchase) can buy any commodity offered in the market at will.

The suppliers of the commodity, by pricing it, can only "propose" a trade which they themselves cannot enforce. They can only revise the price, depending on the response of the market, so as to be able to sell their commodity as quickly and as dearly as possible. The owners of money, representing the force of demand in the market, buy immediately if the price is low and temporise if the price is high. This fact compels the sellers increasingly to adjust their supply prices to the demand prices. Therefore, the equality of demand and supply emerges sooner or later, as the commodity is *actually* bought and sold a great number of times in recurrent trade. It emerges, in other words, as money *measures* the value of the commodity by its repetitive purchases, establishing a *normal price* that measures its value.

The measurement of value thus occurs, when physical money acts as the means of purchase. The price at which the commodity is sold varies from time to time, but eventually settles to a normal level, a level that measures its value. Since a genuine commodity is reproducible, that is to say, it can be supplied in any quantity (in any number of interchangeable samples), its purchase will be repeated until its price settles to a normal level.

What I call a normal price here is, in fact, the same thing as an equilibrium price. The equilibrium price of a commodity in the capitalist market, however, cannot be adequately specified until the real conditions of production, which underlie its demand and supply, are made more explicit. That is why the dialectic speaks of a "normal" price rather than of an "equilibrium" price in this present, abstract context of simple circulation which makes no explicit reference to production. For the same reason, I say that a normal price "measures" the value of a commodity, instead of saying that an equilibrium price "determines" the value of a commodity.[6]

Such dialectical subtlety notwithstanding, the measurement of the value of a particular commodity implies, in the background, the allocation of society's resources for its production relative to that for the production of gold (the monetary commodity). If the commodity is traded at its normal price, that fact implies that it is neither overproduced nor underproduced, and that its production consumes (uses up) just the right quantities of society's resources. It is in this sense that the normal price is said to measure the value of the commodity.

Yet no assertion has so far been made, nor is it generally true, that commodity-values are proportional to normal prices. Suppose that there are two commodities, **A** and **B**, whose normal prices are \$1 and \$2 respectively. This does not imply that, if **A**'s value is x, **B**'s value ought to be $2x$ (for some positive number x). In fact, **B**'s value may well be only $0.5x$. No contradiction exists between the two statements: (1) that only when **B**'s price is twice as much as **A**'s are these commodities produced in the right quantities; and (2) that one unit of **B** then consumes half as much of society's resources as one unit of **A** does. This assertion leads us to the definition of the substance of value.

4. What is the substance of value? Can there be a non-labour theory of value?

Capitalism differs from "simple commodity production" in, among other things, that the former, by virtue of the conversion of labour-power into a commodity, is necessarily indifferent to the production of specific use-values. Unlike the small commodity producer, the capitalist has no stake in the production of particular goods. Capital, in other words, produces *any* commodity if it is profitable to do so (just as money buys *any* commodity if it is desirable to do so). It amounts to saying that capital produces commodities as *value*, i.e., with indifference to their use-values.

The production of commodities as value, which characterises the capitalist economy, however, depends on the conversion of labour-power into a commodity. For only commoditised labour-power can be indifferent to the use-values that it produces.

Labour that produces a use-value (a material object for use or consumption) is called productive. Labour-power is the capacity to perform productive labour which, as is well known, is both concrete-useful and abstract-human. The classical school understood this duality of productive labour only vaguely, which made their labour theory of value inconclusive. It was with the explicit recognition of this duality that Marx removed all ambiguities from the labour theory of value. The fact that, in all societies, productive labour has an abstract-human aspect makes labour-power, in principle, a non-specific factor of production.

This means that, at some finite cost, human labour can always be shifted from one concrete-useful form to another. There may be cases in which the cost is prohibitive, but the capitalist method of production tends to reduce that cost, if not to eliminate it altogether, by the simplification of labour. It is precisely for this reason that capital which, purchases labour-power as a commodity can produce *any* commodity with indifference to its use-value, while labour, on the other hand, becomes an abstract "disutility" to the worker regardless of which concrete-useful form it is rendered in.

Now it is obvious even to a child that there are no such things as "abstract-spatial land" and "abstract-physical capital". Land, though an original factor of production, comes only in various concrete-useful forms (in location, fertility, etc.); moreover, the production of use-values does not "consume (use up)" land, which is a free gift of nature to society.[7]

Capital, in the sense of capital-goods, is not even an original factor of production. Moreover, the fact that every item of capital is a specific assemblage of various elements of production (not unlike the pieces of a meccano set?) explains the inveterate non-malleability and immeasurability of capital. This characteristic of capital caused a great uproar in bourgeois economics (and even led to the invention of that prismatic "standard commodity", which not only fascinates but also spellbinds some comprador Marxists).

Clearly, both a land theory and a capital theory of value are idle bourgeois fantasies with no credible economic foundation.[8] Productive labour alone, which flows from labour-power, forms the substance of value. For, labour-power is the only element of production which is both original and non-specific to use-values.

When commodities are produced in socially necessary (equilibrium) quantities, i.e., are neither overproduced nor underproduced, we say that "socially necessary labour" has been spent for their production.

Hence, a precise statement of the labour theory of value is that socially necessary labour forms the substance of commodity values. Indeed, the capitalist production of commodities as value means nothing other than the production of commodities as embodiments of socially necessary labour. This fact also implies that the magnitude of the value of a commodity is defined (determined) by the quantity of socially necessary labour embodied in it. Socially necessary labour is the only real cost that society incurs in the production of commodities.

5. What is the necessity of the law of value?

A close relation has already been observed between the existence of capitalism (the conversion of labour-power into a commodity) and the validity of the labour theory of value (the production of all commodities as embodiments of socially necessary labour). The law of value says that, when the labour theory of value holds, capitalist society is viable, and vice versa. A society is said to be viable if its direct producers have a guaranteed access to the product of their necessary labour, since with it they can reproduce their labour-power.

Thus capitalism is viable as a historical society, if and only if the money wages paid to workers enable them to "buy back" enough wage-goods for the reproduction of their labour-power. We have to make sure that this condition of viability is consistent with the labour theory of value, i.e., with the capitalist indifference to the production of use-values. The necessity of the law of value means that the viability of capitalism implies and is implied by the validity of the labour theory of value.

Let us assume the following: (1) all workers work for 12 hours a day with the rate of surplus value of $e = 1$; (2) 3 units of **A**, where **A** represents the basket of assorted wage-goods, suffice to reproduce the daily consumption of labour-power; and (3) no fixed capital exists. With these general assumptions consider the following specific case. A capitalist produces, per employment of one worker, 15 units of **A** in a day with the rate of profit of $r = 0.2$; the value and the price of **A** per unit are respectively $\lambda_a = 2$ and $p_a = 1$. Then we are in effect confronted with the situation described in the table below. Obviously the capitalist must pay \$3 as the money wage so that the worker can, with it, buy back 3 units of **A**, which are the product of his necessary labour of 6 hours.

(**A**)	c		v		s		
in labour	18	+	6	+	6	= 30	$\lambda_a = 2$
in money	9.5	+	3	+	2.5	= 15	$p_a = 1$
in quantity	9.5	+	3	+	2.5	= 15	$r = 0.2$

In order for the labour theory of value to hold, so that only socially necessary labour is applied for the production of all commodities, the latter must, of course, be produced in socially necessary quantities. This further implies that the production of all commodities must be equally profitable, and that capitalists are, therefore, indifferent to the use-value aspect of production. So let **B** whose value happens to be $\lambda_b = 1$ be any commodity different from **A** and producible with the rate of profit of $r = 0.2$. Suppose now that another capitalist advances, per employment of one worker, \$9 for the daily production of 24 units of B. Then from the information available, we can construct the following table:

(B)	c		v		s		
in labour	12	+	6	+	6	= 24	$\lambda_b = 1$
in money	6	+	3	+	1.8	= 10.8	$p_b = 0.45$
in quantity	13.33	+	6.67	+	4	= 24	$r = 0.2$

Here again the worker must be paid \$3 with which to buy 3 units of **A** for the reproduction of his labour-power, and that is done. Since **B** represents *any* commodity other than **A**, it follows that capitalism is viable, when all commodities are produced with only socially necessary labour. This establishes *the necessity of the law of value*. For, even though prices are not proportional to values, there clearly exist some prices that ensure both the validity of the labour theory of value and the viability of capitalist society.

That, however, is quite different from claiming a theory of the (quantitative) determination of values and prices. Here we have assumed (λ_a, λ_b, e) and (p_a, r), together with various parameters, and deduced only p_b, although this latter represents all "other" prices. The implication is that a set of equilibrium prices relative to p_a and r exists which appropriately allocates socially necessary labour to the production of all commodities, so as to make capitalist society viable.[9] For the theory of the (quantitative) determination of values and prices, the nature of productive techniques must be known more explicitly.

6. How do you quantitatively determine values and prices?

In the appendix to this essay, I provide the algebra for the simplest case consisting of one capital-good, one wage-good, and one luxury-good (consumption good for capitalists). Here, I would rather illustrate the theory with concrete numbers. Suppose that 150 units of the capital-good are produced with 50 units of the capital-good itself and 20 hours of labour. Let us write this technical and allocational relation as (50, 20) → 150. We shall adopt the same convention for the other two goods, and suppose the following technology complex (T) to correspond to system (1) in the appendix:

$$
(T) \begin{cases} \quad (& 50 & , & 20 &) & \rightarrow & 150 & = X \\ \quad (& 40 & , & 30 &) & \rightarrow & 80 & = Y \\ +) \ (& 30 & , & 40 &) & \rightarrow & 90 & = Z \\ \hline & 120 & , & 90 & & & . \end{cases}
$$

For the system to be meaningful, we must first ascertain that the amount of the capital-good produced (150 units) is not smaller than the amount of it used up (120 units). This condition of self-replacement or productiveness, which in the appendix appears as a weak inequality in (2) is the same thing as what Uno calls "the absolute foundation of the law of value". The operation $\Lambda(T)$, shown as (3) in the appendix, then enables us to find values which in the present case will be $(\lambda_x, \lambda_y, \lambda_z) = (0.2, 0.475, 0.511)$.

To determine the rate of surplus value we must make use of the identity $\lambda_y Y = 90/(1 + e)$, which corresponds to (4) in the appendix. This identity says that the workers "buy back" the output of the wage-good with their necessary labour, a proposition already referred to in connection with the "necessity of the law of value". In the present case we find a positive rate of surplus value, $e = 1.368$. Since a non-positive rate of surplus value is meaningless, T must satisfy the inequality $\lambda_y 80 < 90$ to be capitalistically operable. This and the condition of self-replacement, however, in effect guarantee positive prices and a positive rate of profit.

Now consider the operation $P(T)$, as shown by (5) in the appendix. This system of three equations is clearly under-determined. For even when we assume an arbitrary wage-rate (such as $w = 1$), we still have three prices (p_x, p_y, p_z) and the rate of profit (r) to determine. I, therefore, introduce the identity $p_y Y = w90$, corresponding to (6) in the appendix, which says that the money value of the output of the wage-good is entirely bought by the total wage-bill paid during the period. This identity, which I call "the fundamental constraint of the capitalist market", is clearly a market expression of the viability condition of capitalism. (Hence, unlike Walras' Law, this constraint is not arbitrarily imposed as a postulate. It is derived from the previous theory of the necessity of the law of value.) Prices and the rate of profit can now be calculated, when $w = 1$, as (p_x, p_y, p_z) = (0.5477, 1.125, 1.087) and $r = 0.7338$.

The present theory can be easily generalised to apply to a system containing any number of commodities. It can also allow for fixed capital and differences in the turnover-frequencies of capital. At this point, however, I simply wish to call attention to several points of theoretical importance, a full discussion of which would require more space. (i) All commodities can be categorised into three groups. (ii) The technology complex, T, is specific to the indicated activity levels, implying not only technology in the narrow sense but also an equilibrium allocation of capital. (iii) The outputs (150, 80, 90) emerge at the end of the period, but the inputs (120, 90) must be there at the beginning. Take note, however, that variable capital (w90) is "advanced" only in money terms, not in physical terms as a stock of wage-goods. (iv) A technology complex which does not satisfy the condition of self-replacement with respect to all capital-goods and the condition that $e > 0$ cannot be capitalistically operated. (v) The method of the fundamental constraint is crucial to the solution of the price system, especially when there are more than one wage-good.[10]

7. What is the transformation problem? What is its economic significance?

I would like to emphasize that there are two transformation problems. One involves the dialectical (i.e., qualitative or conceptual) transformation of values into prices and of surplus value into profit. Here there is no question of an inverse transformation. The other has to do with a mathematical (i.e., quantitative or formal-logical) transformation of values into prices, and of the *rate of* surplus value into the *rate of* profit. In this case, the inverse transformation is part of the problem.

In the dialectic, which is the logic of synthesis, the same concept reappears a number of times but each time it is increasingly more specified or concretised, and, therefore, assumes different names. What used to be called A at a more abstract (i.e., less synthetic) level of discussion now appears as B, redefined to fit the new context. When this sort of thing occurs we speak of the conversion (or transformation) of A into B. For example, "the conversion of the value of labour-power into wages" means that what was referred to, in earlier contexts, as the value of labour-power is now specified as money-wages. "The transformation of surplus profit into rent" means that surplus profit which arises in a particular context, i.e., specifically in relation to the differential fertility of land, is called rent. There are, of course, many other instances of such usage in *Capital*.

Such transformations are akin to the transformation of Cinderella into the Crown Princess. The person has not changed but the context has, requiring her to adjust her appearance and demeanour accordingly. In the dialectic of capital, the transformation of values into prices occurs, when one moves from the doctrine of production, in which the production of commodities is strictly viewed as the production of value, to the doctrine of distribution, which takes the distinctness of use-values in the capitalist market into explicit consideration. This statement means that values and prices, which could not be quantitatively determined in the earlier context, may now be completely spelled out, as capital emerges from the underworld of production into the limelight of the capitalist market, permitting the full specification of the technology complex (T).

In the following chart the lateral arrow indicates the qualitative transformation. Prices that remained in the shadow of values in the doctrine of production come to the forefront in the doctrine of distribution, relegating values to the background. That is why we speak of $\bar{\Lambda} \rightarrow P(T)$ rather than $\bar{P} \rightarrow \Lambda(T)$. Here the focus is on the transformation of quantitatively unspecified values and prices into them so specified.

	Doctrine of Production		Doctrine of Distribution	
Explicit	$\Lambda = \bar{\Lambda}$	$\rightarrow$	$P = P(T)$	$\uparrow\downarrow$
Implicit	$P = \bar{P}$		$\Lambda = \Lambda(T)$	

The word "transformation", however, is not monopolised by the dialectic. When it is used in mathematics (as, e.g., linear, power, Laplace transformation, etc.), it means a transplantation of a mathematical point or relation from one space (or system of coordinates) to another. Similarly, we can speak of the mathematical transformations of values into prices and of prices back into values. These are shown by the pair of vertical arrows in the above chart. That is to say, if we first know values and the rate of surplus value, we can get to the corresponding prices and rate of profit, provided that we also have certain information about the value compositions of capital. And under similar conditions we can take the reverse course as well.

To see this, rewrite the first two equations of $\Lambda(T)$ and $P(T)$, assuming $w = 1$, respectively as follows:

$$\begin{cases} \lambda_x 150/20 = [k_x/(1 + e)] + 1, \\ \lambda_y 80/30 = [k_y/(1 + e)] + 1, \end{cases} \qquad (*)$$

and

$$\begin{cases} p_x 150 = 20\,(1 + r)\,(k'_x + 1), \\ p_y 80 = 30\,(1 + r)\,(k'_y + 1), \end{cases} \qquad (**)$$

where $k_x = \lambda_x 50\,(1 + e)/20$ and $k_y = \lambda_x 40\,(1 + e)/30$ are the value compositions of capital, whereas $k'_x = p_x 50/20$ and $k'_y = p_x 40/30$ are the corresponding price compositions of capital. Clearly,

$$k'_x/k_x = k'_y/k_y = p_x/\lambda_x (1 + e).$$

Moreover, $\lambda_y (1 + e) = p_y$ from (4) and (6) of the appendix. Hence, if we know (e, λ_x, k_x, k_y), we can always derive (r, p_x); and if we know (r, p_x, k'_x, k'_y), then we can get (e, λ_x). Here I illustrate just this latter transformation. Write (*) above as:

$$\begin{cases} \lambda_x 150 = 20\,[(k'_x \lambda_x/p_x) + 1], \\ \lambda_y 80 = 30\,[(k'_y \lambda_x/p_x) + 1]. \end{cases}$$

and recall that $(r, p_x, k'_x, k'_y) = (0.7338, 0.5477, 1.369, 0.7303)$. Then we get $\lambda_x = 0.2$ and $\lambda_y = 0.475$. Since the second equation is equal to $90/(1 + e)$ by the viability condition of capitalism, we also get $e = 1.368$. The same results have been obtained from the direct solution of $\Lambda(T)$.

The meaning of this transformation is self-explanatory. It establishes that one point $(\lambda_x, \lambda_y, \lambda_z, e)$ in the value space has a unique corresponding point (p_x, p_y, p_z, r) in the price space and *vice versa*, just as one point in the Cartesian coordinate system has its image in the polar coordinate system and *vice versa*. The same mathematical relations hold differently in different spaces.

8. What is the law of average profit?

When values and prices are quantitatively determined, it turns out that they are not, in general, proportional to each other. Yet the deviation of equilibrium prices from values is by no means arbitrary. The law of average profit claims that the extent to which equilibrium prices (production-prices) depart from value-proportional prices is strictly predetermined by the variability of techniques in the production of individual commodities as use-values, so that equilibrium prices are, as it were, tethered to values. In other words, the law of average profit defines the concrete mode of enforcement of the law of value through the motion of prices in the capitalist market.

The law of average profit, however, is often phrased in a somewhat more specific form, such as: "If it is assumed that the price of the aggregate-social product is equal to its value, then the production-price of the commodity produced with a higher-than-the-social-average value composition of capital exceeds its value-proportional price, and *vice versa.*" This statement applies strictly to the case in which (1) fixed capital does not exist, and (2) there is no more than one capital-good in the system. In other cases small modifications will be necessary. I shall refer to this proposition as the *first law of average profit.*

In chapter XI of *Capital*, volume III, Marx also advances a closely related proposition that: "When wages are raised, the production-price of a commodity produced with a higher(lower)-than-the-social-average value composition of capital falls (rises); and when wages are lowered, the exact reverse occurs." I refer to this latter proposition as the *second law of average profit.*

It can easily be established that, if the rate of surplus value is assumed to be zero (i.e., $e = 0$), i.e., if no surplus labour is performed, values and prices will be proportional. Such a case is, of course, capitalistically meaningless, since a zero rate of surplus value would mean a zero rate of profit (by virtue of the so-called fundamental theorem). However, real wages are at their "theoretical" maximum when the rate of profit is zero and prices are consequently proportional to values. Now from this limiting point, let wages fall, and profits emerge. Prices will then begin to diverge from values; and they will do so the more, the more the rate of surplus value increases. This is the meaning of the second law of average profit. In fact, it combines the first law of average profit with the well-known Ricardian theorem that, given the technology, a gain in the rate of profit is a loss in real wages, and *vice versa.* (The same idea is embodied in the so-called "factor-price frontier" in neo-classical economics.)

In the previous example, we had $(k_x, k_y, k_z) = (1.1842, 0.6316, 0.3553)$. Let us define the social-average composition of capital as $k = (10k_x, + 30k_y, + 40k_z)/90$, using labour-inputs for weights. It turns out that in this particular case $k = 0.6316$ is also, by chance, equal to the value composition of capital in the wage-good producing sector k_y (= 0.6316). On the other hand, in order to equate total value $(\lambda_x X + \lambda_y Y + \lambda_z Z = 114)$ to total price $(p_x X + p_y Y + p_z Z = 270)$, let us apply the conversion rate $\alpha = 2.3683$ to labour values $(\lambda_i, i = x, y, z)$ and obtain value-proportional prices $(q_i = \alpha \lambda_i)$, which are $(q_x, q_y, q_z) = (0.4737, 1.1295, 1.2100)$.[11]

It is now possible to compare equilibrium prices and value-proportional prices, and derive the following conclusion:

$p_x (= 0.548) > q_x (= 0.474)$, since $k_x (= 1.1843) > k (= 0.6316)$;

$p_y (= 1.125) = q_y (= 1.125)$, since $k_y (= 0.6316) = k (= 0.6316)$;

$p_z (= 1.087) < q_z (= 1.210)$, since $k_z (= 0.3551) < k (= 0.6316)$.

This illustrates the first law of average profit.

In order to illustrate the second law, I let the production of the wage good increase from $Y = 80$ to $Y' = 85$. For simplicity, however, I assume: (i) that this is entirely at the expense of the luxury-good and does not affect the output level of the capital-good; (ii) that the total number of hours of current labour is unchanged at 90; and (iii) that the change in the pattern of social demand does not affect the methods of production. We then have the new technology complex:

$$
(T') \quad
\begin{cases}
(\quad 50 \quad , \quad 20 \quad) \rightarrow \quad 150 \quad = X' \\
(\quad 42.500 \quad , \quad 31.875 \quad) \rightarrow \quad 85 \quad = Y' \\
+) \ (\quad 28.594 \quad , \quad 38.125 \quad) \rightarrow \quad 85.781 \quad = Z' \\
\hline
\quad 121.094 \quad , \quad 90
\end{cases}
$$

which satisfies the condition of self-replacement. In this case we have $(\lambda_x, \lambda_y, \lambda_z, e) = (0.2, 0.475, 0.511, 1.229)$, so that values are unchanged but the rate of surplus value has fallen (real wages have risen). The value compositions are, of course, uniformly lower by about 5.87% to reflect the change in the rate of surplus value: $(k_x, k_y, k_z) = (1.1148, 0.5945, 0.3343)$, and their labour-weighted social-average will change to $k = 0.5999$, which is only about 5.02% lower than before. By solving the price equations, we find out that $(p_x, p_y, p_z, r) = (0.5098, 1.0588, 1.0327, 0.6810)$, assuming again that $w = 1$. In this case, we should have $\alpha = (p_x X' + p_y Y' + p_z Z')/(\lambda_x X' + \lambda_y Y' + \lambda_z Z') = 255.06/114.22 = 2.2373$, which implies $v = \alpha/(1 + e) = 1.0038$.[12]

Now, according to the second law of average profit, the fall in the rate of surplus value from 136.8% to 122.9% (which raises v from 1 slightly to 1.0038) should make prices more proportional to values. That is to say, we expect that p_x/p_y falls towards q_x/q_y since $k_x > k$ and that p_z/p_y rises towards q_z/q_y since $k_z < k$. Indeed p_x/p_y which used to be 0.4868 has fallen to 0.4815, coming closer to $q_x/q_y = 0.4210$; and p_z/p_y which used to be 0.9662 has risen to 0.9753, coming closer to $q_x/q_y = 1.0779$. The value ratios q_x/q_y and q_z/q_y are, of course, unchanged by the fall in the rate of surplus value, since the methods of production (technology in the narrower sense) are assumed to be the same.

9. How does the law of market value supplement the law of average profit?

So far it has been supposed that there exists only one technique for the production of a particular commodity. This assumption is surely unrealistic. A use-value is often produced with different techniques, so that in the same industry some firms earn more, and others less, than the average profit. In other words, positive or negative surplus profits are the norm. This multiplicity of techniques, however, does not invalidate the labour theory of value, but we must now take into account the principle of market value, which enables us to identify the value (or equilibrium price) determining technique, or combination of techniques, from among those actually employed by different firms in the industry.

Suppose that, for the production of steel ($X = 150$) with itself and labour, two techniques are simultaneously used as follows, their outputs being $X^{(1)} = 80$ and $X^{(2)} = 70$, respectively.

$$
\begin{array}{rccccl}
(& 30 & , & 8 &) & \rightarrow & 80 = X^{(1)} \\
+) (& 10 & , & 20 &) & \rightarrow & 70 = X^{(2)} \\
\hline
(& 40 & , & 28 &) & \rightarrow & 150 = X
\end{array}
\qquad (***)
$$

Hence, *in toto* 150 units of steel are produced with 40 units of steel itself and 28 units of labour. But (40, 28) → 150 cannot immediately be used to determine the value of steel. In the presence of two (or more) techniques, we cannot know in advance which technique or combination of techniques will be used to respond to an autonomous change in the demand for steel.

When the demand for X increases, it may be $X^{(1)}$ or $X^{(2)}$ or some combination of both, that supplies the required addition. Let us suppose that, when the demand for X increases by 10 units, $X^{(1)}$ increases by 8.205 units and $X^{(2)}$ by 1.795 units. This means that when X must increase overall by 6.667%, $X^{(1)}$ increases by 10.256% and $X^{(2)}$ by 2.564%, so that the elasticity of $X^{(1)}$ at the margin is $\delta^{(1)} = 1.5384$ and the corresponding elasticity of $X^{(2)}$ is $\delta^{(2)} = 0.3846$. The two techniques shown in

(∗∗∗) above must be weighted by these elasticities before being added up to the synthetic value-determining social technique as:

$$
\begin{array}{rcccc}
(& 46.16 & , & 12.31 &) & \rightarrow & 123.08 \\
+) \ (& 3.84 & , & 7.69 &) & \rightarrow & 26.92 \\
\hline
(& 50 & , & 20 &) & \rightarrow & 150
\end{array}
$$

All techniques in (T), as shown earlier in my answer to question 6, are social techniques synthesized in the same fashion.

Refer to the essay on "The Law of Market Value" further down in this volume for a more detailed account of the same principle, including its possible application to the cases of heterogeneous labour and joint production.[13] Here, I wish to reaffirm that values and equilibrium prices are meaningful concepts, if, and only if, resources readily flow *at the margin of* all capitalist industries. Thus, if, as demand shifts from industry **A** to industry **B**, enough resources migrate from **A** to **B** so as to adjust the output levels to the altered conditions of demand, then the law of value is securely preserved. It is by no means necessary that all currently employed resources should actually move between **A** and **B**.

The development of capitalism, with its attendant simplification of labour, ensures an adequate (but never complete) mobility of resources for the marginal adjustment of industrial outputs. The law of value works, even if immobile and non-competing elements persist in the interior of various industries. Such elements give rise to "false social value" and surplus profits (positive or negative) that express it. The law of value that takes such contingent matters into consideration is called the law of market value. It, together with the law of average profit, describes the concrete mode of enforcement of the law of value.

10. How does the presence of landed property bear on the regulation of capitalist society by the law of value?

In collecting differential rent, landed property merely assists capital rather than interfering with its logic. Let us reinterpret the first two lines of (∗∗∗) in such a way as to represent the production of wheat with itself and labour per 100 acres of two different types of land. Land-(1) is more fertile than land-(2), since the net output per unit of labour is only 3 on land-(2) whereas it is 6.25 on land-(1). The differential fertility of land is, however, given by nature, and does not tend to be eliminated by the competition of capitals. Hence, the market-regulating value and production-price of wheat should be equal to the "individual" value and production-price of wheat harvested on the least fertile land-(2).

If we calculate $(p_x/w, r)$ with (30, 8) → 80 = $X^{(1)}$ and (40, 30) → 80 = Y, assuming that the total labour employed in the system is 90, we get $(p_x/w, r)$ = (0.5235, 0.7667). If we use (10, 20) → 70 = $X^{(2)}$ instead, other things being equal we get $(p_x/w, r)$ = (0.6156, 0.6476). These latter numbers are respectively the market regulating production-price of wheat and the general rate of profit. Hence the farmers who produce on land-(1) earn the surplus profit of 0.6156 − 0.5235 = 0.0921 per unit of wheat, which should, of course, be converted into differential rent, if the capitalist market is to guarantee fair competition.

If $X^{(1)}$ and $X^{(2)}$ refer to the outputs of the first and the second instalment of investment on 100 acres of the same land, rather than the outputs per 100 acres of different lands, the formal aspects of the problem remain unchanged. The first instalment is more productive than the second, and, hence, pays a rent proportional to the differential productivity of investment. In collecting differential rent of either kind, landed property has so far not actively interfered with the determination of the rate of profit and production-prices by capital.

The situation changes altogether, when landed property collects absolute rent. By limiting the supply of agricultural land, landed property can raise the price of agricultural products above their production-prices, and thus appropriate part of surplus value produced in agriculture, *before* its capitalist distribution as average profit. Since the value composition of capital in agriculture tends to be lower than the social average, the production-prices of agricultural products are lower than their value-proportional prices, meaning that surplus value normally tends to be transferred from agriculture to non-agriculture.

Now the appropriation of agricultural surplus value by landed property in the form of absolute rent certainly reduces average profit, which is the form of distribution of surplus value to capital. Yet, it does not reverse the flow of surplus value from agriculture (or industries with lower capital composition) to non-agriculture (or industries with higher capital composition).

It is, however, technically possible for landed property to limit the supply of land so drastically as to raise the market prices of agricultural goods above their value-proportional prices. In such a case, landed property would earn monopoly rent in addition to absolute rent, and this would disrupt the operation of the law of average profit. For surplus value would then have to flow from industries with higher capital composition (non-agriculture) to industries with lower capital composition (agriculture), a movement which would be exactly opposite of that established earlier by the principle of the distribution of surplus value as profit, once that principle itself was established by the operation of the law of average profit.

Should this happen, the regulation of capitalist society by the law of value would be suspended, and a Malthusian underconsumption (if not a Ricardian stationary state) could no longer be ruled out as a chimera. Genuine capitalism, however, consists of a "teleological coexistence" of capital and landed property in which the latter, being "satisficed" (an expression due to H. A. Simon to describe the sense of having achieved sufficiency in satisfaction) with increasing wealth, refuses to yield to the bourgeois addiction to maximise revenues.

Appendix

Consider the simplest capitalist economy in which one means of production, or capital-good, (X), one wage-good (Y), and one consumption-good for capitalists, or luxury-good, (Z), are produced and competitively traded. If X_i $(i = x, y, z)$ represent the quantities of the capital-good used, and L_i $(i = x, y, z)$ the number of hours of labour spent, for the production of X, Y, Z, then the technology complex, T, can be written as follows:

$$(T) \quad \begin{cases} (X_x, L_x) & \to \quad X, \\ (X_y, L_y) & \to \quad Y, \\ (X_z, L_z) & \to \quad Z. \end{cases} \tag{1}$$

The component techniques of T are all value-determining "social" techniques synthesized by the method discussed in Section 9 of the text.

In order for this economy to be reproducible, it is necessary that the condition of self-replacement

$$X_x + X_y + X_z \leqq X \tag{2}$$

should hold. This guarantees that all values λ_i $(i = x, y, z)$ are meaningfully positive. The Λ-operation is as follows:

$$\Lambda(T) \quad \begin{cases} \lambda_x X_x + L_x = \lambda_x X, \\ \lambda_x X_y + L_y = \lambda_y Y, \\ \lambda_x X_z + L_z = \lambda_z Z. \end{cases} \tag{3}$$

In order to determine the rate of surplus value (e), the following constraint (the viability condition) must be used:

$$\lambda_y Y \equiv (L_x + L_y + L_z) / (1 + e). \tag{4}$$

This constraint says that the workers are guaranteed to receive the product of their necessary labour.

Write equilibrium prices, or production-prices, as p_i ($i = x, y, z$), the rate of profit and the money wage-rate as r and w. Then the P-operation on T is:

$$\text{P(T)} \begin{cases} (p_x X_x + w L_x)(1 + r) = p_x X, \\ (p_x X_y + w L_y)(1 + r) = p_y Y, \\ (p_x X_z + w L_z)(1 + r) = p_z Z. \end{cases} \tag{5}$$

These equations together with the constraint

$$p_y Y \equiv w (L_x + L_y + L_z) \tag{6}$$

can be solved for an arbitrary w. This "fundamental constraint of the capitalist market" says that the workers do not save, and hence that the total wages bill paid in society should equal the total money value of wage-goods produced in that society. Clearly (6) is the market expression of (4). If, in addition to (2), we also have the condition $e > 0$ in (4), then the prices and the rate of profit are bound to be positive.

Notes and References

[1] "When, at the beginning of this chapter, we said; in common parlance, that a commodity is both a use-value and an exchange value, we were, accurately speaking, wrong. A commodity is a use-value or object of utility, and a value." *Capital*, I (New York: International Publishers, 1967), p. 60.

[2] The problem goes back to the classical school, whose labour theory of value was described as being only about 93% a labour theory of *price*. (See the well known article by G.J. Stigler, "Ricardo and the 93 Per Cent Labour Theory of Va-

lue", in *The American Economic Review*, XLVIII (1958), reprinted in G.J. Stigler, *Essays in the History of Economics* (Chicago: University of Chicago Press, 1965), pp. 326-42. Stigler, of course, is talking about the labour theory of price, not of value, in that essay. Even Marxists, many of whom fail to distinguish between value and exchange value despite Marx's express warning, have unknowingly upheld a labour theory of *price* in the name of the labour theory of *value*.

3 For the argument that "scarcity" does not explain the cause of prices, see the following essay in this volume.

4 See Kôzô Uno, *Principles of Political Economy: Theory of a Purely Capitalist Society*, trans. by T. Sekine (Sussex: Harvester Press, 1980), pp. 32-4, note 2.

5 For details see my "Pricing of Commodities", in *York Studies in Political Economy*, IV (1985), pp. 97-121.

6 I also alert the reader to another (qualitative) usage of the word "determine (*bestimmen*)" as in Marx's expression "socially necessary labour *determines* the value of a commodity". I take this to mean that "socially necessary labour defines or forms the substance of value", rather than that "the magnitude of value is represented by the number of hours of socially necessary labour".

7 Marx simply accepted the Ricardian view that land was an "indestructible" element of production. More recently, however, we have been made keenly aware that the "topsoil" can easily be destroyed by misuse or lack of preservatory care. In theory, the teleological coexistence of private landed property with capital, makes it impossible for the latter to unilaterally spoliate the productivity of land, so that it is *as if* land were indestructible in a genuinely capitalist regime. The fact that agribusiness does not recognise the separation of capital from landed property means that it is *not* a genuinely capitalist industry and hence has no relevance to the law of value.

8 P. A. Samuelson, "Wages and Interest: A Modern Dissection of Marxists Economic Models", in *The American Economic Revue* XLVII (1957), pp. 181-219. E. D. Domar, *Essays in the Theory of Economic Growth* (Oxford University Press, 1957), p. 26, p. 88.

9 See the following essay in this volume for more detail.

10 In the absence of this constraint, the solution of the price system requires the unreasonable assumption that the workers are paid physically prescribed wage-baskets with no option to retrade their contents, i.e., that they are paid "fodder" instead of money wages. Such an assumption which in effect reduces labour-power to an intermediate good, and renders the distinction between "variable" and "constant" capital irrelevant is incompatible with the presuppositions of the dialectic of capital. See "The Transformation Problem, Qualitative and Quantitative", in this volume.

[11] Confirm that $\alpha = 2.3683$ makes total value equal to total price, i.e., $q_x X + q_y Y + q_z Z = 270 = p_x X + p_y Y + p_z Z$. The following discussion, however, does not depend on this particular choice of the "postulate of invariance", so called by F. Seton in his "The Transformation Problem", in *The Review of Economic Studies*, XX (1957), pp. 149-60. In the present case, it so happens that another invariance postulate $q_y Y = 90 = p_y Y$ also holds with the same $\alpha = 2.3683$. That, however, implies that $v = \alpha/(1 + e) = 1$ which is the money wage-rate that would prevail if prices were proportional to values.

[12] See the preceding note 11.

[13] See "The Law of Market Value", in this volume.

The Necessity of the Law of Value, Its Demonstration and Significance

Introduction

In paragraph 31 of his *Principles* (see Appendix with excerpt below) Uno illustrates the labour-and-production process by means of the following numerical example: 6 kg. of raw cotton, one spinning machine, and 6 hours of labour produce 6 kg. of cotton yarn.[1] It is assumed that no surplus labour is performed. It is also assumed that the 6 kg. of raw cotton embody 20 hours of labour, and the current depreciation of the spinning machine is worth 4 hours of labour. Hence the means of production already embody 24 hours of labour. This and the 6 hours of current labour thus produce the 6 kg. of cotton yarn which embody 30 hours of labour.

Further along in paragraph 34 where he explains the process of value formation and augmentation, Uno supposes that the means of livelihood needed for the reproduction of labour-power per day can be produced in 6 hours of labour, and that the money price of the basket is 3 shillings. When the production of cotton yarn illustrated earlier is to be capitalistically operated, Uno supposes furthermore that the constant capital which embodies 24 hours of labour can be purchased for 12 shillings and the 6 kg. of cotton yarn which embody 30 hours of labour can be sold for 15 shillings. Hence the capitalist recovers the 12 shillings that he spent on the means of production by selling four-fifths (or 4.8 kg.) of his output of yarn, and 3 shillings that he paid the worker by selling the remaining one-fifth (or 1.2 kg.) of the same.[2]

The above information may be tabulated as follows, where (**A**) refers to the production of the means of livelihood (wage-good) and (**B**) to that of cotton yarn, per employment of one worker. All numbers in square brackets are supplied additionally by the present writer. Let u stand for the product value, and c, v, s, respectively, for its constant-capital, variable-capital and surplus-value component.

(A)	c		v		s		u	
in labour	[18]	+	6	+	0	=	[24]	$\lambda_a = 3$
in money	[9]	+	3	+	0	=	[12]	$p_a = 1.5$
in quantity	[6]	+	[2]	+	0	=	[8]	$r = 0$

(B)	c		v		s		u	
in labour	24	+	6	+	0	=	30	$\lambda_b = 5$
in money	12	+	3	+	0	=	15	$p_b = 2.5$
in quantity	4.8	+	1.2	+	0	=	6	$r = 0$

From the numbers newly supplied in square brackets it should be inferred that 2 baskets of wage-goods are assumed necessary and sufficient to reproduce a one-day consumption of labour power. The symbols $\lambda_a (p_a)$ and $\lambda_b (p_b)$ denote the values (prices) of the basket of wage-goods and of cotton yarn, respectively; the symbol r denotes the rate of profit.

The problem

Now in paragraph 35, while still discussing the process of value formation and augmentation, Uno lets the spinning capitalist double the scale of his operation, not only by extending the working-day from 6 to 12 hours but also by applying twice the means of production.[3] The situation can, therefore, be tabulated as follows.

(B')	c		v		s		u	
in labour	48	+	6	+	6	=	60	$\lambda_b = 5$
in money	24	+	3	+	3	=	30	$p_b = 2.5$
in quantity	9.6	+	1.2	+	1.2	=	12	$r = 0.11$

If this is the case in the spinning sector, however, it must be supposed that the worker in the sector which produces baskets of wage-goods too must work 12 hours a day, dividing it half and half between the necessary and surplus labour-time. It will be shown presently (see next section) that in this latter sector alone the v-column and the u-column must always remain proportional. Hence, if the same rate of profit of $r = 0.11$ as in the cotton spinning sector (**B'**) must prevail in the expanded wage-goods producing sector (**A'**) as well, the following situation must be obtained.

(**A'**)	c		v		s		u			
in labour	36	+	6	+	6	=	48	λ_a	=	3
in money	18.6	+	3	+	2.4	=	24	p_a	=	1.5
in quantity	12.4	+	2	+	1.6	=	16	r	=	0.11

Are these two situations (**A'**) and (**B'**) mutually consistent? There must be something wrong since the values and prices are proportional ($\lambda_a : p_a = \lambda_b : p_b = 2 : 1$) even though the value composition of capital differs between the sectors (c/v is 6 in **A'** and 8 in **B'**). Such a thing is, of course, impossible. Besides, the capital composition in (**A'**) is 6 in value and 6.2 in price (the latter being about 3.3% higher); but in (**B'**) it is 8 both in value and in price. This cries out for a justification.

Wage-good sector

Let us first establish the reason why only in the sector producing wage-goods the v-column and the u-column must be proportional. Let the number of workers engaged in the production of wage-goods be m, and let A be the total number of the baskets of wage-goods produced in society. Then we have:

$$48m = \lambda_a A, \qquad 24m = p_a A, \qquad 16m = A \qquad (1)$$

necessarily.

Now let n stand for the total number of productive workers in society, L for the total number of hours worked in society, w for the wage-rate per hour, and e for the rate of surplus value. Then we have:

$$6n = L/(1 + e), \qquad 3n = wL, \qquad 2n = A. \qquad (2)$$

Under any circumstances, however, the identities

$$\lambda_a A = L/(1 + e), \qquad p_a A = wL \qquad (3)$$

must hold.[4] Hence in capitalist society as a whole the v-column times n/m should always be equal to the u-column in the production of wage-goods.

Now let us consider the question of capital composition in value and in price. Let only one capital-good **X** be in use in both sectors, and let X_a be the quantity of it in use in the wage-good sector. If L_a is the number of hours of labour spent in that sector, the capital composition in value is $\lambda_x X_a (1 + e)/L_a$ and in price $p_x X_a / wL_a$. Hence, their ratio is $\lambda_x (1 + e) : p_x / w$. In the spinning sector, the same ratio applies inasmuch as the capital composition in value is $\lambda_x X_b (1 + e)/L_b$ and that in price is $p_x X_b / wL_b$ there, with similarly defined symbols X_b and L_b.

In the case in which there are many capital-goods **X**, **X'**, **X"**... in use, it is not reasonable to expect the same ratio between sectors, unless these capital-goods are used in the same fixed proportion everywhere. Though in each sector the ratio is in the form:

$$\text{Average of } (\lambda_x, \lambda'_x, \lambda''_x, ...)(1 + e) :$$
$$\text{Average of } (p_x, p'_x, p''_x, ...) / w,$$

the method of averaging (assigning weights to different capital-goods) differs from one sector to another. Even so, however, one can say the following. If the ratio $\lambda_x^{(t)} (1 + e) : p_x^{(t)}/w$ is the largest with regard to the i-th capital-good $(t = i)$ and the smallest with regard to the j-th capital-good $(t = j)$, then the ratio in any sector must be between these two extremes.

For the problem at hand, however, detail is not important. For simplicity it may be assumed that, if, in the wage-goods sector, the capital composition in price is $x\%$ higher than that in value terms, the same deviation applies in all other sectors, though in reality it varies within limits. In other words, let us assume either only one capital-good to be in use in all sectors or many capital goods in the same mix everywhere.[5]

A reverse solution

At this point, one may ask whether it is possible at all to arbitrarily expand the spinning sector first, and then adapt to it the wage-goods sector, even though the latter has to satisfy the condition of proportionality between the v-column and the u-column. By a trial-and-error experiment, one can easily discover that this is impossible. Perhaps Uno himself tried to construct a plausible example and could not obtain a satisfactory one. Actually, I do surmise that to have been the case, since he keeps the wage-goods sector rather vague without supplying necessary numbers.

At any rate the reason that an extensive debate over Uno's demonstration of the law of value has taken place to no avail is due to the lack of appropriate numbers illustrating the condition of that sector.[6]

With this in mind, I seek a solution by reversing the procedure, i.e., by fixing the conditions of the wage-goods sector as in (**A'**) first, and then adapting the spinning sector to it as in (**B''**) below, rather than doing the reverse. But, as before, I assume in (**B''**) that the one-day output of a spinning worker is 12 kg. of cotton yarn, and that in these are embodied 60 hours of labour. Then the situation in that sector must be the following:

(**B''**)	c		v		s		u		
in labour	48	+	6	+	6	=	60	λ_b = 5	
in money	24.8	+	3	+	3.1	=	30.9	p_b = 2.575	
in quantity	9.63 +		1.17 +		1.2	=	12	r = 0.11	

The numbers previously known are underlined.

Here, 12 of the 60 hours of labour are current, so that 48 hours of labour must be embodied in the means of production. Since the necessary labour-time is 6 hours, the value composition of capital is 8. The price composition of capital must be about 3.3% higher, as in the wage-goods sector. It should then be about 8.267. This requires that the capitalist invests 24.8 shillings in the means of production per employment of one worker. Since he has to realise the general rate of profit of 11% on $c + v$ = 27.8 shillings in order for the labour theory of value to hold, his profit must be 3.1 shillings. Hence the output, the 12 kg. of cotton yarn, must be sold for 30.9 shillings or for the unit price of p_b = 2.575.

In this case the two sectors (**A'**) and (**B''**) are consistent, and the equality:

"2 baskets of wage-goods = 1.17 kg of cotton yarn"

holds unambiguously. For both sides embody 6 hours of necessary labour and can be bought for 3 shillings, which constitute the daily wage.

Necessary and socially necessary labour

Here it is correct to say that 1.17 kg. of yarn are the product of the necessary labour of 6 hours, but not of *socially* necessary labour of 6 hours. Indeed, since the value of yarn is $\lambda_b = 5$, it must follow that 1.17 kg. of yarn must embody only 5.85 hours of socially necessary labour. (It is, of course, part of rudimentary knowledge that "necessary labour" and "socially necessary labour" are two entirely different concepts.) The spinning capitalist, however, recovers the money value of variable capital advanced by selling 1.17 kg. of yarn for 3 shillings. The reason for this is that the worker can buy back 2 baskets of wage-goods for 3 shillings and these are necessary and sufficient for the reproduction of labour-power used up for the day. These 2 baskets of wage-goods are not only the product of the necessary labour of 6 hours, but they also embody 6 hours of *socially* necessary labour.

If this is the case the following famous statement of Uno does not appear to be accurate in this case.

> Suppose, for example, that the spinning capitalist sells 6 labour-hours' worth of his output for 3 shillings. If, despite this, the other capitalist sold only 5 labour-hours' worth of his output for 3 shillings to the worker, then not only would the latter fail to receive sufficient means of livelihood, but the capitalist who produces the means of livelihood would gain more than the capitalist who spins cotton, which would make the production of cotton an altogether futile enterprise for capital.[7]

This statement is correct in the absence of surplus labour (i.e., when $r = e = 0$); and Uno meant it for such a case, for example, as between (**A**) and (**B**) above. Indeed while the spinning capitalist sells 1.2 kg. of cotton yarn which embody 6 hours of labour for 3 shillings, the capitalist who supplies wage-goods cannot sell only 1.67 baskets of them which embody 5 hours of labour for 3 shillings. That would mean that the spinning worker could not reproduce his labour-power. This merely reasserts the fact that, in the absence of surplus labour, values and prices are proportional, and that products embody as much "*socially* necessary" labour as they do "necessary" labour.

In the more general case, with positive surplus labour ($r, e, > 0$), the equivalence of "necessary" and "socially necessary" labour fails. Although every worker performs 6 hours of necessary labour and is paid 3 shillings, the latter enable him to buy back the product of 6 hours of (socially necessary) labour only as wage-goods. In the case of cotton yarn for the production of which a higher value composition of capital than that in the wage-goods sector applies, the wage of 3 shillings enables him to buy back the product of only 5.58 hours of (socially necessary) labour. It enables him to buy back the product of more than 6 hours of (socially necessary) labour, if it is of the sector whose value composition is lower than that in the wage-goods sector.

Suppose that a capitalist produces, per employment of one worker, 10 units of (**C**) which embody 42 hours of labour. Then the value composition of capital (c/v) in this sector is 5 and is smaller than in the sector (**A'**) which produces wage-goods where it is 6. The situation in that case is as follows:

(**C**)	c		v		s		u		
in labour	30	+	6	+	6		= 42	λ_c	= 4.2
in money	15.5	+	3	+	2		= 20.5	p_c	= 2.05
in quantity	7.56	+	1.46	+	0.98		= 10	r	= 0.11

The composition of capital in price is 5.167 or about 3.3% higher than that in value terms. In this case, what the wage of 3 shillings can buy back is 1.46 units of (**C**) in which as much as 6.132 hours of (socially necessary) labour are embodied.

Yet all these industries (**A'**), (**B''**) and (**C**) operate at the uniform profit rate of 11%, so that it should not be, to any one in particular, "an altogether futile enterprise for capital".

The necessity of the law of value

What is the relevance of the above technicalities to the idea of the necessity of the law of value?

In capitalist society the production of commodities is universal and not partial. In other words, all use-values that society needs are produced as value-objects because even labour-power is converted into a commodity. Value-objects tend to embody only socially necessary labour. When all commodities embody only socially necessary labour, they are all produced in quantities that meet the social demand (none being either overproduced or underproduced). This further implies that the allocation of productive labour in society is optimal and a uniform rate of profit obtains in all spheres of production. The law of value, on this ground, claims that all commodities tend to be exchanged at equilibrium prices, which presuppose an optimal social allocation of productive labour, and, consequently, also presuppose the expenditure of only socially necessary labour for the production of all commodities.

The direct producer in a capitalist society cannot live for an extended period of time unless he sells his labour-power at least for its value. If the consumption of his labour-power per day can be made good by 2 baskets of wage-goods, as supposed above, the socially necessary labour for the production of these two baskets is also the necessary labour for the reproduction of his labour-power. Though every worker works for 12 hours, he receives the wage of 3 shillings with which to buy back 2 baskets of wage-goods produced with 6 hours of labour. As soon as this assumption is made, it is possible to deduce the price of any other commodity, i.e., the price at which that commodity must be traded, if its daily output per employment of one worker is known in units of physical quantity and in terms of the labour directly and indirectly spent on it.

Now let us consider a "simple commodity producer" who produces 5 units of (**D**), which are the product of 40 hours of labour, either directly and indirectly. Assume that he too works 12 hours a day and can reproduce his daily consumption of his labour-power with 2 baskets of wage-goods, like the worker employed by a capitalist. In this case, he can continue to sell his product for any price that enables him to recover the advance of his means of production and to pay for his upkeep without getting into any serious trouble. For example, a situation such as,

(**D**)	c		v		s		u			
in labour	28	+	6	+	6	=	40		$\lambda_d = 8$	
in money	14.46	+	3	+	0.88	=	18.34		$p_d = 3.668$	
in quantity	3.94	+	0.82	+	0.24	=	5		$r = 0.05$	

can be repeated endlessly. Here the profit-rate is only 5%. But that may be enough for the small producer to survive. The problem here is that under other circumstances he may also get a profit-rate of 10%, 15%, etc.; and the price of his product (p_d) varies accordingly. In any case, it is not possible to determine a definite price corresponding to the socially necessary labour for the production of (**D**), unless the same commodity is capitalistically produced in the same market.

If, however, this commodity (**D**) is capitalistically produced, then the following situation must necessarily hold per employment of one worker per day:

(**D'**)	c		v		s		u	
in labour	28	+	6	+	6	=	40	$\lambda_d = 8$
in money	14.46	+	3	+	1.92	=	19.38	$p_d = 3.876$
in quantity	3.73	+	0.77	+	0.5	=	5	$r = 0.11$

In this case, society's productive labour is allocated in such a way that, in all branches of production, including the production of (**D**), the uniform profit-rate of 11% obtains.

The fact that the 5 units of (**D**) are sold for 19.38 shillings (i.e., $p_d = 3.876$) confirms the 40 hours of labour spent on them directly and indirectly as that which was socially necessary.

In small commodity production, however, a condition of excess supply can persist for a lengthy period of time in which each producer of (**D**) is obliged to sell its 5 units for only 18.34 shillings and to sustain the low profit-rate of 5%. This would in effect mean that the 8 hours of labour actually spent for the production of (**D**) per unit were not all socially necessary, and that only 94.6% (= 18.34 / 19.38) of 8, or 7.57, hours were formative of value. In other words, value cannot be defined properly unless society's productive labour is (or tends to be) optimally allocated to the production of all commodities.

The above is my interpretation of what Uno meant by the "necessity of the law of value" in capitalist society. The exchange of commodities "according to values" does not mean "at prices proportional to values". It rather means the exchange of commodities "at prices which reflect an optimal allocation of society's productive labour to the production of all commodities".

Appendix

Excerpt of Kôzô Uno, *Principles of Political Economy:*

31. The end-result of a labour-process is its product, and from the point of view of the product the same process can be viewed as a production-process. Here both the means and the objects of labour are called *means of production*; labour-power too is often regarded as one of the two *elements of production* together with the material means of production. Even in the production-process, however, labour-power which is the active factor does not operate in the same way as the means of production which are passive factors. Suppose, for instance, that 6 kg. of raw cotton and a

spinning machine together produce 6 kg. of cotton yarn in 6 hours. In this simplified example, all the means of labour other than the machine are assumed away, and so is the waste of cotton. The 6 kg. of cotton yarn, which in this case are the product of 6 hours of spinning labour, do not embody just 6 hours of labour as such because the production of the 6 kg. of raw cotton as well as the production of the spinning machine must have required some labour. If 20 hours of labour have been spent for the production of the 6 kg. of raw cotton, and if the part of the machine embodying 4 hours of labour wears out during the current production of the 6 kg. of yarn, then 24 hours of labour are already embodied in the means of production quite apart from the 6 additional hours of spinning labour itself. Consequently the 6 kg. of cotton yarn require 30 hours of labour in all to produce. If, however, the productivity of spinning labour doubles, and twice as much yarn can now be produced during the same 6 hours, then there will be 12 kg. of cotton yarn requiring 54 hours of labour, of which 48 hours correspond to the raw cotton used up and the wear and tear of the machine. Of course, from the point of view of the spinning process which produces cotton yarn as the new product, the labour-time required for the production of the spinning machine and of the raw cotton is given in advance; the productivity of spinning labour, however, changes the proportion in which the total labour cost of the new product is divided into the old and the new component. Labour in the spinning process, therefore, functions on the one hand as what Marx calls *concrete-useful labour* in that, as it converts raw cotton into cotton yarn, it also preserves the labour-time already embodied in the means of production such as raw cotton and the spinning machine used up in the process as part of the total labour-time required to produce the yarn. Simultaneously, the same labour functions on the other hand as what Marx calls *abstract-human labour* in that it adds the spinning hours of labour to the labour hours already materialised in the means of production, regarding them as homogeneous components of the total labour-time embodied in the final product. The same labour, in other words, possesses two entirely different aspects, the one being quite specific and the other perfectly abstract. In the present example the former aspect requires that the labour should be suitable for the production of cotton yarn; the latter aspect requires that it should not be different, as the expenditure of human labour, from that which is embodied either in the raw cotton or in the spinning machine. A production-process can furnish various specific products only with labour that possesses this dual character.

[...]

34. Suppose that the means of livelihood needed for the reproduction of labour-power per day can be produced with 6 hours of labour, and that the money price of the basket is 3 shillings. If the production of cotton yarn illustrated in the preceding section is to be capitalistically operated, it may further be supposed that the means of production (such as raw cotton and the spinning machine) which required 24 hours of labour to produce are paid 12 shillings, and that the 6 kg of cotton yarn whose production needed 30 hours of labour in all are sold for 15 shillings. In this case all the commodities are traded at prices proportional to the labour-time required for their respective production. Trade at such prices implies that the capitalist recovers the 12 shillings with which he compensates the use of the means of production by selling four-fifths (or 4.8 kg.) of his output of yarn, and the 3 shillings that he pays out to the worker by selling the remaining fifth (or 1.2 kg.) of his output. It also implies that the worker can buy back, with the 3 shillings that he has received, the equivalent of a fifth of the output of yarn that he has produced with 6 hours of labour in the form of the means of livelihood. The 3 shillings then intermediate this production-process and the commodity-exchange system that revolves around it. The relation of this worker to his yarn-spinning capitalist determines the exchange relation between this capitalist and the capitalist who produces the means of the worker's livelihood. Suppose, for example, that the spinning capitalist sells 6 labour-hours' worth of his output for 3 shillings. If, despite this, the other capitalist sold-only 5 labour-hours' worth of his output for 3 shillings to the worker, then not only would the latter fail to receive sufficient means of livelihood, but the capitalist who produces the means of livelihood would gain more than the capitalist who spins cotton, which would make the production of cotton yarn an altogether futile enterprise for capital. Of course, all capitalists who advance money for the purchase of labour-power and the means of production individually try to maximise their pecuniary gain by selling their product at the highest possible price. But as capitalists they must collectively make sure, under any circumstances, that their workers get the means of livelihood necessary for the reproduction of labour-power. In order to satisfy this condition capitalists must exchange their products according to the labour-time necessary for the production of these goods. The fact, that the capitalists can choose to produce any commodity of their liking merely by purchasing labour-power as well as the means of production as commodities, or, in other words, the fact that the production relation between capitalists and workers is bound by the form of the commodity ensures this result. In the above example, the worker could not directly obtain the product of his 6 hours of labour, even if it consisted of the means of livelihood; he must buy back' the result of his own labour with the 3 shillings that are paid to

him as the price of his labour-power. This necessity does not follow from the mere fact that products of labour are exchanged as commodities; it only follows from the fact that the production-process itself is governed by the form of the commodity. It is a general economic norm rooted in the labour-and-production process that all products are more or less difficult for society to obtain depending on the labour-time needed to produce them. This norm appears in a commodity-economy as the *law of value* which regulates the exchange of these products.

35. The capitalist who purchases labour-power for the day, however, has no reason to limit its consumption to 6 hours and merely to produce 6 kg of cotton yarn. Moreover, the worker who has been compelled to sell his labour-power for the day as a commodity cannot be free to stop working just because he has finished the labour necessary for the production of his own livelihood. If he therefore works 12 hours a day, then his capitalist can produce 12 kg. of cotton yarn which he can sell for 30 shillings. He makes a net gain of 3 shillings, after having paid 3 shillings for the labour-power and 24 shillings for his means of production. He does not make this gain for having bought his commodities cheap, i.e., for having paid less than is due for the means of production and labour-power, nor does he make this gain for having extorted more than is due from the purchasers of his cotton yarn. Capital increases its own value because labour-power for which it has paid the value creates an entirely new and greater value in the production-process of capital. Of course, the capitalist would endeavour to buy the means of production and labour-power as cheaply as possible, and to sell his cotton yarn as dearly as possible; moreover, in practice, surplus value that he earns through his shrewd mercantile activity cannot often be ignored. As mentioned earlier, however, surplus value so earned cannot be more than the private gain of an individual capital offset by someone else's loss. It cannot be a share of the social gain originating in the formation of new value; in other words, it does not theoretically explain the value-formation-and-augmentation process of capital, which gives rise to true surplus value capable of being shared by all the members of the capitalist class. Theory must uncover the ground for the value-augmenting-power of capital, even when all commodities are supposed to be exchanged at prices proportional to their values. That ground lies in the formation of value by labour which is the consumption of labour-power in the production-process of capital; that is to say, it lies in the social relation that divides men into workers and capitalists.[8]

Notes and References

1 Kôzô Uno, *Principles of Political Economy*, translated from the Japanese by Thomas T. Sekine (Sussex: Harvester, 1980), p. 23.

2 Uno, *Principles of Political Economy*, p. 25.

3 Ibid., p. 26.

4 The first relation states the fact that the working-class buys back all the wage-goods produced in society with the necessary labour-time that it performs. The second relation says that all the wage-goods produced in society are entirely purchased by the total wages-bill paid to the workers.

5 This condition may, at first sight, appear to be rather unduly restrictive. However, the same condition is implied by the usual formulation of the law of average profit that the prices of commodities with a higher(lower)-than-the-average value composition of capital are higher (lower) than their value-prices, i.e., prices proportional to values. See Thomas T. Sekine, *The Dialectic of Capital*, vol. II (Tokyo: Toshindo Press, 1986), pp. 115-23.

6 There is enormous literature in Japanese which is devoted to trying to figure out what exactly it was that Uno tried to establish in those enigmatic paragraphs of his *Principles* (1980).

7 Uno, *Principles of Political Economy*, p. 25.

8 Ibid., p. 23-7.

The Transformation Problem, Qualitative and Quantitative

Introduction

The transformation of values into production-prices has always been a controversial issue in Marxian economic theory; it is also of utmost theoretical importance to the dialectic of capital.[1] In a book recently published in English, Professor Kôzô Uno treats the conceptual significance of the problem flawlessly. But his illustrations remain technically as unsatisfactory as those of Marx, which have given rise to persistent criticisms for over a century. The present paper aims at reinforcing Uno's views on the transformation of values into prices with a technically more defensible apparatus. Since, the so-called transformation problem was originally posed by Ladislaus von Bortkiewicz in the non-Marxian tradition of mathematical economics, many works in the area have neglected the dialectical significance of the problem and trivialised it in consequence. For example, the common practice (originated by Bortkiewicz himself) of physically specifying the worker's consumption basket renders the transformation problem altogether meaningless. This essay explores a few important points of the dialectic of capital related to the transformation problem, and intends to offer a new solution to it free from the Bortkiewiczian aberration.

The contradiction between value and use-value[2]

(a) The dialectic of capital may be said to consist of solving (or overcoming) the contradiction between value and use-value which is first recognised in the form of the commodity. Here, the socially uniform quality of value cannot exist by itself, but only correlatively with a specific use-value. As if to be released from this restriction, the value of the commodity suppresses its own correlative use-value by expressing itself in the use-value of another commodity. This method of overcoming the contradiction is called the dialectic of *transition* or *becoming*. It consists of solving the existing contradiction by seeking another form, or passing from one form to another. It is this method that characterises the Doctrine of

Circulation, the first of the three parts of the dialectic of capital.[3] Thus, the commodity in which value is only immanent develops into money, which openly exhibits value by transcending specific use-values. But value is stationary in money which may only measure, realise, and store value. As if to break out of this captivity, money develops into capital in which value sets itself into motion and augments itself. But even capital is a "metamorphosis of value" in the sense that it alternately assumes and discards the forms of money and of the commodity. Hence, the motion of capital cannot as yet be free from the restrictions of particular use-values, through which value must travel. This restriction is finally lifted in the form of industrial capital which, in principle, can produce and circulate *any* use-value of its choice, so long as it can purchase labour-power as a commodity. The form of industrial capital, therefore, realises the "absolute indifference" of value to use-values, to adopt the Hegelian mode of expression.[4]

(b) But once the form of industrial capital is thus established, a completely new contradiction between value and use-value arises. This is the contradiction between "capital" as the commodity-economic form of value augmentation, and supra-historic "real economic life" which consists of use-value production in general. It is this kind of contradiction that must be settled in the second part of the dialectic of capital called the Doctrine of Production. Here, the contradiction cannot be resolved by discovering a new dwelling place for value. The solution requires the dialectic of *reflection* or *grounding*; that is to say, the solution consists in the assimilation (subsumption or absorption) of real economic life by the chrematistic operation of industrial capital. If the production of use-values common to all societies is capitalistically operated, all use-values must be produced as values, i.e., as mere embodiments of socially necessary labour, because capital is a form absolutely indifferent to the use-values of commodities. The price mechanism that enables capitalist society to produce all socially desired commodities in appropriate quantities is held implicit, i.e., assumed but not analysed, in the Doctrine of Production. Instead, the production of commodities as value that contains surplus value is studied in all aspects, i.e., inside the factory (the production-process of capital), outside the factory (the circulation-process of capital), and as the continuing activity of the aggregate-social capital (its reproduction-process). The purpose of this doctrine is to establish that the capitalist mode of production secures itself as the "absolute actuality" of Hegel, that is to say, as a self-dependent system of commodity production consistent with the general (supra-historic) norms of real economic life. Alternatively, it may be said that the Doctrine of Production demonstrates that capitalism is a historic (historically existent) society rather than an imaginary one.

(c) Now that its historical existence is guaranteed, capital further proceeds to develop its own market, the capitalist market. Although all commodities have been produced as value, and this fact always remains, these commodities are, of course, distinct use-values requiring different techniques of production. Even the same use-value may be produced with several alternative techniques. Thus, the contradiction between value and use-value arises again in yet another form. This time it is a contradiction between the capitalist indifference to use-values and the unavoidability of technical variations in their production. Such a contradiction must be settled by the dialectic of *development* or *unfolding* in the Doctrine of Distribution, which constitutes the last part of the dialectic of capital. Here, capital adapts to the variability of use-value production by differentiating and specialising itself. The formation of the production-prices and the general rate of profit must be evaluated in this light. It is by wisdom and cunning that capital lets the market determine its equilibrium, *as if such things as value and surplus value never existed*, while yet covertly abiding by the production of commodities as value.

Two transformation problems

Since the dialectic proceeds by describing the same thing, X, at different stages of synthesis, X^a, X^b, ..., X^*, it is not surprising that the same concept returns a number of times and increasingly more specific each time, i.e., more concretely determined, sometimes even under different names. When this occurs, one talks of a transformation or conversion of A into B. For example, "the conversion of the value of labour-power into wages" means that what used to be called the value of labour-power appears in a new context as wages, the new context being richer in concrete specifications. "The conversion of surplus profit into rent" means that surplus profit arising in a particular context, i.e., specifically in relation to the differential fertility of land, is called rent. There are many instances of such usage in *Capital*.[5] The same applies to the "transformation of surplus value into profit". What used to be called surplus value, from the point of view of the production-process of capital, now appears as profit in the capitalist market, in which surplus value is distributed as profits to individual units of capital. This is a change in the self-conceptualisation of capital, and may be called a conceptual or qualitative transformation. This transformation must not be confused with another transformation that arises in consequence, namely the mathematical or quantitative transformation of one set of numbers into another. Non-Marxists have consistently ignored the qualitative transformation, while Marxists who tend to sneer at quantitative transformation theories do not themselves appear to have fully grasped the dialectical significance of the qualitative transformation. Indeed, some of their pragmatic spokesmen have gone so far as to produce the monstrosity of a "historical" transformation. The relation between the qualitative and the quantitative transformation can be properly understood only in the context of the dialectic of capital.

In the Doctrine of Production, capitalist commodity production was strictly viewed as the production of value, i.e., as the expenditure of socially uniform productive labour. The diversity of use-value production represented by a particular technology complex, T, was not relevant, and was never made explicit, in that doctrine. Only when capital develops its own market in the Doctrine of Distribution must the distinctness of use-values be taken into explicit consideration. This requires a quantitative specification of technology as T. It is true that value was said to be "determined" by socially necessary labour. But this latter was not quantitatively specified with reference to any particular complex, T, of techniques. It only meant a qualitative determination. For example, the value of labour-power could be arbitrarily assumed to be six hours a day, or three hours a day, without changing the argument. Thus, if Λ is a set of values and the rate of surplus value, any consistent set of numbers $\bar{\Lambda}$ could be used to support the arguments of the Doctrine of Production. Correspondingly, a consistent set, $\bar{P}$, of equilibrium prices and the rate of profit could be presupposed. This is not the case in the Doctrine of Distribution, which explicitly specifies a complex of technology, T. Both prices and values must now be "quantitatively" determined as $P(T)$ and $\Lambda(T)$. But if this is the case, a new problem of relating $P(T)$ with $\Lambda(T)$ necessarily emerges, a problem which was absent in the Doctrine of Production.

The following chart pictorially illustrates the relation between the two transformation problems.

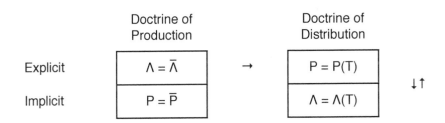

	Doctrine of Production		Doctrine of Distribution	
Explicit	$\Lambda = \bar{\Lambda}$	$\rightarrow$	$P = P(T)$	$\downarrow\uparrow$
Implicit	$P = \bar{P}$		$\Lambda = \Lambda(T)$	

In the conceptual transformation, which is shown here by the lateral arrow, there is no question of an inverse transformation. The conceptual transformation simply means that $\Lambda(T)$ is more concretely specified or more synthetic than $\bar{\Lambda}$. One talks of $\bar{\Lambda} \rightarrow P(T)$ rather than $\bar{\Lambda} \rightarrow \Lambda(T)$ or $\bar{P} \rightarrow P(T)$ simply because the price mechanism which was deliberately held implicit in the Doctrine of Production is now made explicit to play the principal part in the Doctrine of Distribution. The same consideration does not apply to the mathematical transformation which is here depicted by the set of vertical arrows. In this case, the inverse transformation is part of the problem. Since both $P(T)$ and $\Lambda(T)$ are determined in reference to T, there is no question of which is prior to the other. There is no reason why $\Lambda(T)$ should first be known before $P(T)$ may be calculated, or the other way around. Indeed, $\Lambda(T)$ is not there to derive $P(T)$ from, nor $P(T)$ to derive $\Lambda(T)$ from. Both systems exist on their own. But this does not mean that they are unrelated or that the relation is such as to make one of them redundant or otiose.

The price system and the value system

Let us consider a very simple capitalist economy in which only three goods are produced: X (the means of production), Y (the wage-good), and Z (the consumption-good for capitalists). The price equations are written as follows:

$$\begin{cases} (p_x X_x + w L_x)(1 + r) = p_x X, \\ (p_x X_y + w L_y)(1 + r) = p_y Y, \\ (p_x X_z + w L_z)(1 + r) = p_z Z, \end{cases} \tag{1}$$

where X_x, X_y, X_z, are the means of production consumed, and L_x, L_y, L_z labour directly spent, for the current production of X, Y, Z; and p_x, p_y, p_z, w, r are the money prices, the money wage-rate, and the general rate of profit.[6] In order to solve these equations for p_x/w, p_y/w, p_z/w and r, one more equation must be introduced. The historical viability of capitalism established in the Doctrine of Production, however, requires that the workers should be paid the money wage necessary and sufficient to reproduce their labour-power. In the present context, this fact can be stated by

$$w(L_x + L_y + L_z) \equiv p_y Y, \tag{1'}$$

the relation that I wish to call the fundamental constraint of capitalism.[7] Moreover, the four variables can be positively solved if and only if,[8]

$$0 \; < \; \frac{L_x}{X - X_x} \; < \; \frac{L_x + L_z}{X_y} \; . \tag{2}$$

The first inequality, requiring $X - X_x > 0$, is guaranteed by the condition of reproduction, $X \geq X_x + X_y + X_z$ (which is what Marx's $\parallel c \leq \mathrm{I}(v + s)$ means).[9] This is also established in the Doctrine of Production. The second inequality implies that the rate of surplus value (e) is positive, as can be easily seen in the value system:

$$\left\lgroup \begin{array}{l} \lambda_x X_x + L_x = \lambda_x X, \\ \lambda_x X_y + L_y = \lambda_y Y, \\ \lambda_x X_z + L_z = \lambda_z Z, \end{array} \right. \tag{3}$$

$$(L_x + L_y + L_z)\,\frac{1}{1 + e} \; \equiv \; \lambda_y Y, \tag{3'}$$

where λ_x, λ_y, λ_z are the values of the three commodities.[10] This system of equation (3) and (3') is also positively solved for λ_x, λ_y, λ_z and e, if and only if the inequalities of (2) hold.

This means that $P(T) = \{p_x/w,\, p_y/w,\, p_z/w,\, r\}$ and $\Lambda(T) = \{\lambda_x,\, \lambda_y,\, \lambda_z,\, e\}$, both depending on the same technological complex:

$$(T) \left\lgroup \begin{array}{l} (X_x, L_x) \to X, \\ (X_y, L_y) \to Y, \\ (X_z, L_z) \to Z, \end{array} \right.$$

are, in fact, very closely related.[11] It is a simple matter to prove the following proposition, which only rephrases Morishima's Fundamental Theorem in a simpler context, though perhaps in a more striking fashion.[12]

If $(\lambda_x, \lambda_y, \lambda_z, e) > 0$ in (3) (3'), then (1) (1') can be solved for a $(p_x/w, p_y/w, p_z/w, r) > 0$. Conversely, if $(p_x/w, p_y/w, p_z/w, r) > 0$ in (1) (1'), then (3) (3') must imply a $(\lambda_x, \lambda_y, \lambda_z, e) > 0$.

What this means is that no commodity can be capitalistically produced except as a value-object and that no value-object can fail to be profitably produced.

The mathematical transformation

Values (λ_i, $i = x$, y, z) have so far been defined in terms of labour embodied and prices (p_i, $i = x$, y, z) in terms of money. It is convenient to express values too in terms of money so as to enable their direct comparison with prices. The conversion rate (α) of embodied labour into money can be chosen in many different ways. But if v stands for the monetary expression of the value of labour-power, the relation $v = \alpha/(l + e)$ always holds, since $1/(1 + e)$ is the "real wage" or the proportion of necessary labour to total labour.[13] Applying the same α to all λ_i, ($i = x$, y, z) and writing $\alpha\lambda_i \equiv q_i$, one may rewrite (3) (3') as,

$$\left\{ \begin{array}{l} q_x X_x + v L_x(1 + e) = q_x X, \\ q_x X_y + v L_y(1 + e) = q_y Y \quad \equiv v(L_x + L_y + L_z), \\ q_x X_z + v L_z(1 + e) = q_z Z. \end{array} \right. \qquad (4)\ (4')$$

The particular choice of α has been called by F. Seton the postulate of invariance.[14] For example if,

$$\alpha' \equiv \frac{p_x X + p_y Y + p_z Z}{\lambda_x X + \lambda_y Y + \lambda_z Z},$$

total value (in q) is equal to total price. It is also possible to choose an α such as to make total surplus value (in q) equal to total profit. If α is so chosen as to let the value (in q) of the wage-good equal to its price, one should have,

$$\alpha'' \equiv \frac{p_y Y}{\lambda_y Y} = \frac{p_y}{\lambda_y} \quad \text{so that} \quad \lambda_y \alpha'' = q_y = p_y. \qquad (5)$$

But the fundamental constraint of capitalism (1') or (4') always implies,

$$L_x + L_y + L_z \equiv \frac{q_y Y}{v} = \frac{p_y Y}{w}.$$

Hence, the proposed invariance postulate (5) is simply satisfied by the assumption, $v = w = 1$. This postulate will be adopted in the following if only for arithmetical convenience.

To introduce the transformation problem, define the organic composition of capital in each industry in two ways:

$$k_i \equiv \frac{q_x X_i}{v L_i}, \quad k'_i = \frac{p_x X_i}{w L_i} \qquad (i = x, y, z). \tag{6}$$

Then, clearly,

$$k'_i = \frac{(p_x/w) k_i}{q_x/v}, \qquad k_i = \frac{(q_x/v) k'_i}{p_x/w}, \tag{6'}$$

for all $i = x, y, z$. Rewrite (1) (1') and (4) (4') respectively as follows, using (6):

$$\left\{ \begin{array}{l} p_x X = w L_x (k'_x + 1) (1 + r), \\ p_y Y = w L_y (k'_y + 1) (1 + r), \\ p_z Z = w L_z (k'_z + 1) (1 + r), \\ \qquad \text{******} \\ p_z Y \equiv w (L_x + L_y + L_z), \end{array} \right. \tag{7}$$

$$\left\{ \begin{array}{l} q_x X = v L_x (1 + e + k_x), \\ q_y Y = v L_y (1 + e + k_y), \\ q_z Z = v L_z (1 + e + k_z), \\ \qquad \text{******} \\ q_y Y \equiv v (L_x + L_y + L_z). \end{array} \right. \tag{8}$$

If $w = v = 1$ is assumed by the adopted invariance postulate, it is easy to derive from (7) and (8) that,

$$\frac{p_x}{q_x} = \frac{(k'_x + 1) (1 + r)}{1 + e + k_x}, \tag{9}$$

and

$$\frac{p_y}{q_y} = \frac{(k'_y + 1) (1 + r)}{1 + e + k_y} = 1. \tag{10}$$

The last ratio is equal to one in view of the adopted invariance postulate. But if (6') is now considered, (9) and (10) can also be written either as,

$$\frac{p_x}{q_x} = \frac{1 + r}{1 + e - r k_x}, \tag{9'}$$

and
$$\frac{p_x}{q_x} = \frac{k_y + e - r}{k_y(1 + r)} ;$$
(10')

or as
$$\frac{p_x}{q_x} = \frac{1 + r(k'_x + 1)}{1 + e} ,$$
(9")

and
$$\frac{p_x}{q_x} = \frac{k'_y}{k'_y + (k'_y + 1) - e} .$$
(10")

It is, therefore, obvious that (9') and (10') implicitly determine (p_x, r), if (q_x, e, k_x, k_y) are known and that (9") and (10") implicitly determine (q_x, e), if (p_x, r, k'_x, k'_y) are known.[15] In other words, if $\alpha\Lambda(T) \equiv Q(T)$ or (8) is previously solved, the crucial components (p_x, r) of P(T) can be automatically derived; and, if P(T) or (7) is previously known, the crucial components, (q_x, e) of Q(T), can be automatically derived. Undoubtedly, this is a complete solution of the mathematical transformation problem in the very simple context of three commodities.[16]

A caveat emptor

The above theory can be easily generalised to apply to a capitalist economy with any number of commodities. The general case will be discussed in the Appendix. Here, I wish to stress an important matter of methodology which is often overlooked in discussions of the transformation problem. If, as in the present model, only one wage-good Y is allowed, the fundamental constraint amounts to defining a real wage-rate, $w/p_y \equiv Y/L$, where L is the total expenditure of direct labour in all industries (in the present case $L \equiv L_x + L_y + L_z$). But, if more than two wage-goods are introduced, such a simple definition of the real wage-rate is impossible. Practically all writers on the transformation problem since von Bortkiewicz have resorted, in such a case, to defining a so-called "commodity-complex which forms the real wage-rate",[17] which amounts to specifying a physical assortment of wage-goods. They have technologically interpreted the consumption of wage-goods by workers as the "production of labour" by means of wage-goods. That is to say, they have adopted the view that labour too is an intermediate good, considering the human worker in the same way as a "beast of burden". I strongly object to this "labour-feeding technology" approach,[18] or the "fodder method" for short, on conceptual grounds. But before stating my objections, here is an example which shows that my method of the fundamental constraint solves P(T) differently from the fodder method.

Suppose that there are two wage-goods Y and Y'. Let the technology complex be,

$$
\begin{array}{llll}
X_i & L_i & & \\
(30, & 20) & \to X & = & 100 \\
(24, & 24) & \to Y & = & 80 \\
(24, & 12) & \to Y' & = & 120 \\
\underline{+)\ (11, & 44)} & \to Z & = & 110 \\
89 & 100 & & &
\end{array} \qquad \text{(T)}
$$

First, I solve P(T) with the method of the fundamental constraint. Let

$$(p_x 30 + w20)\,(1 + r) \qquad\qquad = p_x 100\,, \qquad\qquad \text{(a)}$$
$$[p_x\,(24 + 24) + w\,(24 + 12)]\,(1 + r) = w100\,. \qquad \text{(b)}$$

If $w = 1$, these two equations determine $r = 0.5594$, and $p_x = 0.58604$. Other prices are determined by,

$$(p_x 24 + w24)\,(1 + r) = p_y 80 \quad, \qquad\qquad \text{(c)}$$
$$(p_x 24 + w12)\,(1 + r) = p_{y'} 120 \,, \qquad\qquad \text{(d)}$$
$$(p_x 11 + w44)\,(1 + r) = p_z 110 \quad. \qquad\qquad \text{(e)}$$

Assuming $w = 1$ again, they are $p_y = 0.74198$, $p_{y'} = 0.33871$, and $p_z = 0.71514$.

With the fodder method I must solve P(T) otherwise. First, I eliminate w from (a), (c), and (d) above by means of,

$$w = p_y \left(\frac{Y}{L}\right) + p_{y'} \left(\frac{Y'}{L}\right) = p_y 0.8 + p_{y'} 1.2 \,. \qquad \text{(f)}$$

The result is the following system of homogenous linear equations:

$$
\begin{bmatrix}
100\varrho - 30 & -16 & -24 \\
-24 & 80\varrho - 19.2 & -28.8 \\
-24 & -9.6 & 120\varrho - 14.4
\end{bmatrix}
\begin{bmatrix}
p_x \\
p_y \\
p_{y'}
\end{bmatrix}
=
\begin{bmatrix}
0 \\
0 \\
0
\end{bmatrix},
$$

where $\varrho \equiv 1 / (1 + r)$. If $w = 1 = 0.8\,p_y + 1.2\,p_{y'}$, the solutions are $r = 0.60623$, $p_x = 0.61996$, $p_y = 0.78058$, $p_{y'} = 0.31295$. With those numbers known, it is easy to determine from (e) that $p_z = 0.74207$. Thus, it is clear that the same technology complex, T, gives rise to different solutions of P(T), depending on whether one uses the method of the fundamental constraint or the Bortkiewiczian fodder method.[19] The question naturally arises as to which solution corresponds to the true equilibrium of the capitalist market.

The importance of the fundamental constraint

I am absolutely certain that the capitalist market never solves the price system P(T) with the fodder method. For the substitution of (f) in (a), (c), (d), and (e) means that every hour of labour regardless of where and by whom it is performed is paid the physical wage consisting of 0.8 units of Y and 1.2 units of Y'.[20] Such a ridiculous assumption amounts to claiming that the capitalist market is somehow endowed with an invisible Stalinist authority which medically, nutritionally, biologically or politically pre-scribes a wage-basket of fixed composition to all workers, and allows no retrading of wage-goods among them. The workers are, therefore, obliged to convert their money wages into, say, a package of cigarettes, whether they smoke or not, a bottle of vodka, whether they drink or not, a lipstick and a few razor blades, whether they are male or female, some school supplies and a box of disposable diapers regardless of the ages of their children.[21] Such complete nonsense cannot possibly occur in the capitalist commodity-economy. Even in the remotest event that wages were paid in kind in the first instance, in what way could the capitalist market prohibit the retrading of wage-goods? But if retrading is permit-ted, the prices of wage-goods that the fodder method determines are in general bound to change, and all other prices as well as the rate of profit will change in consequence.[22] The fodder method determines false equi-librium prices and a false rate of profit which do not reflect the reality of the capitalist market. If so, all transformation theories, supposed to be internally consistent and logically unassailable, which depend on the Bortkiewiczian fodder method, must be judged invalid without exception.[23] For what is the point of converting values and the rate of surplus value into false production-prices and a false rate of profit, which the capitalist market never determines, and back again?[24]

Some recent authors, particularly those who call themselves Sraffi-ans, are unabashedly remiss on this point. Not only do they naïvely ac-cept the Bortkiewicz-type solution to the transformation problem but, on the ground that it is formally consistent, they insist on its superiority to Marx's unfinished solution.[25] All theories must of course be formally consistent, but formal consistency (which many neo-classical economic propositions also satisfy) is not a sufficient condition for the validity of a theory. The uncritical acceptance of the Bortkiewiczian fodder method suggests the danger of approaching the mathematical transformation problem without being supported by the conceptual transformation problem. For the fodder method not only determines wrong prices and a wrong rate of profit but also throws the concept of the capitalist mode of production overboard. Since labour-power is a commodity inseparable from its natural owner, it cannot be reproduced in the production-process of capital (i.e., within the factory). Labour-power must be reproduced through the individual consumption-process of the workers themselves (i.e., through their family life). But, when therefore they appear in the capitalist market to buy wage-goods, they act no differently from any other purchaser of capitalistically produced commodities. The only constraint to which they are subject is that they spend only the money wages that they earn in exchange for their labour-power (wL) to purchase only as great a quantity of wage-goods as necessary and sufficient for the reproduction of their labour-power ($p_y Y + p_{y'} Y'$). But this is precisely what the fundamental constraint of capitalism stipulates. The capitalist market competitively determines a general rate of profit and production-prices subject to the fundamental constraint, and not subject to an arbitrarily prescribed wage-basket.[26]

The significance of the value theory

A valid solution to the mathematical transformation problem $\Lambda(T) \rightleftarrows P(T)$ does not imply that one of the two systems is redundant[27] or that the transformation is a trivial non-problem.[28] These misguided opinions too derive from the uncritical acceptance of the Bortkiewiczian fodder method. Both the Samuelsonians and the Marxo-Sraffians believe that $P(T)$ is sufficient to establish a theory of "exploitation" similar to Marx's. But their theory of exploitation, directly drawn from T, including physical wages, unlike Marx's, applies to human and non-human "workers" with the same formal consistency. All intermediate commodities such as horses, cows, hens, hogs, other animals, and plants which neither form nor augment value can be "exploited" in the same way as the direct producers. In fact, I cannot think of any productive element that is not "exploited" in their sense. It is only by a subjective labelling that the letter L in their model is made to stand for human labour exclusive of non-human services. (What economic justification do they offer that "being exploited" is an exclusively human privilege not to be shared by creatures of lesser intelligence?) But even if that particular name-giving is accepted in place of a valid concept formation, their letter, L, can still include unproductive labour, which produces neither value nor surplus value. Such an inaccurate and empty theory of exploitation may indeed serve partisan politics but it does not expose the objective logic of capitalist society at all.

The dialectic of capital does not proceed in such a haphazard fashion. First, the circulation-form of industrial capital is shown to require a commodity called labour-power, whose use-value consists in being able to produce *any* (humanly producible) use-value. Only the labour-power of productive workers, not of horses and cows, can satisfy this essential condition. Next, it is shown that when capital produces all commodities as value, i.e., indifferently to use-values, appropriating surplus labour only in the form of surplus value, *no exercise of extra-economic compulsion* is needed to reduce the productive workers to a position similar to that of "the beasts of burden". That crucial fact, which is prior to the formation of the capitalist market, cannot be demonstrated except by the theory of value. The fundamental constraint of capitalism must be deduced from this previously established theory, and not "out of thin air", i.e, like Walras' law, as a convenient axiom. Indeed, it is easy for the reader to confirm that the value system, $\Lambda(T)$, can be solved equivalently, whether with the method of the fundamental constraint or with the Bortkiewiczian fodder method, even when there are many wage-goods.[29] This means that the workers are, *as producers*, indifferent to the use-values of wage-goods, even though, *as consumers*, they are not. That is to say, it implies that the workers whose labour-power is incorporated in variable capital lose their personality and human dignity and are reduced to "beasts of burden" in the production-process of capital, even though, in the capitalist market, they continue to function as free, equal, and independent traders. The essence of capitalism lies in this fact, that capital produces all commodities indifferently to use-values, i.e., as value, by means of labour-power converted into a commodity, which however must not be sold "rump and stump, once for all".[30] The law of value would indeed be unnecessary, if capitalist society itself were "unnecessary" being reducible to a collection of convict-labour camps or of cattle farms.[31]

Those who believe that the value system is either redundant or merely derivative of the physical conditions of production simply refuse to learn what the capitalist mode of production objectively is, clinging to their subjective conception (often *naïve*, if not make-believe, horror story) of capitalism. Once their ideological aims are satisfied with the grotesque theory of animal exploitation and the chimerical profit-rate and

production-prices, they ask for no more. I have no alternative but to conclude that, if anyone suffers from "obscurantism", they do. "And that is
that" or at least "voilà"![32] If, in their own style, an extra dose of offense
must always be added in order to sound more convincing.

Appendix

Assume that there are m means of production, q - m wage-goods, and s -
q consumption-goods for capitalists, where m, q, s are integers, $0 < m < q$
$< s$. Let the technology of producing the means of production be written
as,

$$(T_x) \begin{cases} (x_{11}, & x_{12}, & ..., & x_{1m}, & L_1) & \to & x_1 , \\ (x_{21}, & x_{22}, & ..., & x_{2m}, & L_2) & \to & x_2 , \\ \\ (x_{m1}, & x_{m2}, & ..., & x_{mm}, & L_m) & \to & x_m , \end{cases}$$

and the technology for the production of wage-goods as,

$$(T_y) \begin{cases} (x_{m+1,1}, & x_{m+1,2}, & ..., & x_{m+1,m}, & L_{m+1}) & \to & y_{m+1} , \\ (x_{m+2,1}, & x_{m+2,2}, & ..., & x_{m+2,m}, & L_{m+2}) & \to & y_{m+2} , \\ \\ (x_{1q}, & x_{q2}, & ..., & x_{qm}, & L_q) & \to & y_q & , & (+ \\ (x_{y1}, & x_{y2}, & ..., & x_{ym}, & L_y) \end{cases}$$

The technology complex, T_z, of consumption goods for capitalist, can be
similarly written, though without the additive operation as in T_y. If

$$L = \sum_1^s L_j$$

is the total expenditure of current labour, it is possible to determine p_1, ...,
p_m and r from the following price system (in which it will be assumed that
$w = 1$ for simplicity):

$$\left\{ \begin{array}{l} (p_1x_{11} + p_2x_{12} + \ldots + p_mx_{1m} + wL_1)\,(1+r) = p_1x_1 \ , \\ (p_1x_{21} + p_2x_{22} + \ldots + p_mx_{2m} + wL_2)\,(1+r) = p_2x_2 \ , \\ \quad \ldots \\ (p_1x_{m1} + p_2x_{m2} + \ldots + p_mx_{mm} + wL_m)\,(1+r) = p_mx_m, \\ \quad ****** \\ (p_1x_{y1} + p_2x_{y2} + \ldots + p_mx_{ym} + wL_y)\,(1+r) \equiv wL \ . \end{array} \right. \tag{11}$$

The solutions of (11) enable the further determination of $p_{m+1}, \ldots, p_q$ as well as $p_{q+1}, \ldots, p_s$. The last identity of (11) is, of course, the fundamental constraint of capitalism.

The corresponding value system will be written as,

$$\left\{ \begin{array}{l} q_1x_{11} + q_2x_{12} + \ldots + q_mx_{1m} + vL_1\,(1+e) = q_1x_1 \ , \\ q_1x_{21} + q_2x_{22} + \ldots + q_mx_{2m} + vL_2\,(1+e) = q_2x_2 \ , \\ \quad \ldots \\ q_1x_{m1} + q_2x_{m2} + \ldots + q_mx_{mm} + vL_m\,(1+e) = q_mx_m, \\ \quad ****** \\ q_1x_{y1} + q_2x_{y2} + \ldots + q_mx_{ym} + vL_y\,(1+e) \equiv vL \ . \end{array} \right. \tag{12}$$

Assuming $v = 1$ again (i.e., adopting the same invariance postulate as in the text), one may solve (12) for $q_1, \ldots, q_m$, and e, which further enable the determination of $q_{m+1}, \ldots, q_q$ as well as $q_{q+1}, \ldots, q_s$.

Let us now define the value composition of capital both in value and in price terms as:

$$k_i = \frac{q_1x_{i1} + \ldots + q_mx_{im}}{L_i}, \quad k'_i = \frac{p_1x_{i1} + \ldots + p_mx_{im}}{L_i} \qquad (i = 1, \ldots, m, y). \tag{13}$$

The relation between k_i and k_i' can then be stated either by,

$$k'_i = [\gamma_{i1}\,(\frac{p_1}{q_1}) + \ldots + \gamma_{im}\,(\frac{p_m}{q_m})]\,k_i \ , \tag{14}$$

$$\gamma_{ij} \equiv \frac{q_jx_{ij}}{q_1x_{i1} + \ldots + q_mx_{im}} \qquad (i, j = 1, \ldots, m, y),$$

or by

$$k_i = [\beta_{i1} \left(\frac{p_1}{q_1}\right) + \dots + \beta_{im} \left(\frac{q_m}{p_m}\right)] \, k'_i ,$$

$$\beta_{ij} \equiv \frac{p_j x_{ij}}{p_1 x_{i1} + \dots + p_m x_{im}} \qquad (i, j = 1, \dots, m, y),$$

(14')

with (13) one can restate both (11) and (12) quite simply as,

$$\left\{ \begin{array}{l} L_1 (k_1' + 1) \, (1 + r) \equiv p_1 x_1, \\ L_2 (k_2' + 1) \, (1 + r) \equiv p_2 x_2, \\ \qquad \dots \\ L_m (k_m' + 1) (1 + r) \equiv p_m x_m, \\ \qquad ****** \\ L_y (k_y' + 1) \, (1 + r) \equiv L. \end{array} \right. \quad (11')$$

$$\left\{ \begin{array}{l} L_1 (k_1 + e + 1) \equiv q_1 x_1, \\ L_2 (k_2 + e + 1) \equiv q_2 x_2, \\ \qquad \dots \\ L_m (k_m + e + 1) \equiv q_m x_m, \\ \qquad ****** \\ L_y (k_y + e + 1) \equiv L. \end{array} \right. \quad (12')$$

Now eliminate $k_1', \dots, k_m'$ and k_y' from (11') by means of (14) to obtain,

$$\left\{ \begin{array}{l} \displaystyle [(\gamma_{11} \frac{p_1}{q_1} + \dots + \gamma_{1m} \frac{p_m}{q_m}) \, k_1 + 1] \, (1 + r) = p_1 \frac{x_1}{L_1}, \\[2em] \displaystyle [(\gamma_{21} \frac{p_1}{q_1} + \dots + \gamma_{2m} \frac{p_m}{q_m}) \, k_2 + 1] \, (1 + r) = p_2 \frac{x_2}{L_2}, \\[1em] \qquad \dots \\[1em] \displaystyle [(\gamma_{m1} \frac{p_1}{q_1} + \dots + \gamma_{mm} \frac{p_m}{q_m}) \, k_m + 1] \, (1 + r) = p_m \frac{x_m}{L_m}, \\[1em] \qquad ****** \\[1em] \displaystyle [(\gamma_{y1} \frac{p_1}{q_1} + \dots + \gamma_{ym} \frac{p_m}{q_m}) \, k_y + 1] \, (1 + r) \equiv \frac{L}{L_y}. \end{array} \right. \quad (15)$$

If the value system (12') is previously solved, so that $q_1, \dots, q_m$ and $k_1, \dots, k_m, k_y$ are already known, this system can clearly determine $p_1, \dots, p_m$ and r, and hence all other prices. Conversely eliminate $k_1, \dots, k_m$ and k_y from (12') by means of (14') to obtain,

$$\left\{ \begin{array}{ll} (\beta_{11} \dfrac{p_1}{q_1} + \ldots + \beta_{1m} \dfrac{p_m}{q_m}) \, k'_1 + e + 1 & = \quad q_1 \dfrac{x_1}{L_1}, \\[2em] (\beta_{21} \dfrac{p_1}{q_1} + \ldots + \beta_{2m} \dfrac{p_m}{q_m}) \, k'_2 + e + 1 & = \quad q_2 \dfrac{x_1}{L_2}, \\[1em] \qquad \ldots & \\[1em] (\beta_{m1} \dfrac{p_1}{q_1} + \ldots + \beta_{mm} \dfrac{p_m}{q_m}) \, k'_m + e + 1 & = \quad q_m \dfrac{x_m}{L_m}, \\[0.5em] \qquad\qquad ****** & \\[1em] (\beta_{y1} \dfrac{p_1}{q_1} + \ldots + \beta_{ym} \dfrac{p_m}{q_m}) \, k'_y + e + 1 & \equiv \quad \dfrac{L}{L_y}. \end{array} \right. \tag{16}$$

If the price system (11') is already solved, so that p_1, ..., p_m and k'_1, ..., k'_m, k'_y are known numbers, the present system determines q_1, ..., q_m, e, and consequently all the rest of the value system.

$$* \quad * \quad * \quad * \quad * \quad *$$

Perhaps a numerical example is helpful to exhibit the working of this transformation theory. Let the technology complex be,

		x_{j1}	x_{j2}	L_j				
(T_x)	{	(38,	22	20)	→	183	=	x_1
		(40,	10	30)	→	190	=	x_2
(T_y)	{	(18,	40	15)	→	120	=	y_3
		(5,	30	40)	→	75	=	y_4
(T_z)	{	(10,	20	5)	→	20	=	z_5
		(20,	10	5)	→	30	=	z_6

The price system,

$$\left\{ \begin{array}{l} (p_1 38 + p_2 22 + w20)\,(1+r) = p_1 183, \\ (p_1 40 + p_2 10 + w30)\,(1+r) = p_2 190, \\ \qquad\qquad ****** \\ (p_1 23 + p_2 70 + w55)\,(1+r) = \quad 115 \, , \qquad w = 1 \end{array} \right. \tag{17}$$

determines

$$r = 0.3671, \quad p_1 = 0.2843, \quad p_2 = 0.3226,$$
$$k'_1 = 0.8950, \quad k'_2 = 0.4866, \quad k'_y = 0.5295.$$

Although p_i, ($i = 3, ..., 6$) can be immediately calculated, they are not particularly relevant to the present theory. Let us compute instead the β-coefficients as follows:

$$\beta_{11} = 0.6035, \quad \beta_{21} = 0.7790, \quad \beta_{y1} = 0.2245,$$
$$\beta_{12} = 0.3965, \quad \beta_{22} = 0.2210, \quad \beta_{y2} = 0.7755.$$

Similarly, the value system,

$$
\begin{cases}
q_1 38 + q_2 22 + v20 \,(1 + e) = p_1 183 , \\
q_1 40 + q_2 10 + v30 \,(1 + e) = q_2 190 , \\
\qquad\qquad ****** \\
q_1 23 + q_2 70 + v55 \,(1 + e) = 115 , \quad v = 1
\end{cases}
\tag{18}
$$

can be solved for,

$$e = 0.5715, \quad q_1 = 0.2654, \quad q_2 = 0.3209,$$
$$k_1 = 0.8573, \quad k_2 = 0.4609, \quad k_y = 0.5194.$$

Again, instead of obtaining q_i, ($i = 3, ..., 6$), let us calculate the λ-coefficients as follows:

$$\lambda_{11} = 0.58825, \quad \lambda_{21} = 0.7679, \quad \lambda_{y1} = 0.2137,$$
$$\lambda_{12} = 0.41175, \quad \lambda_{22} = 0.2321, \quad \lambda_{y2} = 0.7905.$$

Now, let us first deduce p_1, p_2, and r indirectly from the value system without solving the price system (17). Simply rewrite (17) as,

$$
\begin{cases}
20 \,(k_1' + 1)\,(1 + r) = p_1 183 , \\
30 \,(k_2' + 1)\,(1 + r) = p_2 190 , \\
55 \,(k_y' + 1)\,(1 + r) = 115 ,
\end{cases}
\tag{17'}
$$

and apply the γ-transformations

$$k'_i = [\gamma_{i1} (\frac{p_1}{q_1}) + \gamma_{i2} (\frac{p_2}{q_2})] \ k_i \ (i = 1, 2, y)$$

to eliminate k'_i ($i = 1, 2, y$) from (17'). The result is,

$$\begin{cases} [(\gamma_{11} \dfrac{p_1}{q_1} + \gamma_{12} \dfrac{p_2}{q_2}) \ k_1 + 1] \ (1 + r) = p_1 \ \dfrac{183}{20}, \\[4mm] [(\gamma_{21} \dfrac{p_1}{q_1} + \gamma_{22} \dfrac{p_2}{q_2}) \ k_2 + 1] \ (1 + r) = p_2 \ \dfrac{190}{30}, \\[4mm] [(\gamma_{y1} \dfrac{p_1}{q_1} + \gamma_{y2} \dfrac{p_2}{q_2}) \ k_y + 1] \ (1 + r) = \dfrac{155}{55}. \end{cases}$$

Since γ_{ij}/q_j ($i = 1, 2, y; j = 1, 2$) and k_i ($i = 1, 2, y$) are already known, the present system becomes,

$$\begin{cases} [(2.2163 p_1 + 1.28311 p_2) \ 0.8573 + 1] \ (1 + r) = 9.15 p_1, \\ [(2.8930 p_1 + 0.7233 p_2) \ 0.4609 + 1] \ (1 + r) = 6.33 p_2, \\ [(2.8051 p_1 + 2.4634 p_2) \ 0.5194 + 1] \ (1 + r) = 2.091. \end{cases}$$

Whence follows approximately $r = 0.368$, $p_1 = 0.2823$ and $p_2 = 0.3201$, which are close enough to the direct solutions of the price system (17).

Conversely, let us calculate e, q_1, q_2 indirectly from the price system without solving the value system (18). Simply rewrite (18) as,

$$\begin{cases} 20 \ (k_1 + e + 1) = q_1 183, \\ 30 \ (k_2 + e + 1) = q_2 190, \\ 55 \ (k_y + e + 1) = 115, \end{cases} \tag{18'}$$

and eliminate k_1 with the β-transformations

$$k_i = [\beta_{11} (\frac{p_1}{q_1}) + \beta_{12} (\frac{p_2}{q_2})] \ k'_i \qquad (i = 1, 2, y).$$

The result is,

$$\left\{ \begin{array}{l} (\beta_{11} \dfrac{q_1}{p_1} + \beta_{12} \dfrac{q_2}{p_2})\ k'_1 + e + 1\ =\ q_1 \dfrac{183}{20}, \\[3mm] (\beta_{21} \dfrac{q_1}{p_1} + \beta_{22} \dfrac{q_2}{p_2})\ k'_2 + e + 1\ =\ p_2 \dfrac{190}{30}, \\[3mm] (\beta_{y1} \dfrac{q_1}{p_1} + \beta_{y2} \dfrac{q_2}{p_2})\ k'_y + e + 1\ =\ \dfrac{155}{55}. \end{array} \right.$$

Since β_{ij}/p_j ($i = 1, 2, y; j = 1, 2$) and k'_i ($i = 1, 2, y$) are already known, this system can be numerically stated as,

$$\left\{ \begin{array}{l} (2.1228\,q_1 + 1.2291\,q_2)\ 0.8950 + e + 1\ =\ 9.15\,q_1, \\ (2.7401\,q_1 + 0.6851\,q_2)\ 0.4866 + e + 1\ =\ 6.33\,q_2, \\ (0.7897\,q_1 + 2.4039\,q_2)\ 0.5295 + e + 1\ =\ 2.091\ . \end{array} \right.$$

Whence follows: $e = 0.5698$, $q_1 = 0.2689$, $q_2 = 3212$, which are again close enough to the direct solutions of the value system.

Notes and References

[1] By the "dialectic of capital" I mean a synthesis of the economic theories of *Capital* into the dialectical system of a purely capitalist society, following the method of the late Professor Kôzô Uno. See K. Uno, *Principles of Political Economy* (The Harvester Press, 1980); Thomas T. Sekine, "Uno Riron: A Japanese Contribution to Marxian Political Economy", *Journal of Economic Literature*, XIII (1975), pp. 847-877; Brian MacLean, "Uno's Principles of Political Economy, A Review Article", *Science & Society*, XLV (1981), pp. 212-227.

The purpose of the present paper is limited to the discussion of the transformation problem from the point of view of the dialectic of capital. I, therefore, consciously avoid a survey of the voluminous literature on the problem.

[2] This section is an extremely condensed summary of the system of the dialectic of capital, and may be found difficult by the reader if he is not previously acquainted with Hegel's *Logic* or with Uno's book, quoted in the preceding footnote. In that case he may skip this section and directly go to the next in his or her first reading.

[3] The dialectic of capital consists of the three Doctrines of (Simple) Circulation, Production, and Distribution. The Doctrine of Circulation roughly corresponds to the first six chapters (Parts I and II) of *Capital*, Volume I, and the Doctrine of Distribution to the whole of *Capital*, Volume III. The remainder of *Capital* falls within the scope of the Doctrine of Production.

[4] The reference is to Hegel's *Logic*. See A. V. Miller, *Hegel's Science of Logic*, (London: George Allen & Unwin Ltd., 1969); and W. Wallace, *Hegel's Logic*, with Foreword by J. N. Finlay, (Oxford: The Clarendon Press, 1975).

[5] Other examples are as follows: the conversion of money into capital; the conversion of labour-power into a commodity; the conversion of commodity-capital into commercial capital; the conversion of capital itself into a commodity. In none of these cases can the conversion or transformation (*Verwandlung*) mean a mathematical function or change of coordinates. Notice also that Marx talks of the conversion of surplus value into profit *and* not of the conversion of the rate of surplus value into the rate of profit except in very special cases.

[6] The uniformity of the general rate of profit in all industries in (1) implies that all goods are produced in equilibrium quantities. In other words, the table of parameters expressed by (T) towards the end of this section represents the existing technology in the neighbourhood of an equilibrium, i.e., together with the allocation of capital in that neighbourhood. I, of course, do not assume technology to be globally linear homogeneous.

[7] Empirically, this means that "the workers do not save". But in the dialectic we cannot simply accept (1') as a "realistic" assumption or as an axiom. Such a fundamental proposition, which is not a mere expository device, must be adopted in view of an earlier development of economic theory in the Doctrine of Production. I have shown elsewhere that capitalist society would be impossible if productive workers either saved or dissaved permanently. See my "The Necessity of the Law of Value", *Science & Society*, XLIV (1980), pp. 289-304. The content of this essay is mostly incorporated in the first two of *Theoretical Essays* of this volume.

[8] From (1) and (1') we have,

$$\frac{p_x}{w} = \frac{L_x}{X(1+r)^{-1} - X_x} \text{ and}$$

$$\frac{p_x}{w}(X_y + L_y)(1+r) = L_x + L_y + L_z \ .$$

Hence, if $p_x / w > 0$, $r > 0$, then (2) follows immediately. But if (2) is assumed,

$$0 \; < \; \left(\frac{L_x}{X - X_x} \right) X_x + L_y \; < \; L_x + L_y + L_z .$$

Hence, it is always possible to find an $r > 0$ such that,

$$(1 + r) \left[\frac{L_x}{X(1 + r)^{-1} - X_x} \right] X_x + L_y \; = \; L_x + L_y + L_z ,$$

and $\quad X(1 + r)^{-1} - X_x \; > \; 0 .$

Consequently, the price system can be positively solved.

[9] The so-called intersectoral condition of the reproduction schemes, $IIc \le I(v + s)$ is often misunderstood to be an equilibrium condition. In fact, it is only a constraint. If C stands for the output of the first sector, $I(v + s) \equiv C - Ic$. Hence, the condition states $Ic + IIc \le C$. If there is only one means of production, X, as presently assumed, this means $X_x + X_y + X_z \le X$.

Since the reproduction schemes describe the circular flow of capitalist society, its equilibrium being held implicit and not directly analysed, the intersectoral condition merely specifies a feasible set, and not a particular point in the set.

The fundamental constraint (1') must hold whether the condition of reproduction is satisfied with an equality or with an inequality sign. That is to say (1') must hold whether the capitalist economy maintains a simple reproduction or it involves an accumulation of capital. The numerical example presented later, in which $\Sigma X_i = 89 < 100 = X$ implies an expanded reproduction.

[10] This system simply defines values on the assumption that X, Y, and Z are produced in socially desired quantities. In the price system (1) (1'), these outputs are bound to be socially desired quantities because of the uniform profit-rate, r. See footnote 6 above. That is why P(T) must be written first before a corresponding Λ(T) is introduced. This also means that even Λ implicitly presupposes an equilibrium of the market, P.

[11] See footnote 6 above. It may be remarked here that the pattern of the social demand (X, Y, Z) is determined largely by cultural and historical conditions independently of the market. Price theory can explain only small variations in the neighbourhood of a given (X, Y, Z). For example, the fact that orientals traditionally eat more rice than wheat is not explained by economic theory, though the latter may show the direction into which the substitution of one for another occurs when they are confronted with small change in prices.

[12] Michio Morishima, *Marx's Economics* (Cambridge UP, 1973). It seems to me that Professor Morishima previously assumes the positivity of prices and values before proving the theorem. A more general version of the following theorem is proved in my *Dialectic of Capital*, Volume II (Tokyo: Toshindo Press, 1986), pp. 103ff.

[13] If $e = 100\%$ and if one hour of labour produces \$6 ($a = 6$), then the money-wage (v) must be \$3 because $1/(1 + e) = \frac{1}{2}$.

[14] Francis Seton, "The Transformation Problem", *The Review of Economic Studies*, XX (1957) pp. 149-60.

[15] More generally (9') (10') and (9") (10") can be written as four transformers:

$$
\begin{cases}
\dfrac{p_x}{w} = F_1 \left(k_x, k_y, \dfrac{q_x}{v}, e \right) , \\[2ex]
r = G_1 \left(k_x, k_y, \dfrac{q_x}{v}, e \right) , \\[2ex]
\dfrac{q_x}{v} = F_2 \left(k'_x, k'_y, \dfrac{p_x}{w}, r \right) , \\[2ex]
e = G_2 \left(k'_x, k'_y, \dfrac{p_x}{w}, r \right) .
\end{cases}
$$

[16] See the appendix to this essay for a more general case involving more than three commodities.

[17] L. von Bortkiewicz, "Value and Price in the Marxian System", *International Economic Paper* No.2 (1952), p. 21.

[18] "The consumption of food by a beast of burden is nonetheless a necessary factor in the process of production" (*Capital* 1, New York: International Publishers, 1967, p. 572). Morishima, *op. cit.*, p. 54, refers to "labour-feeding input coefficients".

[19] Some may find it strange that the same set of equations (a), (c), (d), (e) and

$$ w = p_y 80 + p_{y'} 120 \qquad \text{(g)} $$

gives rise to two entirely different solutions. But we are here faced with a system of non-linear equations which we propose to reduce to a system of linear equations by assigning a proper value to the parameter, $\varrho \equiv 1/(1 + r)$. The first method amounts to a claim that ϱ is the Frobenius root of matrix A and the second method to a claim that ϱ is the Frobenius root of matrix B, where,

$$
A \equiv \begin{bmatrix} 0.3 & 0.2 \\ 0.48 & 0.36 \end{bmatrix}
\quad \text{and} \quad
B \equiv \begin{bmatrix} 0.3 & 0.16 & 0.24 \\ 0.3 & 0.24 & 0.36 \\ 0.2 & 0.08 & 0.12 \end{bmatrix}
$$

But the Frobenius root of A is 0.6412876 which, as can easily be confirmed, is not even an eigenvalue of B. The question of choosing a right ϱ for the solution of the price system is therefore not a mathematical matter. It involves economic theory as I wish to show in the following section.

20 This amounts to postulating identical tastes on the part of each worker. Not much is gained by introducing a utility function if this unreasonable postulate is not overcome. See Leif Johansen, "Labour Theory of Value and Marginal Utilities", *Economic of Planning*, III (1963), pp. 89-103, reprinted in *A Critique of Economic Theory*, edited by E. K. Hunt and J. G. Schwartz (Penguin Education), 1972.

21 It is true perhaps that not all workers have children to raise. But the working class as a whole must reproduce itself not only year by year but also over generations. Hence, the consumption of the worker, through which he reproduces labour-power, must always allow for wherewithal to raise children.

22 In fact, the equilibrium rate of profit falls, as from 60.6% to 55.9% in the above example, because the retrading of wage-goods means that the profit maximisation of the capitalists must now allow for the civil rights of the working consumers. This may be interpreted as a special case of P. A. Samuelson's so-called Le Chatelier principle.

23 All discussions of Marxian price theory, whether specifically related to the transformation problem or not, have become thoroughly dependent on the fodder method. The only exception that I know is John E. Roemer, "Marxian Models of Reproduction and Accumulation", *Cambridge Journal of Economics*, II (1978), pp. 37-53, and Alain Lipietz, "The So-called Transformation Problem Revisited", CEPREMAP, no. 7902BIS, duly credits Roemer's contribution. I cannot, however, follow Roemer's method because it requires a previous solution of the value system in order to solve the price system. Specifically, "the social rate of exploitation" "must be taken as given to some level, e^*" before one undertakes to solve the price system. But the capitalist, market, in fact, determines the rate of profit and production-prices without any knowledge of values and surplus value. The dialectical significance of Marxian price theory, as I see it, is to show that the rate of profit and production-prices that the capitalist market determines *as if values and surplus value never existed* are actually not independent from them.

24 The fodder method, therefore, imposes such a stringent constraint on the capitalist market as to make it completely meaningless. Surely this is worse than assuming an identical organic composition of capital in all industries, which makes the transformation problem unnecessary.

25 The most blatant example is I. Steedman, *Marx after Sraffa* (London: NLB, 1977), where anyone who complains of the emptiness of formal logic is summarily executed, ayatullah style, with a charge of obsucrantism.

26 Even on a purely formal basis, the fundamental constraint is less binding than the fodder requirement and yet solves the transformation problem effectively without recourses to pretentious mathematics.

27 P. A. Samuelson, "Understanding the Marxian Notion of Exploitation", *Journal of Economic Literature*, XI (1971), pp. 399-431.

28 Steedman, *op. cit.*, pp. 14, 52.

[29] Consider the value system,

$$
\begin{cases}
q_x 30 + 20v\,(1 + e) &= q_x 100, \\
q_x 24 + 22v\,(1 + e) &= q_y\ 80, \\
q_x 24 + 12v\,(1 + e) &= q_{y'} 120, \\
q_x 11 + 44v\,(1 + e) &= q_z\ 110, \\
100v \equiv q_y 80 + q_{y'} 120, \quad v \equiv 1.
\end{cases}
$$

The method of the fundamental Constraint determines (q_x, e) from

$$
\begin{cases}
q_x 30 + 20\,(1 + e) = q_x 100 \\
q_x 48 + 36\,(1 + e) = 100
\end{cases}
$$

as $\qquad e = 1.0115, \qquad q_x = 0.5747.$

According to the fodder method, we first construct the system,

$$
\begin{cases}
q_x 30 + (1 + e)\,(16\ \ q_y + 24\ \ q_{y'}) &= q_x 100, \\
q_x 24 + (1 + e)\,(19.2 q_y + 28.8 q_{y'}) &= q_y 80, \\
q_x 24 + (1 + e)\,(9.6\ \ q_y + 14.4 q_{y'}) &= q_{y'} 120.
\end{cases}
$$

But it can easily be confirmed that, with $e = 1.0115$, the above can be reduced to a system of linear homogeneous equations in $q_x, q_y, q_{y'}$ whose coefficient matrix is singular.

[30] *Capital*, I, p.168.

[31] About the significance of the law of value, see Thomas T. Sekine, "The Necessity of the Law of Value", *Science & Society*, XLIV (1980), pp.289-304. See note 7 above.

[32] See literature quoted in footnotes 25 and 27 above.

The Law of Market Value

Introduction

In 1973 professor Michio Morishima claimed that Marx's labor theory of value "gets into difficulties" if (i) the choice of techniques, (ii) heterogeneous labor, or (iii) joint production, is considered.[1] This brilliant neoclassical discovery was instantly copied by the Sraffian Marxists, who have ever since obstreperously campaigned for "a materialist account of capitalist societies" unfettered by "irrelevant" labor values. Morishima's *Einführung* in his Marx-appreciation is well known and hardly disguised. It is not surprising that a neoclassical economist like him, intent upon discovering early signs of the von Neumann-type theory in the history of economic thought, should read Marx in a somewhat original fashion. And if the labor theory of value "as Marx formulated it" appears to serve no useful purpose, it is only natural for him to insouciantly discard it for its *alleged* limitations. One can only admire the articulate way in which Morishima challenged the Marxian tradition. What is not so easily comprehensible is the remarkable alacrity and enthusiasm with which those who openly profess to be Marxists have seized upon this particular piece of neoclassical creativity, and turned it against their own tradition. Surely there must be an explanation for this pathological phenomenon. Its cause may, in part, be traced back to certain weaknesses in Marx's own formulation of the law of value.[2]

As Rosdolsky has pointed out,[3] Marx appears to define the concept of "socially necessary labor" as the determinant of commodity values in two ways. Sometimes his definition seems to be purely "technological"; sometimes it seems to explicitly allow for demand conditions. There is, of course, no contradiction in this. Since the dialectic does not specify any concept completely at one stroke, but concretizes a preliminary definition step by step as the level of abstraction is changed, Marx may in one context specify the value of a commodity "technologically", i.e., taking the demand for it for granted, and in another context introduce the market mechanism by which the supply of the commodity is adjusted to the demand for it. Yet this has been a source of enormous confusion among Marxists, who generally tend to cling to the first, less synthetic definition of value, presumably for the relative ease of quoting the text in its support. Even Rosdolsky, who is keenly aware of the dialectical need to define the same concept at different abstraction levels until it is fully synthesized, does not always appear to be at ease with the law of value. The difficulty that has plagued generations of Marxists as well as their critics originates in the incompleteness of the theory of market value which Marx exposed in Chapter X of *Capital*, Volume III. As Itoh and Yokokawa have recently observed,[4] the text of this chapter reproduces the uncertain mixture, peculiar to Marx, of the technological and the demand-oriented concepts of value. Clearly a textual interpretation no longer solves the problem. A more positive reconstruction of the theory of market value originally presented, but not completed, by Marx is necessary in order to adequately comprehend the working of the law of value. It was the late Professor Kôzô Uno who applied himself to this important task.[5]

In the present paper I intend to examine Morishima's challenge to the Marxian tradition from the point of view of Uno's reformulation of the theory of market value, and to demonstrate the integrity and the impregnability of the labor theory of value under each of the above-mentioned three considerations.

The concept of market value

Perhaps the best way to begin our discussion is to recall Marx's well-known reference to the introduction of power-looms into England,[6] although that is a rather special case of the application of the principle of market value. Marx claims that the introduction of power-looms almost immediately halved the value of cloth, despite the fact that a sizeable portion of the output of cloth still continued to be hand-woven. How is this possible? Let us suppose that a unit of cloth embodies two hours of socially homogeneous labor when hand-loomed, and only one hour when power-loomed. If the value of cloth were calculated by some average of these two extreme cases, it would not fall from two to one, unless and until the hand-loom production of cloth was completely eliminated, contrary to Marx's supposition. Clearly the market value of cloth cannot be determined by any statistical average. It must instead be determined by the technique or combination of techniques that is capable of adjusting the output to changes in the demand for cloth. Suppose, for example, that the demand for cloth suddenly increases by 10%. One cannot *a priori* conclude how the output of cloth increases correspondingly by 10%. It may be that the hand-weavers who are already fully employed are unable to increase their supply at all, at least not immediately (i.e., within the previously specified market period). But a 10% increase in total output may be an easy matter for capitalist factories equipped with power-looms and capable of hiring the required addition to unskilled labor. If that is the case, the power-loom technique determines the value of cloth, and the hand-loom technique does not participate in the value determination at all.

Of course, that is not the only possible case. It is also possible that the hand-weavers too respond to the increased demand to some extent, expanding the total output by, say 3%, while the power-looming capitalist factories take care of the remaining 7%. In that case the value of cloth is determined 30% by the hand-loom technique and 70% by the power-loom technique, i.e., as $1.3 = 0.3(2) + 0.7(1)$. If on the other hand the power-loom technique is only experimentally used, and cannot expand the total output of cloth by more than 1%, while the remaining 9% must and can be effected by the hand-loom technique, then the market or social value of cloth will be $1.9 = 0.9(2) + 0.1(1)$.

If a technical change is involved as in the present example, the value of cloth eventually falls from the one that is determined by the older technique to the one that is determined by the new technique, i.e., from 2 to 1 (in the number of hours of social labor), as the use of power-looms becomes more and more widespread. The process of switching techniques from one to another as innovation occurs will be studied by a special theory of market value, i.e., by the theory of surplus profit that specifically represents an extra surplus value.[7] Such a theory, like the theory of differential rent (which is also a special form of surplus profit), presupposes a general theory of surplus profit or of market value. Before exploring this theory in the following pages, I would like to emphasize two things. First, even in a purely capitalist society,[8] there is no need for any given use-value to be produced by one and the same technique. Second, if several techniques are simultaneously employed to produce an identical use-value, the value-determining technique or combination of techniques cannot be *a priori* specified. These two facts are certainly not defects of the theory of value; they are indications of the contradiction between value and use-value, i.e., of the reality of the capitalist market,[9] which the theory of value is meant to overcome.

Capital produces commodities as *value* indifferently to their use-values. But this does not mean that capital can produce value without at the same time producing a specific use-value. The production of a use-value is always exposed to contingencies, i.e., to circumstances not explainable by the logic of the commodity-economy. For example, no one industry consists of identical firms, each firm being different in size, in location, in managerial organization, and in the technical method of production that it employs. Although some of these factors tend to be standardized or made uniform by competition, the development of capitalism does not ensure a complete elimination of the individualities of different productive units even within the same industry. A theory of value that becomes inoperative because of such circumstances cannot be said to have overcome the contradiction between value and use-value. Also, when the market demand for a particular commodity varies, the way in which different firms respond to it by adjusting their outputs depends on such contingent factors as the geographical location of the new demand, the system of communication by which the information is spread, or the degree of dependence on skilled labor by different firms. These are real parameters that underlie and constrain the operation of the capitalist market, and the theory cannot ignore them by simply pronouncing them them to be absent. Instead, a true dialectical theory must prove itself to be workable whatever may be the combination of these parameters. *The law of market value is the law of value that takes such contingent elements of use-value production explicitly into consideration.*

The principle of the determination of market value

Suppose that there are two industries, A and B. If the demand shifts from A to B, but if resources (i.e., direct and indirect labor) do not correspondingly shift from A to B, so that the outputs of these two industries fail to conform to the new pattern of social demand, then it is impossible to unambiguously determine the values of their products. For the outputs of these two industries are not in socially necessary quantities, nor is labor directly or indirectly spent on them. Socially necessary labor for the production of a commodity which defines its value is the flow of labor directly or indirectly required for its production in the socially necessary quantity. Only when it is *assumed* that all commodities are produced in equilibrium quantities is it warranted to say that the value of a commodity is commensurate with the amount of technically necessary labor for its production. Marx's "technological" definition of socially necessary labor in Volumes I and II of *Capital* suggests that he does indeed assume such a situation there. In *Capital*, Volume III, in which the formation of production-prices is examined, however, such an assumption is clearly out of place. A uniform rate of profit presupposes a free mobility of resources and the consequent provision of all use-values in the socially necessary quantities. Although in the equilibrium of the capitalist market the production-prices of commodities are not proportional to their values, this does not contradict the fact that an optimum allocation of labor is accomplished only by the formation of production-prices and a general rate of profit.

Thus, value and production-prices are meaningful concepts only when they tend to settle to definite levels in view of *an adequate mobility of resources.* But an adequate mobility of resources does not mean that *all* currently employed productive resources should change industries at the slightest variation of all the demand condition. It means only that the supply of all commodities can be adjusted to their demand in such a way as to maintain the given levels of their values and production-prices. (In the language of neoclassical price theory this is equivalent to saying that all industries are "constant-cost industries" because a sufficient number of marginal firms move from one industry to another.)[10] In fact, the presence of fixed capital and other circumstances makes it impossible for well-established firms to easily switch industries at short notice. Even theoretically unambiguous definitions of values and production-prices require only a small reallocation of resources, ensuring the adaptation of supplies to a small change in the pattern social demand.[11] In other words, the concept of values and production-prices is meaningful if, and only if, resources readily flow at the margins of all capitalist industries. Thus if, as the demand shifts from industry A to industry B, enough resources migrate from A to B so as to adjust the new output levels to the altered conditions of demand, the integrity of the law of value is securely preserved.[12]

But this also means that the value (and the equilibrium price) of a commodity is determined only at the margin of its productive adjustment. For example, if hand-looms and power-looms are simultaneously employed for the production of cloth, but if the burden of marginal productive adjustment falls entirely on the power-loom technique, it is the quantity of labor required by that technique which determines the value of cloth, regardless of the proportion in which the two techniques are employed to produce the total output of cloth. Suppose, for example, that 100 units of cloth are socially demanded and that the hand-weavers who produce 80 units cannot flexibly adjust their output. The total labor-time actually spent for the production of the 100 units of cloth is $80(2) + 20(1) = 180$ hours. But these cannot be immediately regarded as the hours of "socially necessary labor". Since one additional unit of cloth is produced by the power-loom technique with one hour of labor, 100 units of cloth are produced with 100 hours of socially necessary labor. To say that a unit of cloth is produced with one hour of *socially* necessary labor implies that the same amount of labor is withdrawn from alternative uses for the production of cloth. Marx expresses this fact, somewhat clumsily, by saying that "the labor-time socially necessary is that required to produce an article *under the normal conditions of production*,[13] i.e., by the technique capable of marginally adjusting the industry's output. The difference between the quantities of socially necessary and actually spent labor, 100 - 180 = -80, will be called negative rent or negative "false social value".[14]

Market value and the market regulating production-price

Suppose that there are two processes which produce a commodity X (say steel) with the same commodity X and labor, as follows:

	steel	labor					
	(12 ,	3)	→	65	=	$X^{(1)}$	technique (1)
+)	(3 ,	12)	→	100	=	$X^{(2)}$	technique (2)
	(15 ,	15)	→	165	=	X	total.

It is clearly impossible to calculate the value of X as $\lambda_x = 0.1$ from the equation $\lambda_x 15 + 15 = \lambda_x 165$ because that would make no economic sense. In order to correctly calculate the market value, we must know how these two techniques respond to a variation in the social demand for X. If the demand for this commodity changes by dX and the responding changes in the output of the two techniques are $dX^{(1)}$ and $dX^{(2)}$ respectively, then the value of X is meaningful if and only if $dX^{(1)}/dX + dX^{(2)}/dX = 1$, i.e., if and only if X is a capitalistically reproducible commodity.[15] Let us call $dX^{(i)}/dX$, $(i = 1,2)$, the marginal response ratio of technique (i), and also define what may be called the supply elasticity of technique (i) by $\delta^{(i)} = (dX^{(i)}/dX)(X/X^{(i)})$, $(i = 1,2)$. Suppose that the marginal response ratios of the two techniques are both ½. Then clearly $\delta^{(1)} = 1.269$ and $\delta^{(2)} = 0.825$. In that case the market value can be calculated as follows. Multiply each technique by its supply elasticity and add them together to obtain the value-determining social technique:

	(15.2,	3.8)	→	82.5	=	$\delta^{(1)} \times$ technique (1)
+)	(2.5,	9.9)	→	82.5	=	$\delta^{(2)} \times$ technique (2)
	(17.7,	13.7)	→	165	=	social technique.

Then, $\lambda_x 17.7 + 13.7 = \lambda_x 165$ determines $\lambda_x = 0.093$ as the market value of X. What Marx calls the "individual values" of the two techniques are then determined by the equations $0.093(12) + 3 = \lambda_x^{(1)} 65$ and $0.093(3) + 12 = \lambda_x^{(2)} 100$ as $\lambda_x^{(1)} = 0.0633$ and $\lambda_x^{(2)} = 0.1228$. These individual values contribute 50% each to the determination of the market or social value of X. If, however, the marginal response ratios are $dX^{(1)} / dX = 0.25$ and $dX^{(2)} / dX = 0.75$, so that $\delta^{(1)} = 0.6346$ and $\delta^{(2)} = 1.2375$, then the value determining social technique of X is (11.33, 16.75) → 165. Hence we have $\lambda_x = 0.1090$, $\lambda_x^{(1)} = 0.0663$, $\lambda_x^{(2)} = 0.1233$. In this case $\lambda_x^{(1)}$ contributes 25% and $\lambda_x^{(2)}$ 75% to the determination of λ_x.[16]

These exercises show that the existence of multiple techniques in an industry causes no problem in the determination of a unique market value for its product, *provided that the marginal response ratios are known*. These ratios reflect the real parameters of the market, as already mentioned. But they are not in the nature of fixed aggregators that can be *a priori* specified. For example, a 10% increase in the demand for steel does not always occur in the same way. Sometimes it is an expansion of the automobile industry which induces it, sometimes it is a large construction project undertaken in a given geographical region, sometimes it is the opening of a new export market, sometimes it is the need to build up military hardware, etc. Surely, we cannot expect that the marginal response ratios of the existing techniques to be the same in all these cases. They are subject to contingencies and cannot be predicted by either technical or commodity-economic terms. But their unpredictability is a fact of life and the theory cannot be blamed for failing to pretend otherwise. All that the theory is expected to do is to show how the commodity value can be uniquely determined *whatever may be the combination of these contingent factors*. The theory of market value, therefore, need not go any further than specifying the method of synthesizing the value-determining social technique from the concurrently employed multiple techniques, once given any arbitrary set of the marginal response ratios.[17]

The same social technique can be used to determine the market regulating production-price. Thus if the general rate of profit is 40%, and if the marginal response ratios of the two techniques are both ½, the market-production-price (p_x) in terms of the wage (w) is calculated from

$$(p_x\ 17.7 + w\ 13.7)\ (1 + 0.40)\ =\ p_x\ 165$$

as $p_x / w = 0.1368$. The individual production-prices are $p_x^{(1)} / w = 0.100$ and $p_x^{(2)} / w = 0.1737$ in that case.[18] If the general rate of profit is 25% and if the marginal response ratios are 0.25 for technique (1) and 0.75 for technique (2), the market regulating production-price is found to be $p_x / w = 0.1388$ from $(p_x\ 11.33 + w\ 16.75)\ (1 + 0.25) = p_x\ 165$, and the individual production-prices are $p_x^{(1)}/w = 0.0897$ and $p_x^{(2)}/w = 0.1552$.[19] Moreover, the same method of synthesizing the social technique can be applied to basic goods and non-basic goods alike. I show in the appendix how the value calculating operation, Λ, and the production-price calculating operation, P, can be applied to a technological complex, T. All the component techniques of T which are unique with respect to a given use-value are the synthesized social techniques.

The problem of heterogeneous labor

According to Marx,

> "the different proportions in which different sorts of labor are reduced to unskilled labor as their standard is established by a social process that goes on behind the backs of the producers, and, consequently, appear to be fixed by custom".[20]

But this rather strange "social process" is, in fact, nothing other than the working of the law of market value. So far the existence of skilled labor, or what Marx enigmatically calls "intensified or multiplied simple labor", has been neglected on the ground that capitalism in itself possesses a tendency to simplify and standardize the labor-process. The development of the capitalist method of production, through the dialectic of co-operation, manufacture and mechanization accomplishes the simplification of labor. Although this fact is undisputed, it does not mean that skilled labor must be completely eliminated in a purely capitalist economy. For the presence of skilled labor does not in any way affect the validity of the labor theory of value, as long as the mechanization of industry increasingly substitutes unskilled for skilled labor. In that case the marginal output of any industry will tend to be produced with unskilled labor only, which, of course, is much more mobile inter-industrially than labor with specific skills. If this were not the case with all industries, it would not be possible to say that capital produces commodities as value indifferently to their use-values, or that productive labor can be applied indifferently through capital to the production of any commodity. The existence of capitalist society, of course, presupposes that the marginal supply of all commodities is a product of simple (and indifferent) labor. Bur that presupposition does not imply that no part of the current output of any use-value should be produced with skilled labor.

Suppose that knives are either machine-made with unskilled labor or hand-made with skilled labor. If machine-made knives and hand-made knives are qualitatively identical, the individual value of machine-made knives is most likely to regulate the market value. For when the demand for knives increases, the output of hand-made knives cannot as flexibly respond to the increased demand as that of machine-made knives. If hand-made knives are qualitatively superior to machine-made knives, the skilled knife-makers earn, on top of their wages, a rent proportional to the supply inelasticity of their skill. But the existence of no society, capitalist or otherwise, depends on the availability of a skill that produces high-quality or luxury knives, since two or three ordinary knives will probably do the same job as one luxury knife in any case.

The problem of joint production

Joint production is another case to which the application of the theory of market value is essential. But this problem has of late become more controversial than others, requiring a somewhat lengthy treatment in what follows.

In 1975 Steedman produced the following example.[21] Suppose that two commodities X_1 and X_2 are jointly produced by themselves and labor L in two processes as follows:

	The inputs of				The outputs of			
	X_1	X_2	L		X_1	X_2	L	
	(25,	0,	5)	→	(30,	5,	0)	process (1)
+)	(0,	10,	1)	→	(3,	12,	0)	process (2)
	(25,	10,	6)	→	(33,	17,	0)	total

It is also assumed that "the reproduction of labor" requires the following consumption-process.[22]

$$(3, 5, 0) \quad \rightarrow \quad (0, 0, 6).$$

Steedman calculates "values" as $\lambda_1 = -1$, $\lambda_2 = 2$ by a strange system of equations:

$$\lambda_1 25 + 5 = \lambda_1 30 + \lambda_2 5,$$
$$\lambda_2 10 + 1 = \lambda_1 3 + \lambda_2 12. \qquad [1]$$

Since for the labor of $t = 6$ hours the workers receive the value wage of $v = \lambda_1 3 + \lambda_2 5 = 7$, the rate of surplus value $e = (t - v)/v$ may be calculated to be negative as $-\frac{1}{7}$. Steedman also calculates the Sraffa-type prices and the rate of profit to be all positive, i.e., as $p_1 = \frac{1}{3}$, $p_2 = 1$, $r = 0.2$. If instead we employ the von Neumann-Morishima type equations:

$$
\begin{aligned}
(p_1 2 \ + \ w5)\,(1 + r) \ &= \ p_1 30 \ + \ p_2 5, \\
(p_2 10 + w5)\,(1 + r) \ &= \ p_1 3 \ \ + \ p_2 12, \\
w6 = p_1 3 + p_2 5, \qquad &\quad w = 1,
\end{aligned}
\qquad [2]
$$

we also get positive prices $p_1 = 0.2457$, $p_2 = 1.0526$, and a positive rate of profit $r = 0.134$.

This example gives the spurious impression that capitalism can produce X_1 and X_2 *profitably*, despite the fact that they are not value-objects (since they embody negative surplus value). Such an irrational result follows from Steedman's complete disregard of the law of market value. Systems of equations such as [1] and [2] above have, in my view, absolutely no economic meaning. They are merely invented and postulated by mathematical economists to suit their fancy; capitalism does *not* actually solve such imaginary systems of equations. Why, for one thing, should the rate of profit be uniform in system [2]? If equilibrium outputs $(X_1, X_2) = (33, 17)$ are produced by two non-joint-production processes, a uniform rate of profit does make sense. For suppose that by a new allocation of resources a little less than 33 units of X_1 and a little more than 17 units of X_2 are produced. Then the excess demand for X_1 raises p_1 and the profit-rate of that sector, and the excess supply of X_2 lowers p_2 and the profit-rate of that sector. Consequently, resources will flow from the X_2-sector to the X_1-sector until the profit-rates are equalized. This fact is unambiguous. The same argument, however, does not in general apply to the present joint-production example.

Suppose that the activity level of process (1) is reduced to $(20, 0, 4)$ → $(24, 4, 0)$ and the activity level of process (2) expanded to $(0, 20, 2)$ → $(6, 24, 0)$. Then the outputs $(X_1, X_2) = (30, 28)$ are not in equilibrium relative to the social demand indicated by $(X^*_1, X^*_2) = (33, 17)$. But does the excess demand for X_1 by 3 units (which raises p_1) necessarily make process (1) more profitable, and the excess supply of X_2 by 11 units (which lowers p_2) necessarily make process (2) less profitable? One cannot in this case conclude that resources must flow from process (2) to process (1) until their profit-rates are equalized. Suppose that in view of the excess demand for X_1 by 3 units, $p_1 = 0.2457$ is raised by 0.06 to $p_1 = 0.3057$. Then $6 = p_1' 3 + p_2' 5$ requires that $p_2 = 1.0526$ should now be lowered to $p_2' = 1.01658$. In that case, the profit-rate of process (1) is calculated to be 12.75% and that of process (2) to be 17.47%. Hence resources flow in the wrong direction, indicating the meaninglessness of the uniform profit-rate of 13.40% originally calculated from equations system [2]. Since this system does not meaningfully determine a general rate of profit and production-prices, neither does the corresponding system [1] determine proper values.

Since there are two technical processes in the present case, the law of market value tells us from the beginning that the given data are insufficient for the determination of values and prices. The four marginal response ratios $dX_j^{(i)}/dX_j$ ($i = 1,2$; $j = 1.2$) must, in this case, be known in order to calculate proper values and prices. Let us, in the first instance, suppose these ratios to be all equal to ½. Now suppose that the demand for X_1 varies ($\Delta X_1 \neq 0$) but that the demand for X_2 is unchanged ($\Delta X_2 = 0$). Then in order to supply ΔX_1, the two techniques must be combined with the supply of elasticities $\delta_1(1) = 0.55$ and $\delta_1(2) = 5.5$, so that the synthesized technique for the production of X_1 is (13.75, 55, 8.25) → (33, 68.75*, 0). Here the starred entry $X_2 = 68.75$ is evidently irrelevant, since no change has occurred in the demand for X_2. This technique is, therefore, valid in the neighborhood of $X_1 = 33$ but not of $X_2 = 68.75*$. That is to say, its unit expression (0.417, 1.67, 0.25) → (1, 2.083*, 0) is meaningful but not (0.2, 0.8, 0.12) → (0.48,* 1, 0). Hence, the determination of values and prices must entirely disregard $X_2 = 68.75*$ as a free bonus or rent of some sort to society. Suppose now that the demand for X_1 remains constant ($\Delta X_1 = 0$) but that the demand for X_2 varies a little ($\Delta X_2 \neq 0$). In this case the supply elasticities of the two techniques are $\delta_2(1) = 1.7$ and $\delta_2(2) = 0.7083$. Hence, combining the given data with these elasticities, we find that the social technique for the production of X_2 to be (42.50, 7.08, 9.21) → (53.12*, 17, 0). Here again, $X_1 = 53.12*$ is entirely irrelevant for the determination of values and prices and must be ignored. The calculation of values by

$$\lambda_1 13.75 + \lambda_2 55 + 8.25 = \lambda_1 33,$$
$$\lambda_1 42.50 + \lambda_2 7.08 + 9.21 = \lambda_2 17,$$

[3]

yields $\lambda_1 = -0.274$ and $\lambda_2 = -0.246$. If the consumption process is considered,

$$6 = (\lambda_1 3 + \lambda_2 5)(1 + e)$$

determines $e = -3.924$.

Clearly, this is an impossible situation. Neither X_1 nor X_2 can be capitalistically produced as value-objects if the marginal response ratios are all equal to ½. This fact should also mean that the production of X_1 and X_2 cannot then be profitable either. Indeed, the corresponding price system,

$$(p_1 13.75 + p_2 55 \quad + w 8.25)\,(1 + r) \quad = \quad p\,133,$$
$$(p_1 42.5 \quad + p_2 7.08 + w 9.21)\,(1 + r) \quad = \quad p_2 17, \qquad [4]$$
$$6w = p_1 3 + p_2 5, \qquad w = 1,$$

determines either $p_1 = 0.2969$, $p_2 = 0.6658$, $r = -0.8$ or $p_1 = -3.4944$, $p_2 = 3.2966$, $r = -1.815$. One reason why neither the value nor the price system can be positively solved is that the conditions of self-replacement are not satisfied at the margin of the present activity levels. Indeed in order to produce $X_1 = 33$ and $X_2 = 17$, as much as 56.25 units of X_1 and 62.08 units of X_2 are being consumed by the two activities. As a matter of fact, the matrix of coefficients does not even satisfy the Hawkins-Simon condition, which Morishima calls the "productiveness" of the technology.[23] This condition is weaker than what I call the conditions of self-replacement.

For any means of production (X), the condition of self-replacement is $X \geq X_I + X_{II}$, where X is the current output of (X), X_I is part of X that is currently consumed for the production of means of production, and X_{II} is part of X which is currently consumed for the production of articles of consumption. If, as in the present case, (X) is also directly consumed, that amount (X_{III}) must be added on the right-hand side of the inequality: $X > X_I + X_{II} + X_{III}$. If equality holds, (X) is simply reproduced; if strong inequality holds, (X) will be accumulated. If $X_{II} + X_{III} > 0$, the condition of self-replacement is $X > X_I$ even in simple reproduction. Sraffa refers to the same condition as $X \geq X_I$, assuming $X_{II} + X_{III} = 0$.[24]

In order for the economy to be reproducible, the conditions of self-replacement must hold for all means of production such as (X) at the margin of the present activity levels. A value system that is reproducible can be *meaningfully* solved for positive values. If in addition the rate of surplus value is positive, the price system too can be *meaningfully* solved for positive prices and a positive rate of profit. Even when values and prices are positive because of the satisfaction of the Hawkins-Simon conditions, if the economy is not even reproducible, such positive values and prices are *meaningless*. Marx's famous intersectoral condition $II\,c < I\,(v + s)$ of the reproduction schemes is automatically satisfied if the conditions of self-replacement hold for all means of production, since it is a value-weighted sum of $X > X_I + X_{II}$ over all (X)'s.

The question naturally arises as to whether or not a more appropriate set of marginal response ratios exists, which enables positive solutions of the value and the price system based on Steedman's technology. This problem must now be faced. In order for the system to yield meaningfully positive values, the output of each commodity must not be smaller than the productive consumption of that commodity by the two processes *plus* its designated level of consumption by the workers. This, in the present numerical example, amounts to the constraints:

$$(\delta_I^{(1)} + \delta_2^{(1)})\, 25 \;\leq\; 33 - 3,$$
$$(\delta_I^{(2)} + \delta_2^{(2)})\, 10 \;\leq\; 17 - 5. \qquad\qquad [5]$$

On the other hand, since, in the production of each commodity, the marginal response ratios of available techniques must add up to one, the following equalities must also hold:

$$\delta_I^{(1)} \frac{30}{33} + \delta_I^{(2)} \frac{3}{33} = 1,$$
$$\delta_2^{(1)} \frac{5}{17} + \delta_2^{(2)} \frac{12}{17} = 1. \qquad\qquad [6]$$

Thus eliminating $\delta_I^{(2)}$ and $\delta_2^{(2)}$ from [5], we may restate the constraints as:

$$\delta_I^{(1)} + \delta_2^{(1)} \;\leq\; 1.2\;,$$
$$24\,\delta_I^{(1)} + \delta_2^{(1)} \;\geq\; 26.92\;. \qquad\qquad [5']$$

This implies that $\delta_I^{(1)} = 1.118$. But the first equation of [6] shows that even the smallest admissible $\delta_I^{(1)}$ renders $\delta_I^{(2)}$ a negative number, an obvious impossibility. Hence, it must be concluded that Steedman's technology *can never be capitalistically operated*. To pretend to refute the labor theory of value (or anything else for that matter) by presupposing the capitalistically impossible is indeed a brilliant piece of sophistry.

Further remarks on joint production

In order to illustrate the determination of values and prices under joint production, we must presuppose a technology that is at least in principle capitalistically operable, that is to say, a technology which satisfies the conditions of self-replacement when synthesized with *some* supply elasticities of its component techniques. For example, consider the following terminology:

	The inputs of				The outputs of		
	X_1	X_2	L	$\rightarrow$	X_1	X_2	L
	(20,	3,	5)	$\rightarrow$	(30,	6,	0)
+) (	2,	5,	1)	$\rightarrow$	(3,	12,	0)
(	22,	8,	6)	$\rightarrow$	(33,	18,	0)
(	2,	1,	0)	$\rightarrow$	(0,	0,	6)

In order for this technology to be capitalistically operable, (α) values must be meaningfully positive, and (β) the rate of surplus value must also be positive.

The first condition (α) requires that

$$\begin{aligned}
[\delta_1^{(1)} + \delta_2^{(1)}]\,20 \;+\; [\delta_1^{(2)} + \delta_2^{(2)}]\,2 &\;\leq\; 33 - 2, \\
[\delta_1^{(1)} + \delta_2^{(1)}]\,3 \;+\; [\delta_1^{(2)} + \delta_2^{(2)}]\,5 &\;\leq\; 18 - 1.
\end{aligned} \qquad [7]$$

Since the marginal response ratios of the two techniques for each commodity must add up to one, the following must also hold:

$$\begin{aligned}
\delta_1^{(1)}\,\frac{30}{33} \;+\; \delta_1^{(2)}\,\frac{3}{33} &= 1, \\
\delta_2^{(1)}\,\frac{6}{18} \;+\; \delta_2^{(2)}\,\frac{12}{18} &= 1.
\end{aligned} \qquad [8]$$

Eliminating $\delta_1^{(2)} + \delta_2^{(2)}$ from [7] and [8], we obtain

$$\begin{aligned}
19\,\delta_2^{(1)} &\;\leq\; 6, \\
0.5\,\delta_2^{(1)} &\;\leq\; -45.5 + 47\,\delta_1^{(1)}.
\end{aligned} \qquad [9]$$

But in view of the non-negativity of the elasticities, [8] also requires that

$$\delta_1^{(1)} \leq 1.1 \qquad \text{and} \qquad \delta_2^{(1)} \leq 3. \qquad [8']$$

Thus [8'] and [9] define the area from which $(\delta_1^{(1)}, \delta_2^{(1)})$ can be chosen to satisfy condition (α).

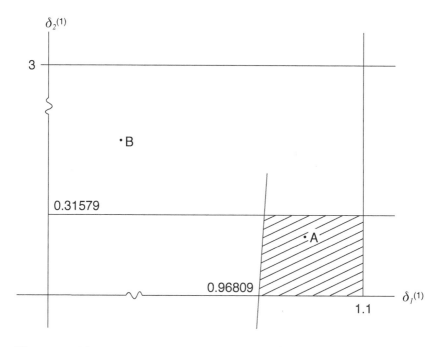

Thus, consider, for example, point A at which $\delta_1^{(1)} = 1$ and $\delta_2^{(1)} = 0.2$ (this implies that $\delta_1^{(2)} = 1$, $\delta_2^{(2)} = 1.4$). In this case, values are meaningfully positive as $\lambda_1 = 1.36$ and $\lambda_2 = 1.12$. Moreover, these values satisfy condition (β) as $e = 0.5625$. The fundamental Marxian theorem, therefore, predicts that the price-system too can be meaningfully solved in positive numbers. Indeed, it will be found that $r = 0.04878$, $p_1 = 2.12056$, $p_2 = 1.75890$. But if one takes point B at which $\delta_1^{(1)} = \delta_2^{(1)} = 0.5$ (this implies $\delta_1^{(2)} = 6$, $\delta_2^{(2)} = 1.25$), neither the value system nor the price-system can be positively solved. This is expected because point B does not satisfy condition (α). Thus, it must be concluded that the existing technology is capitalistically operable under some combinations of supply elasticities but not under other combinations. It is interesting to note that the Steedman method applied to the present technology *always* yields positive values and a positive rate of surplus value as $\lambda_1 = 0.4776$, $\lambda_2 = 0.0746$, $e = 4.8261$. Similarly, the von Neumann-Morishima method *always* generates positive prices and a positive rate of profit from this technology as $p_1 = 3.3736$, $p_2 = 0.1453$, $r = 0.40$.

The question that now arises is why the law of market value makes the same technology complex sometimes capitalistically operable and sometimes not. To answer this problem, normalize the two techniques for the unit production of X_1. Then from

technique (1) : (0.666 ,   0.1   ,   0.1666)   → $X_1^{(1)}$,

technique (2) : (0.666 ,   1.666,   0.3333)   → $X_1^{(2)}$,

it is found that (1) is the more productive technique. Similarly normalize the two techniques for the unit production of X_2. Then from

technique (1) : (3.333 ,   0.5   ,   0.8333)   → $X_2^{(1)}$,

technique (2) : (0.1666,   0.41666,   0.08333)   → $X_2^{(2)}$,

it is found that (2) is the more productive technique for the purpose. From this it can be surmised that the viability of the economy depends on its ability to respond to an autonomous change in the demand for a use-value by a preponderant adjustment of the more productive technique for its production.

To verify this hypothesis in the present example, write

$$
D \; = \; \begin{bmatrix} dX_1^{(1)} \,/\, dX_1 & dX_1^{(2)} \,/\, dX_1 \\ dX_2^{(1)} \,/\, dX_2 & dX_2^{(2)} \,/\, dX_2 \end{bmatrix},
$$

and consider the two points A and B. Then it can be readily confirmed that

$$
D_A \; = \; \begin{bmatrix} 0.91 & 0.09 \\ 0.06 & 0.93 \end{bmatrix} \qquad D_B \; = \; \begin{bmatrix} 0.45 & 0.55 \\ 0.17 & 0.83 \end{bmatrix},
$$

at A and B respectively. Thus, the marginal response ratios of the more productive techniques (the diagonal terms) are greater at capitalistically operable point A than at B, which is not capitalistically operable. Indeed, [8'] and [9], which can be alternatively written as

$$1 \geq \frac{dX_1^{(1)}}{dX_1} \geq 0.9090906 - 0.0290133 \frac{dX_2^{(2)}}{dX_2},$$

$$1 \geq \frac{dX_2^{(2)}}{dX_2} \geq 0.8947369.$$

[10]

are satisfied by point A but not by point B. This means that only a matrix, D, that satisfies [10] under the given technology enables the capitalist economy to viably respond to autonomous changes in the demand for commodities.

The economic meaning of this fact can perhaps be explained heuristically as follows. Consider a nation consisting of two regions. Although both regions produce X_1 and X_2, let us suppose that region I, equipped with technique (1), is more productive in X_1 and region II, with technique (2), is more productive in X_2. Clearly, the viability of this economy depends on the way the two regions respond to autonomous variations in the demand for the two commodities. Specifically, if the demand for X_1 varies, region I must bear most of the burden of adjustment; and if the demand for X_2 varies it is region II that should do the same. Suppose that this does not occur or occurs insufficiently for political or geographical reasons. Then it is perfectly possible that the economy in possession of the above technology will fail to adequately supply X_1 and X_2 in accordance with the social demand. What the theory of market value in effect says is that there is no commodity-economic ground to expect political, cultural, and other contingent conditions to be one way rather than another. If such contingent factors exist (and there is no reason to believe that they do not), theory must take them into consideration rather than pretending them to be absent, as do the methods of Steedman and von Neumann-Morishima.

It may be remarked that the synthesized technology at point A, which is

$$
\begin{array}{llllll}
(22 , & 8 , & 6) & \rightarrow & (33 , & 18^*, & 0) \\
+) \ (\ 6.8, & 7.6, & 2.4) & \rightarrow & (10.2^*, & 18 , & 0) \\
\hline
(28.8, & 15.6, & 8.4) & \rightarrow & (33 , & 18 , & 0) ,
\end{array}
$$

indicates that 10.2* units of X_1 and as much as 18* units of X_2, arise costlessly in the course of providing society with $(X_1, X_2) = (33, 18)$ in accordance with the demand. These do not participate in the determination of values and production-prices. This, of course, does not mean that they should be physically discarded and should not be consumed by anyone in society. But there is no rational commodity-economic principle that regulates their distribution. Some capitalists may wish to donate use-values that accrue to them costlessly to a philanthropic organization; others may try to dispose of them for whatever market price they may be worth. In either case, the market prices of commodities may deviate substantially from production-prices. Such deviations which arise because of the contingencies of use-value production may indeed obstruct the equilibrating mechanism of the market.[25] Yet it is impossible for costlessly and unintentionally produced use-values to have social value. They must be regarded as free gifts of nature which may have high market prices but no value. Instances of pure joint production are, however, exceptional to the production of use-values in general. An overwhelming majority of use-values are produced under capitalism as the single product of well-specialized capitalist enterprises and the extent to which joint production obstructs the convergence of market prices to market production-prices is limited. The only significance of the study of joint production in the present context lies in that it provides a particularly drastic example of the contradiction between the production of commodities *as value* and the production of commodities *as use-values*. It is enough for theory to show how the market value and the market production-price are uniquely and consistently determined even under joint production. It is not for theory to tell to what extent the capitalist market deviates from the system of production-prices because of each exceptional instance of joint production.

The reason why exaggerated attention is nowadays paid to joint production is that the von Neumann-Morishima type models "appear" to circumvent the complexities of fixed capital. The fact that the depreciation of the value of fixed capital does not exactly coincide with the diminution of its present use-value, however, is another striking instance of the contradiction between value and use-value. It is, in my view, altogether incorrect to simply pretend that such a contradiction does not exist, by "theoretically" postulating that capitalists should do what they actually do not. No capitalist "produces" an old machine as a commodity indifferently to its use-value, i.e., as value. A capitalist who employs a one year-old machine for one more year ends up with a two year-old machine, whether he likes it or not. If the machine lasts for more than two years, it still retains part of its old value unconsumed. But the quantity of the remaining value can be only *conventionally* calculated because it can in no way be socially measured. Even if there is an active market for two year-old machines of the same type, its "market value" is phoney, just as the value of any "simply produced" use-value is phoney in the sense of having no commodity-economic rationality.[26] It is, therefore, impossible to abolish fixed capital by axiomatically translating concrete production-processes into "standardized abstract processes of unit time duration".[27] Capital instead faces the problem in its own way and lets the law of relative surplus population prevail over the contingencies of use-value production. If indeed the complexities of fixed capital could be so easily swept under the rug by means of the accounting procedure proposed by von Neumann and Morishima, capitalism would be spared from its periodic crises.[28]

Conclusion

Thus, it is established that the labor theory of value does *not* "get into difficulties" in any of the three cases mentioned by Morishima. Since Marxists are themselves quite remiss in their grasp of the law of value, Morishima and other neoclassical economists cannot be blamed for the simple-minded conception of Marxian "values" upon which their criticism of the labor theory is based.[29] What I hope to have emphasized in this paper is that the dialectical concept of value is much richer and subtler than is immediately apparent from several passages quoted at random from Marx's text. An adequate comprehension of "value" as well as of other basic economic concepts laid out in *Capital*, but not necessarily fully elaborated there, can be achieved only in the context of the dialectical theory of a purely capitalist society. It is because of their characteristic insensitivity, to the dialectical subtleties of economic theory that the Sraffian Marxists have paid an exorbitant price to Morishima's patent without even realizing its consequences. In their eagerness to climb on the neoclassical bandwagon, they voluntarily surrendered the indispensable foundation of Marxian economic knowledge to its foes, while making themselves slaves to the tyranny of formal logic, or what Hegel called the method of "understanding".

Appendix

Consider the simplest capitalist economy in which one means of production (X), one wage-good (Y), and one consumption-good for capitalists

(Z) are produced and competitively traded. If X_i $(i = x, y, z)$ represents the quantities of the means of production, and L_i $(i = x, y, z)$ the number of hours of labour, spent for the production of X, Y, Z, then the technology complex can be written as follows:

$$\text{T} \quad \text{or} \quad \begin{cases} (X_x, L_x) & \rightarrow & X\,, \\ (X_y, L_y) & \rightarrow & Y\,, \\ (X_z, L_z) & \rightarrow & Z\,. \end{cases} \tag{1}$$

The component techniques of T are all value-determining "social" techniques synthesized by the method discussed in the text.

In order for this economy to be reproducible, it is necessary that the condition of self-replacement,

$$X_x + X_y + X_z \leq X\,, \tag{2}$$

should hold. This guarantees that all values λ_i $(i = x, y, z)$ are meaningfully positive. The Λ-operation is as follows:

$$\Lambda(\text{T}) \quad \text{or} \quad \begin{cases} \lambda_x X_x + L_x & = & \lambda_x X\,, \\ \lambda_x Y_y + L_y & = & \lambda_y Y\,, \\ \lambda_x X_z + L_z & = & \lambda_z Z\,. \end{cases} \tag{3}$$

In order to determine the rate of surplus value (e), the following constraint must be used:

$$\lambda_y Y \;\equiv\; (L_x + L_y + L_z) \,/\, (1 + e)\,, \tag{4}$$

This constraint says that the workers receive the product of their necessary labor.

Write production-prices as p_i $(i = x, y, z)$, the rate of profit and the rate of money wage respectively as r and w. Then the P-operation on T is:

$$\text{P(T)} \quad \text{or} \quad \begin{cases} (p_x X_x + w L_x)\,(1 + r) & = & p_x X\,, \\ (p_x X_y + w L_y)\,(1 + r) & = & p_y Y\,, \\ (p_x X_z + w L_z)\,(1 + r) & = & p_z Z\,. \end{cases} \tag{5}$$

These equations together with the constraint

$$p_y Y \equiv w(L_x + L_y + L_z), \tag{6}$$

which says that the workers do not save can be solved for an arbitrary w. Clearly (6) is a market expression of (4). If in addition to (2), we have $e > 0$ in (4), then the prices and the rare of profit are positive.

Notes and References

[1] Michio Morishima, *Marx's Economics* (London, 1973), p. 9.

[2] The labor theory of value, according to which the value of a commodity is determined by the quantity of socially necessary labor for its production, is an aspect of the law of value. See Thomas T. Sekine, "The Necessity of the Law of Value", *Science & Society* (Fall 1980), pp. 289-304.

[3] Roman Rosdolsky, *The Making of Marx's "Capital"* (London, 1977), pp. 88-95.

[4] M. Itoh and N. Yokokawa, "Marx's Theory of Market Value", in Diane Elson, ed., *Value: The Representation of Labour in Capitalism* (Atlantic Highlands, N.J., 1980), pp. 102-104.

[5] Kôzô Uno, *Principles of Political Economy, Theory of a Purely Capitalist Society* (Sussex, 1980), Part III, Chapter I, Sec. 2. About the importance of the late Professor Uno's work, see Thomas T. Sekine, "Uno-Riron: A Japanese Contribution to Marxian Political Economy", *Journal of Economic Literature*, XIII (1975), pp. 847-877. In his book, Uno reconstructs the economic theories of *Capital* as a dialectical system of purely capitalist society. In this paper, as in other writings of mine, I faithfully follow Uno's dialectical method, although I feel free to build on and extend his theoretical contribution as best I can.

[6] "The introduction of power-looms into England probably reduced by one-half the labor required to weave a given quantity of yarn into cloth. The hand-loom weavers, as a matter of fact, continued to require the same time as before; but for all that, the product of one hour of their labor represented after the change only half an hour's social labor, and consequently fell to one half its former value". *Capital* (New York, 1967), I, p. 39. All quotations from *Capital* in this paper are from the same edition.

[7] Firms that employ the value-determining technique tend to earn an average profit, i.e., a profit equal to the money value of total capital advanced multiplied by the general rate of profit. Other firms realize either a positive *surplus profit* on top of their average profit or a negative surplus profit by earning less than their average profit. A surplus profit, therefore, is the difference between the firm's average profit and the profit that it actually earns.

[8] As suggested in footnote 5 above, the present approach defends economic theory only within the context of a purely capitalist society.

9 The dialectical theory of a purely capitalist society consists of specifying and overcoming a contradiction between value and use-value recurring in different forms at all levels of abstraction. That is to say, the theory formulates the reality of the capitalist mode of production in terms of this fundamental contradiction. The "capitalist market" is the market in which all capitalistically produced commodities and labor-power are traded.

10   The theory of a purely capitalist society deals with peculiarities of non-constant-cost industries in the theory of rent.

11   The global pattern of social demand should be taken to be given autonomously. For example, economic theory alone cannot explain why rice instead of wheat is the staple food in Asia. But economic theory should be able to explain comparative static problems such as the one presently under investigation.

12   If resources flow adequately between A and B, I say that each of these industries possesses an "open face". The optimum allocation of resources, which is an important aspect of the law of value, tends to be maintained if, and only if, all industries possess open faces. It is not necessary for any one industry to be wholly open. The value-determining technique or combination of techniques is the technique employed by the open face of the industry. The techniques employed by the closed face of an industry are irrelevant to the determination of market values.

13   *Capital*, I, p. 39, my italics. Although that passage is followed by the phrase: "and with the average degree of skill and intensity prevalent at the time", I believe that it is unwarranted to interpret "the normal conditions of production" in the sense of "the average conditions of production". Marx uses this latter expression frequently in Chapter X, *Capital*, III. For example, "Market value is to be viewed... as the individual value of the commodities produced under average conditions of their respective sphere and forming the bulk of the products of that sphere" (p. 178). Such a specification of market value is in general incorrect, and that is what I wish to establish in this paper. See Itoh and Yokokawa, *op. cit.*, pp. 104-5.

14   Marx introduces the concept of a "false social value" in connection with the first form of differential rent, saying: "This arises from the law of market values, to which the product of the soil is subject". *Capital*, III, p. 661. Suppose that the producers of wheat on a superior land spend 100 hours of labor for a quarter of wheat. But if on the least fertile land a quarter of wheat is simultaneously produced with 180 hours of labor, "society in its capacity of consumer" (*ibid.*) pays the equivalent of 180 hours of labor for a quarter of wheat. Hence, the producers on the superior land earn a positive rent or positive "false social value" of $180 - 100 = 80$ hours of labor.

15   A commodity that is not capitalistically reproducible cannot have its value measured by being repetitively purchased by money. Money measures the value of a commodity by establishing its normal price. A normal price is not a mere market-clearing price but one that implies that any number of samples of the commodity can be supplied in response to the demand for it. A production-price is a normal price with more synthetic specifications.

[16] The "individual values" of a commodity always depend on the market value of its means of production. Although Marx does not seem to make this point clear, it is impossible to know the individual value of a commodity without first ascertaining the market value of its means of production.

[17] Some Marxists may already be shocked by my application of "marginal analysis", suspecting it to be a camouflaged neoclassical trap. But the neoclassical marginal analysis is only a very special case of the present theory in which the marginal response ratio of the least productive technique is always equal to one, and other marginal response ratios are consequently zero by definition. Such a drastic assumption is warranted only when multiple techniques are imposed by the differential fertility of land. In the case of an innovation the opposite is the case. Marx's theory of market value contains the germs of a more general, and economically more meaningful, marginal analysis, such as the one presented here. Although Volume III of *Capital* was published only in 1894, most of it had been written by 1867, i.e., a little earlier than the much glorified Marginal Revolution.

[18] These "individual" production prices are calculated as follows:

$$(p_x 12 + w3)(1.4) \;=\; p_x^{(1)} 65 \;\rightarrow\; p_x^{(1)}/w \;=\; 0.100 \;\text{ and}$$

$$(p_x 3 + w12)(1.4) \;=\; p_x^{(2)} 100 \;\rightarrow\; p_x^{(2)}/w \;=\; 0.1737 \;.$$

The difference between the market and the individual production-price measures the surplus profit (positive or negative) earned by the technique per unit of the commodity. The "individual" rates of profit as opposed to the general rate of profit can be calculated as follows:

$$(p_x 12 + w3)(1 + r^{(1)}) \;=\; p_x 65 \;\rightarrow\; r^{(1)} \;=\; 91.56\% \;\text{ and}$$

$$(p_x 3 + w12)(1 + r^{(2)}) \;=\; p_x 100 \;\rightarrow\; r^{(2)} \;=\; 10.22\% \;.$$

[19] In this case the "individual" rates of profit are $r^{(1)} = 93.37\%$ and $r^{(2)} = 11.79\%$.

[20] *Capital*, I, p. 44.

[21] I. Steedman, "Positive Profits with Negative Surplus Value", *Economic Journal* (1975), 85, pp. 114-123. The same example is reproduced in his book, *Marx after Sraffa* (London, 1977), pp. 150-162.

[22] I have elsewhere called the practices of physically specifying the basket of wage-goods Bortkiewiczian "fodder method" and argued against it. See my "The Transformation Problem, Qualitative and Quantitative," mimeographed, York University, 1981. See the preceding essay in this volume. For the present purpose, however, I swallow my objection so as not to unnecessarily complicate the following exposition.

[23] Morishima, *op. cit.*, p. 22.

24 Piero Sraffa, *Production of Commodities by Means of Commodities* (London, 1960), p. 6.

25 In agriculture, forestry, and fishery, the production of use-values is particularly exposed to natural contingencies. Even the most sophisticated statistical method cannot always "average out" all acts of God. Sometimes drought, locust plague, forest fire, etc., have devastating effects on production; sometimes good weather materializes unexpected bumper crops. Hence, the market prices of agricultural and similar commodities often deviate from their production-prices for a lengthy period of time. There is no reason for economic theory to "panic" each time such deviations occur.

26 See footnote 15 above for the significance of the measure of value. Since second-hand machines of a given vintage cannot be produced in any number of samples in response to demand, they cannot have a normal price that measures their value. They retain only *some* of the value that they had when they were new, i.e., when they were capitalistically produced indifferently as any other commodity. About "simply produced" commodities, see my "Necessity of the Law of Value", quoted in note 2 above.

27 Morishima, *op. cit.*, p. 174. The same thesis is repeated in M. Morishima and G. Catephores, *Value, Exploitation and Growth* (London, 1978), pp. 25-29. The proposed procedure amounts to attributing the same degree of "liquidity" to all items of the capitalist's real assets. Thus, half-used machines, goods-in-pipeline, and finished commodities are all supposed to be monetizable on equal terms. It is true that they are all value-objects and can be sold for money, but not on *equal* terms. The form of industrial capital, M - C ... P ... C' - M', is characterized by the interruption of its circulation by the production-process, C ... P ... C', i.e., by the fact that M - C cannot be immediately followed by C' - M', as in the case of merchant capital. This means that industrial capital purchases its productive elements, C, for consumption *as use-values* with which to produce its output, C', as a commodity. Whereas capital cannot be indifferent to the use-values of C, it is so to the use-value of C'. That is why industrial capital returns to circulation in the phase, C' - M'. (See Thomas T. Sekine, "The Circular Motion of Capital", *Science & Society*, Fall 1981, pp. 288-305.) In other words, only commodity-capital, C', is ready to have its value measured socially, whereas items of productive capital such as half-used machines and goods-in-progress will have to be arbitrarily priced if they are to be sold under *force majeure*. They cannot have capitalistically rational prices to represent their values. Hence, their values can be only conventionally assigned.

28 The decennial crises peculiar to capitalism occur because of the recurrence of the excess of capital. But the excess of capital does not recur with periodicity in the absence of fixed capital. See Uno, *op. cit.*, paras. 84, 85.

29 "Values are determined only by technological coefficients [and] are independent of the market". Morishima, *op. cit.*, pp. 14-15.

Arthur on Money and Exchange

Mr. Christopher Arthur has taken the trouble to critique the Unoist approach to value-form theory,[1] while elaborating on his own reformulation of Marx's seminal contribution to this important subject.[2] Though I greatly respect Arthur's philosophical acumen, I believe that he is largely on the wrong track with regard to this particular issue. For, he altogether misses the *economics* of value-forms, while being overly keen to state his "dialecticized" exposition in *hegelese* (which has its own pitfalls). I nevertheless welcome his overture, as it points to some possible flaws in my previous formulation of Unoist value-form theory. Perhaps I did not spell out a few crucial details with sufficient clarity, thus unwittingly leading Arthur to his misunderstandings.

Specifically, in my previous formulation of the *simple* and *expanded* *value-forms*, I may have given the false impression that the commodity-seller was an *active* consumer[3] irrevocably interested in the use-values of the equivalent (or *desired*) commodities[4]. I adopted the image of the "consumer" as a heuristic device, intending that it would fade away gradually as the theory progressed, until, in the end, it was replaced by the other, more appropriate image of the genuine "merchant". But I was overly optimistic. For the first impression, once engraved upon the mind of the reader, was not so easily blotted out, as Arthur's criticisms of the Uno-school approach demonstrates. I, therefore, take this opportunity to address that problem in some depth.

I also wish to comment on Arthur's proposed dialectic of money as "actualized value", especially as he formulated it in Part I of his paper. There he inherits Marx's unfortunate failure to clearly separate "the commodity's *value expression*" from "money's *measurement of value*", thus perpetuating a stunted economic theory in both fields.

The economic meaning of value-forms

The economic theory of value-forms (or value-expressions) has to do with the *pricing of the commodity*. The commodity is an *object for sale*. Therefore, whoever owns a commodity must *sell* it, for which the first step is to *price* and market it. That alone is what the "value-expression" is concerned with. Like Arthur, I presuppose a fully developed capitalist society as the object of study of the dialectic of capital (though, unlike him, I am not referring to its degenerate, contemporary version still popularly believed to be "capitalist"[5]). For me, therefore, the commodity-seller is, in fact, nothing other than the most abstract (least specified) representation of the capitalist who must sell a capitalistically-produced commodity in his possession.

Now, the commodity is not only a *use-value* (concrete-specific and material wealth, which satisfies a finite want of some individuals) but also *value* (part of the abstract-general, mercantile wealth of society, the demand for which is unbounded). The commodity as use-value or object of consumption is *desired* by individual consumers (direct and productive) only up to a *satiation-point*. That is why, in a pre-capitalist economy, in which use-values do not generally take the commodity-form, there was no such thing as an unbounded pursuit of wealth (except perhaps as a pathological aberration). Capitalist society, in contrast, is predicated upon a boundless pursuit of abstract-general wealth, i.e., wealth as value. But, within the commodity, its *value* is inextricably tied to the correlative *use-value*. It becomes, therefore, necessary to "release" value from that constraining use-value, by converting the commodity into *money* which, as a more direct representation of abstract-general wealth, will be demanded by all commodity-sellers in *any* amount. This is what the *selling* of the commodity involves.

Money, too, since it is itself a commodity, consists of value and use-value. But it is distinct from other commodities, in that its material-sensuous use-value has been *attenuated* to the extent of becoming secondary to its "social" or "formal" (i.e., commodity-economically acquired) use-value of being the direct *means of purchase*. It is in this form that wealth (as value) can be accumulated for some time. Indeed, if too much money is earned, since it cannot all be dissipated in the pursuit of a sybaritic life, it necessarily becomes "idle funds" convertible into capital, in which form then it can be accumulated forever.

No one can sell a commodity without first *pricing* it. Pricing (or the value expression) is, therefore, the first step that its owner must take. His commodity is actually sold for money, however, when someone already in possession of *physical* money presents him/herself in the market to execute his/her *purchase plan*. However, before we reach the point where we may legitimately investigate the theory of the uses of *physical* money, commodities must already be in the market, waiting to be purchased with their *supply prices* indicated. In the dialectic of capital, therefore, the first discourse on "the commodity" should deal *only* with what its owner (seller) must do, *before* he/she actually confronts the buyer (money-owner), and receives real money to complete the sale. In other words, in the theory of the commodity one should be concerned only with *ideal* or imagined money, sought after subjectively, i.e., in the mind of the commodity-seller, and not with *physical* money already present in the hands of the commodity-buyer, ready to be used as the means of purchase. For, we are here not yet concerned with an *exchange* as such, but only with a *call for* an exchange.

Commodities, of course, cannot be exchanged directly in capitalist society, but only with the mediation of money. There were certain ambiguities on this point in Marx's exposition, which may have led to his writing two chapters (first on "Commodities" then on "Exchange") at the beginning of *Capital*, volume I. Maybe Marx wanted to explain the *logic* of money's birth in his chapter 1, and the *fact* of commodity exchange in the following chapter 2. If so, the owners (or the "guardians" as he calls them) of commodities that Marx introduces, at the outset of his chapter 2, are really "empirical" merchants *with physical money already in their pockets*, rather than the strictly "conceptual" commodity-seller with only *imagined* money in his head. I wish to emphasize that we do need this "conceptual commodity-owner (the capitalist in the abstract)" in order to be able to trace the logic of the emergence of money from out of the nature of the commodity itself. For, otherwise, we would be deducing the necessity of money *arbitrarily*, i.e., in the absence of the capitalist (who enacts the logic of capital), and that would not fail to end in a completely futile, if vicarious, exercise in idle speculation.[6]

Arthur overlooks this point completely, as he makes no distinction between the *empirical* and the *conceptual* commodity-owner. But insensitivity at such a critical juncture renders his "dialectical" argument highly suspect. Indeed, much of what Marx deals with in his chapter 2 has to do with empirical-historical (i.e., illustrative) facts pertaining to commodity exchanges *already mediated by money*, and not with a strictly logical derivation of money from the nature of the commodity. Unoists, therefore, believe that Marx's chapter 2 on "Exchange" should be regarded as an appendix (or a set of footnotes) to his chapter 1 on "Commodities".

An introductory overview in the reverse order of value-forms

Let us now see what the commodity-seller must do, before actually meeting a purchaser (who is still hiding, invisible and *anonymous*, in the background of the open market). Suppose that, as a capitalist, I have 200 yards of linen (X) and I want to sell them for, say, $100 of gold money. In my estimation and hope, it is a good price for my linen, i.e., as much gold as I can realistically hope to earn by selling it. But I am not sure if the market will accept my *proposal*. I am stating here my *supply price* in gold money of $100 (or $0.5 per yard) tentatively to test the market and I stand ready to revise it, depending on how the market responds to my offer. Although, in stating my price, I must have surveyed the market in advance and have taken into consideration how other sellers of linen in it are behaving and performing, I am in no position to guess with any accuracy the value of linen that the market will in the end determine. This sort of thing is familiar to all capitalists in their daily experience, and the *money-form of value* must take that experience into account.

But suppose that gold is not yet established (or socially recognized) as money, and that *there is no other single commodity present in the market to act in its place as the universal equivalent*. Then, my sale of 200 yards of linen must take quite a different form. Since I can no longer propose a supply price of my linen in money terms, I must instead express the value of linen in coats, sugar, tea, iron, etc. (i.e., in a coat-price, a sugar-price, etc.), where these commodities may be supposed to be of some interest to me as *use-values* (that is to say, something I would like to have, or do not mind having, in some definite quantities in return for my linen). In other words, I must propose to *sell* my linen for these various other commodities directly, circumstances permitting. The latter are supposed to be available in the market, and so are all deemed *value-objects* (forming part of society's mercantile wealth). By proposing an exchange of my linen for such commodities I am merely reasserting the fact that my linen too is a commodity and, as such, *commensurate with* them. Now that I have multiple "equivalents" for my linen, it is as though I have become a "consumer" in the usual sense of the term, actively interested in their use-values.

But it is not said anywhere that these use-values must be "consumed" by me as soon as they are acquired. (I am not even sure if, in fact, they will be acquired.) Some of them I may demand quite urgently for immediate consumption, but others I may seek less urgently as a temporary stopgap pending still-uncertain future projects. In the former case, the use-values are more distinctly "material-sensuous", and I have a fairly definite *satiation-point* for each of them. (In some cases, my satiation-point may be so low that I may not be interested in acquiring them at all.) But, in the latter case, the use-values are more "neutral" or "speculative" than material-sensuous, so that I will not be so easily satiated (or their satiation-points are practically irrelevant). In such cases, the commodities I seek may be deemed *asset-items* in which I wish to hold my savings, rather than *goods-items* which satisfy my need for immediate consumption. (For instance, tickets to buy bread as you need it, valid for one year, should have a more distant satiation-point than bread itself.) I mention here the two different kinds of use-values, even though the distinction between them may not always be so obvious, since one and the same thing (like gold) can be wanted for either purpose.

Let us then suppose that there are n commodities (A, B, C, ..., N) in the market, and that $(a_x, b_x, c_x, ..., n_x)$ are their specific quantities in which I am (the X-owner is) interested as a consumer, in the broad sense explained in the above paragraph. Of course, these are non-negative quantities, such that, if any of these quantities are zero (e.g., $d_x, f_x, k_x, m_x = 0$), I am *not* interested in acquiring them (D, F, K, and M). These specific quantities certainly need not make up an "optimum" basket or combination of the use-values concerned, such as would maximize my "utility function". I explicitly insert this waiver so as to avoid giving the impression that I am considering myself as an *active* consumer of the type familiar to us in the neoclassical theory of consumer preference. For, I am here hoping to *sell* my linen (X), for definite quantities of use-values: $(a_x$ of A), $(b_x$ of B), $(c_x$ of C), ..., $(n_x$ of N) *once these are given for whatever reason*, by counter-offering the appropriate quantities $a^x, b^x, c^x, ..., n^x$ of my X in each case, until the supply of my linen is exhausted $(a^x + b^x + c^x + ... + n^x = 200$ yards). If I then tabulate all these sales-proposals, I will have the following form.

$$\left\{ \begin{array}{l} (a^x \text{ of X}) \text{ for } (a_x \text{ of A}), \\ (b^x \text{ of X}) \text{ for } (b_x \text{ of B}), \\ (c^x \text{ of X}) \text{ for } (c_x \text{ of C}), \\ [\, (d^x \text{ of X}) \text{ for } (d_x \text{ of D}) \,], \\ ..., \\ (n^x \text{ of X}) \text{ for } (n_x \text{ of N}). \end{array} \right. \qquad (1)$$

Here, I put the entries corresponding to D, F, K, M in square brackets, meaning that they (being "0 for 0") may just as well be suppressed from my *expanded form of value*.

The expanded form of value is *not* a set of proposals to *buy* A, B, C, ..., N in the definite quantities (respectively, of $a_x, b_x, c_x, ..., n_x$) with my linen, X, considered as the means of purchase (my budget constraint being: $a^x + b^x + c^x + ... + n^x = 200$ yards), *since my linen has not yet become a universal means of purchase, or money*. To suddenly claim here the contrary would contradict my own hypothesis, just a few paragraphs back, that *gold is not yet socially recognized as money* and that *there is no other single commodity which can play the rôle of money in place of gold*. I, therefore, cannot interpret the above tabulation (1) as a collection of the consumer's *purchase plan*, with linen acting as money. I must instead accept that it is a set of the linen-owner's *sales*-proposals. Yet, *one does not know how the linen-owner, who desires those commodities* (A, B, C, ..., N), *arrives at the definite quantities, respectively, (a_x, b_x, c_x, ..., n_x,), where d_x, f_x, k_x, $m_x = 0$, of them.* In other words, (a_x of A), (b_x of B), (c_x of C), ..., (n_x of N) must be given *parametrically*, before the linen-owner assigns the appropriate amount of his linen, as (a^x of X), (b^x of X), (c^x of C), ..., (n^x of X), thus expressing the value of his commodity (X), correspondingly.

There are important reasons for this point to be highlighted, and they will be discussed in more detail in the next section. In the meantime, given the expanded value-form, (1), any one entry in it, such as, say, (a^x of X) for (a_x of A), constitutes my (the linen-owner's) *simple value-form.* For instance, if (a^x of X) stands for "20 yards of linen", and (a_x of A) for "one coat", we have the familiar example of Marx: "20 yards of linen are worth one coat".

Simple value-form

So far we have examined the problem of value-forms in the *reverse order*, starting from the money-form, then retracing our steps quickly to the simple value-form. But the "dialectical" exposition of the theory of pricing must abide by the rule of advancing *from abstract to concrete,* beginning with the simple value-form before proceeding, through the expanded and the general, to the money-form of value. Let us, therefore, begin this time with the *simple value-form*

$$(a^x \text{ of X}) \text{ for } (a_x \text{ of A}), \tag{2}$$
or   "20 yards of linen for one coat",

where "for" is an abbreviation of my proposal: "are yours for". In this case, as far as the coat is concerned, the quantity of it that I need or want is just one, *not* two, three or more. Once a definite quantity of the equivalent commodity, (a_x of A), is decided upon *in one way or another,* my next move is to offer (a^x of X) in return for that, and it is a proposal to *sell* X for A, not a proposal to *buy* A for X.

But, how can one be so sure that it must be the case? For, by merely looking at the formula, (a^x of X) for (a_x of A), from the outside, it can be interpreted in both ways with equal likelihood. One should be able to say just as well that it is my *selling* of (a^x of X) for (a_x of A) as that it is my *buy-*

ing of (a_x of A) with (a^x of X). It seems as if there is no compelling reason why it should be the one or the other. But it is precisely here that one must recognize *the fundamental difference between formal logic and the dialectic.* Unlike formal logic, the dialectic knows where the whole argument will lead one to in the end, and that determines the "orientation" in the beginning[7]. In the present case, the simple value-form is meant to lead to the money-form of value, in which the linen-owner will be selling 200 yards of linen for $100. If, however, one interpreted the simple value-form as a *buying* rather than a *selling* operation, one would never arrive at the money-form of value.[8] The desired end: "200 yards of linen for $100" is arrived at, *only* when "(a^x of X) for (a_x of A)" is understood as the selling of X for A, and *not* as the buying of A with X. In the above, I deliberately adopted the reverse order in introducing the subject of value-forms, so that I may highlight this important point.

Indeed, the crucial point in the formulation of the simple value-form is to understand that it has to do with the *selling* operation of the commodity, which involves the designation of (a^x of X), once (a_x of A) is given, not the other way round. But, there is a strong liberal tradition in economics, going back to Adam Smith, to *want* to see the origin of trade in the legendary barter between the beaver trapper and the deer hunter, which is a pure fantasy, a fairy tale. Today, we know that the real origin of trade goes back to *silent trade,* a typical example of which was masterfully recounted by Herodotus.[9] In ethnographic studies one finds many examples of silent trade in different times and places.[10] An even more appealing case of the spontaneous formation of a commodity-exchange market in a POW camp is found in R. A. Radford's article.[11] Marx himself is quite explicit in stating that the exchange of commodities does not arise "inside a primitive society based on property in common". "The exchange of commodities [...] first begins on the boundaries of such communities at their point of contact with other similar communities, or with members of the latter".[12] Commodities are originally "alienable objects" which a self-sufficient community may trade away for things not internally available, and which will bring *additional* convenience or comfort to it, but on which its bare survival does not depend. In Radford's example as well, the war prisoners' essential living needs are already more or less secured by the camp authorities, when small items like "tinned milk, jam, butter, biscuits, bully, chocolate, sugar etc., and cigarettes" first became tradable commodities.[13] It is, therefore, quite appropriate to see in the simple value-form an atavism of the silent trade (between two alien communities, occurring in a designated place, where their inhabitants never see each other face to face), rather than a negotiated barter between the imaginary deer-hunter and the beaver-trapper.

These references are useful for avoiding needless concern with the why of (a_x of A). In fact, all we can, and need to, say here is that it is the definite quantity of a commodity other than X, in the use-value of which the X-owner is interested *in one way or another*. No doubt he has to be a "consumer" in the broad sense, but it is best to leave it at that. For by needlessly delving into the motives shaping his/her consumption plan, which is not at issue here, we run the risk of confusing the *selling* of X with the *buying* of A. If we lack discretion at this point, moreover, we can easily be led to Marshallian offer-curves, behind which lies the neoclassical theory of consumer preference. But the terms of trade which the neoclassical price theory discovers at the intersection of the offer-curves are matters of the least pertinence to Marxian theory of value-forms. The adoption of the overly restrictive theory of individual consumption only narrows one's vision, and makes one blind to at least *two* factors, which, though beyond the purview of neoclassical consumer theory, must not be glossed over in the simple value-form.

In the first place, commodity-A that the linen-owner *desires* may be either urgently needed for immediate consumption, or speculatively selected as a convenient medium in which to "park" temporary savings. *In the second place,* there is no compelling reason to believe that there is only one linen-owner in the market to start with. If there are several others, each one of them must take into consideration the competitors' behaviour and performance in the same market, or may even join them to form a united front or an enterprise called "the linen-owner" (with "& co." abbreviated), in which case (a_x of A) will be the *collectively* (not individually) desired quantity of a use-value other than linen, against which the amount (a^x of X) must also be collectively counter-offered as saleable. Therefore, a theory of consumer demand of the neoclassical type (which does not even permit the interpersonal comparison of utilities) is neither fit nor adequate to account for the meaning of the simple value-form: (a^x of X) for (a_x of A).

Moreover, it must be stressed that, in the simple value-form, commodity-X and its owner are *real,* whereas commodity-A and its owner are *latent,* in the sense that they are, at this point, existing only in the head (mind) of the X-owner. It is in that sense that X is *active* and A *passive.* Yet, once the exchange-proposal, in the simple value-form, is made public, that enables whomsoever possesses (a_x of A) to *buy* (a^x of X) at a moment's notice, if he/she so wishes. This is when the owner of A *can* enter the scene (as the buyer of X) for the first time. For, if someone is offering 20 yards of linen for one coat, the owner of the one coat is as good as having a "little money" to purchase the 20 yards of linen thus offered, if willing to accept the terms of the offer. From the economic point of view, this is the important point. For, it provides *the first clue to the existence of money* as means of purchase.

From expanded to general value-form

Let us now return to the *expanded value-form,* (1), with many equivalents (that is to say, consisting of many simple value-forms). The non-negative parameters $(a_x, b_x, c_x, ..., n_x)$, where, for example, $d_x, f_x, k_x, m_x = 0$, are *exogenously* given. In the absence as yet of the universal equivalent, the linen-owner expresses the value of linen (X) in *some* (many but not all) of the other commodities available in the market: A, B, C, ..., N. In some cases, they are items for immediate consumption; and, in other cases, they are harmless vehicles in which to hold his/her temporary savings. They differ in use-value from X, but are commensurate with it as value-objects (commodities). The only thing that strikes us as bizarre in this value-form is that the linen-owner must propose to *sell* his/her commodity for a variety of equivalents, using their bodies as the value-reflectors (standards of price) of X. But, by virtue of this "bizarre" value-form, these equivalents have all become "little monies" capable of purchasing linen at the quantitative ratios indicated. If so, however, all other commodities should equally be able to generate *many* equivalents, since their owners can each state their own expanded value-form. At this point it becomes obvious that the commodity-economy points to, or aims at, a unitary (single and general) equivalent in which all commodities may reflect their values in common. We must, therefore, explain the *economics* of progressing from the expanded to the general value-form, whereby the commodity-economy overcomes the multiplicity of the equivalents (each of which can act as a "little money" with a variety of qualitative and quantitative restrictions), and generates a *single* general equivalent.

The general equivalent cannot be a commodity in which commodity-sellers happen to take an interest individually *as consumers,* but must be one in which they are *all* equally interested *as merchants,* and not in some restricted quantity but in as great a quantity as can be earned. Such a commodity should have a very special use-value, which is more "social" than "individual", that is to say, more abstract-general (commodity-economic or mercantile) than material-sensuous (directly desirable as object of individual consumption). Or, to put it otherwise, the material-sensuous use-value of the general equivalent commodity must be *attenuated* to the extent of becoming secondary to the "commodity-economic" or "social" use-value of being the direct means of purchase. The Unoist procedure for arriving at the commodity of such use-value unfolds in two steps. *First,* it invites not only the linen-owners, but also the owners of all other commodities in the market to formulate their expanded value-forms of type (1). Supposing that all owners of each commodity are already somehow aggregated into one, we should have N expanded value-forms side by side, which can be obtained by our rewriting $x = a,\ b,\ c,\ \dots,\ n$, bearing in mind that any $x^x = x_x = 0$ for all x. Arthur calls it the procedure of *overlap* as opposed to Marx's procedure of *reversal.*[14]

Thus, if I write out here the first two such expanded value-forms, they will be as follows.

$$
\left\{
\begin{array}{l}
[\ (a^a \text{ of A}) \text{ for } (a_a \text{ of A})\ ], \\
(b^a \text{ of A}) \text{ for } (b_a \text{ of B}), \\
(c^a \text{ of A}) \text{ for } (c_a \text{ of C}), \\
\quad \dots \ \dots \ \dots \\
(n^a \text{ of A}) \text{ for } (n_a \text{ of N}).
\end{array}
\right.
\qquad
\left\{
\begin{array}{l}
(a^b \text{ of B}) \text{ for } (a_b \text{ of A}), \\
[\ (b^b \text{ of B}) \text{ for } (b_b \text{ of B})\ ], \\
(c^b \text{ of B}) \text{ for } (c_b \text{ of C}), \\
\quad \dots \ \dots \ \dots \\
(n^b \text{ of B}) \text{ for } (n_b \text{ of N}).
\end{array}
\right.
\qquad (1')
$$

Here, in the first column, the owner of A is expressing A's value in a number of equivalents, B, C, ..., N, so that the first entry in square brackets is empty ("0 for 0") and may be ignored. Likewise, in the second column, the owner of B is expressing B's value in another set of equivalent commodities, A, C, ..., N, so that the square bracketed second entry is empty and may be ignored. (In each column, there can be other empty entries, if the seller remains uninterested in the use-value of any equivalent.) The best way to visualize this situation is to refer back to R. A. Radford's account of the emerging market in a POW camp, with "an Exchange and Mart notice board in every bungalow, where under the headings 'name', 'room number', 'wanted' and 'offered', sales and wants were advertised. When a deal went through, it was crossed off the board".[15] From their rations and Red Cross food parcels, etc., all soldiers received a series of articles such as "tinned milk, jam, butter, biscuits, bully, chocolate, sugar, cigarettes, etc.", many of which would become "commodities" or something to trade away, e.g., cigarettes for non-smokers, sweets for drinkers, etc. They were thus offered in return for some other things wanted on the notice-board of the Exchange or Mart.

Secondly, the Unoist procedure finds in the "set of sets", as Arthur calls (1'), many equivalent commodities recurring on the right-hand side of expanded value-forms. Some of these commodities may be more "popular" than others, in the sense of appearing as equivalents in the expanded value-form of a great many commodity-sellers. They are candidates for the general equivalent of the system. But it is crucially important here to understand the reason for this popularity. If a commodity appears most frequently on the right-hand side of each column in (1'), because it is widely appreciated for immediate consumption, it will *not* become a general equivalent. For instance, if cigarettes are the most popular item because an overwhelming majority of the commodity-owners are heavy smokers, they will not serve as a general equivalent, since, as soon as they are obtained, they will be consumed. The fact that in Radford's POW camp, "the cigarette became the standard of value" and "the normal currency" shows that there were, in fact, many non-smokers or moderate smokers among the soldiers in the camp, and that they did use them not for their own consumption but as means of obtaining other commodities later.

This brings us back to the important fact that there are among the N commodities in the market, ones that are relatively remote from day-to-day consumption, and which are more likely to serve as merely convenient vehicles in which to hold one's temporary savings. They are not of the kind that the neoclassical theory of consumer preference is interested in. The cigarette for non-smokers in Radford's camp was probably one of the commodities demanded for such a purpose, i.e., as a "temporary abode of purchasing power" (to borrow this poetical expression from Milton Friedman), especially when one had to wait overnight or more, until the market was restocked with a new array of desired goods. Its "popularity" was guaranteed by its liquidity (in the sense here of easy saleability[16]), which was reinforced by virtue of the fact that its holding cost as an asset was negligible. Though instructive, however, a POW camp is a special society. As commodity-exchanges developed in real history, a variety of monies emerged. Thus, according to Marx, "The money-form attaches itself either to the most important articles of exchange from the outside, and these, in fact, are primitive and natural forms in which the exchange-value of home products finds expression; or else it attaches itself to the object of utility that forms, like cattle, the chief portion of indigenous alienable wealth".[17]

The selection of one general equivalent as money from among several possible alternatives depends on the nature of the trading community as well as on the physical fitness of the commodity itself, both involving use-value considerations. But every trading community ends by generating a single monetary commodity as the general (unitary) reflector of values, or, in other words, one such commodity is bound to be excluded from the rest to serve as money. Its special status is predicated on the fact that the monetary commodity is *no longer an object for sale,* i.e., that it will never again occupy the position of the "relative" value-form. *Money only buys and will never be sold as a commodity.* Only at this point can one claim that the expanded value-form has been irrevocably replaced by the *general value-form,* in which all commodities are sold for *the* general equivalent. The latter is no longer demanded in a specific quantity, but in as great a quantity as possible.

This indicates the fact that its use-value is no longer sought for "consumption in the usual sense of the term", but rather for its ability to serve as the standard of price (general reflector of value), and hence as the means of purchase. In the simple and expanded value-form, the use-value of an equivalent commodity may be regarded, at least to some extent, as being material-sensuous in the sense of having a definite satiation-point. But the *material-sensuous* character of the use-value of the equivalent commodity must be *attenuated* so as to become secondary to the "commodity-economic" and "social" use-value, in order for that commodity to become *the* general equivalent in the market for commodity-exchanges. The process of attenuation (which occurs as we pass from the expanded to the general value-form) involves, in fact, a search for a use-value that is *least constraining of value,* in the sense that its urgency of consumption is relatively remote. Other considerations would include that it be relatively easily "saleable" (liquid) and entail a low holding cost. The reason why the word *attenuation* is appropriate here is that even in the monetary commodity the original, material-sensuous use-value never completely disappears, as the persistence of demand for gold for non-monetary uses demonstrates.[18]

Furthermore, the fact that the process of attenuation (which is an automatic process occurring in the market during the search for an appropriate monetary commodity) involves use-value considerations does not make it a wholly empirical-historical matter. It does involve logical judgment on the part of capital. Thus, even if the commodity-owner starts with a consumer-like behaviour, in the first instance, selecting a definite quantity of the use-value of another commodity for the purpose of stating the supply price of his/her own commodity in its terms, that behaviour will steadily be *attenuated* and will transform itself into a merchant-like one, as the selection of the equivalent commodity proceeds automatically within the market, made up of commodity-sellers (capitalists) themselves, until one single general equivalent is isolated.

Arthur's "Dialectical Understanding" of the form of value

In the above explication of value-forms, I have followed Uno's approach, which is different from Marx's. We believe that Marx, despite his truly penetrating insight into the question of value-forms, failed to develop an adequate theory thereof himself, due mainly to his premature reference to the substance of value (socially necessary labour), and that a theory of "value-forms" must first be developed in full, before they can be filled with a "value-substance". Arthur seems to concur with us on this point,[19] yet he defends Marx's inadequate formulation of value-forms, by rejecting the Unoist approach on two counts. *First,* he believes that, contrary to our view, value-form theory can be stated without referring to the (conceptual) commodity-owner (or letting him be the subject of the dialectic). *Second,* he defends Marx's procedure of *reversing* the expanded value-form to obtain the general value-form, finding some obscure "dialectical" significance in it. These two points are related. Here I will begin with the second, following Arthur's argument which is stated in Section I: "The actuality of value" of his paper.[20]

Marx's expanded (or rather "total") value-form, which Arthur inherits "as is", can be restated in our notation, as follows:

$$(a^x \text{ of } X) \text{ for } (a_x \text{ of } A), \text{ or for } (b_x \text{ of } B), \text{ or for } (c_x \text{ of } C), ..., \& \text{ endlessly.} \quad (3)$$

Here Arthur claims, with Marx, that the value of "20 yards of linen", $(a^x$ of X), is "expressed" not only in one coat, $(a_x$ of A), but also in 10 lbs. of tea, $(b_x$ of B), 1 quarter corn, $(c_x$ of C), etc. However, so far as the *expression of the value* of linen (X) in terms of the use-value of other commodities (A, B, ...) is concerned, this is a meaningless statement. The pricing of linen does not mean that its owner may simply assert the "equivalence" of 20 yards of his/her linen with one coat, or 10 lbs. of tea, or 1 quarter corn, etc., especially if these are *not,* as according to Arthur[21], the definite quantities of the other commodities that he/she *desires.* If it is not the linen-owner (whose existence Arthur, in any case, repudiates) that makes this assertion, *WHO* is it? *WHOSE* evaluation is it that "20 yards of linen" should have the same value as all these other things in the stated quantities? In Marx's case, they are all supposed to be products of the same quantity of abstract labour, though, of course, performed in different concrete-specific forms. That is how Marx justified his total value-form (3).

However, if that much (i.e., the fact that all the terms in the total value-form contain the same value magnitude) is *already* known, then the value expression is a forgone conclusion. For the magnitude of value cannot be determined without money's having functioned as *measure of value.* The capitalist market measures commodity-values through its price-mechanism, the working of which requires that these values be first expressed in *money-prices.* The purpose of the value-form theory is to show why all commodities appear in the market with their supply prices *in money,* if tentatively, attached. Yet commodity values do not become *objective* until *physical money* appears in the market and mediates the exchange of commodities. Only then can they be *repetitively* purchased until their prices tend towards *normal* (or equilibrium) levels, at which point the demand for and the supply of them are equated. Only then can we claim that values have been *measured* (not just *expressed*) by the prevailing normal prices (not just in still tentative supply prices). In other words, if the capitalist market did not let (physical) money *measure* values, it would be idle to talk of any value-substance, labour or otherwise, since the magnitude of value itself (the commodity-economic form that may contain real-economic substance) cannot be determined.[22] Thus, we cannot even begin to talk about the price mechanism of the capitalist market, until we first learn the crucial fact that, in order to sell the commodity, *its owner must price it,* that is to say, must express its value in a money-price. For, until that is done, commodity-exchanges themselves cannot even begin.

The problem with Marx's approach here is that he simply dictates the conclusion without in the least showing us how to get there, i.e., skipping the necessary dialectical steps leading to it (which is akin to assuming equilibrium in order to prove its existence), though pretending otherwise (*en jetant de la poudre aux yeux des crédules, as it were*). In Uno's estimation, Marx's failure to strictly abide by his own "method of exposition" resulted in the unsatisfactory development in his theories both of value-forms and of the measure-of-value function of money.[23]

Arthur, like us, wants to develop his value-form theory without reference to the substance of value, which stance is beyond reproach. But how much of the above caveat in economic theory does he heed (or understand)? For he says:

> "From the observation that all commodities are exchangeable, directly or indirectly, in definite proportions arises the postulate that all the many exchange values possessed by a commodity spring from a unitary essence, an inherent power of exchange. [...] if such a presupposition were to be posited in commodity relations themselves, as is shown in the dialectic of the forms of value below, then the issue of its further grounding could be pursued."[24]

Though not perfectly clear to me, he seems to be saying that he starts with the "observation" of the market, in which commodities are (already) mutually exchanged at a variety of exchange-ratios (relative prices).

Since these prices, in his view, spring from the fact that in all commodities is an inherent "power of exchange" or "unitary essence", which he calls "value", he wants to bring out the logic of the "commodity relations themselves", in which the power of exchange (value) of commodities (somehow already immanent) comes out in the open in commodity-prices in the market.

I do not necessarily object to his initial "observation" as such, but the dialectical logic that inheres in the "commodity relations themselves" must be studied *from within*, not from without. That is to say, the subject (or the agent) of the dialectic must be located within the commodity itself as its owner-seller who incarnates the logic of capital. Now, Arthur seems to believe, in unwise imitation of Marx, that he can continue to stay at arm's length from the commodity-exchange market, in which, somehow, the dialectic of the "commodity relations themselves" unfolds, making armchair commentaries of a disinterested "observer" on it. This blurs the focus with regard to the entire issue, which begins to take its toll immediately with his development of the flawed conception of the simple value-form. Though he studiously claims that, in "(a^x of X) for (a_x of A)", the first term in the "relative value-form" is *active* and the second in the "equivalent value-form" is *passive,* he does not seem to realize that X is a *real* commodity firmly in the seller's hands, whereas A is, for the seller, an *imagined* one, existing in his head only, as something which he desires to obtain circumstances permitting.

Here we find the germ of his later discussion on the *reversal,* which he tries to justify by invoking Hegel's dialectic of *force and expression.* He reasons as follows. If X expresses its value (its "power of exchange") in A, X exerts "a special *force* of attraction" on A. Now A that suffers its effect, will exert its own *force* on X, such that A *solicits* X to be its equivalent. "The first force and the soliciting force are therefore merely two moments of a whole relation, and share a common content".[25] Quite apart from the question of pertinence of the application of Hegel's category of "force" to this context, Arthur now clearly places commodity X (which is real) and commodity A (which is latent) on an equal footing, both as active-passive and exchangeable one for the other in the market. The economics of *selling* the commodity thus disappears behind a Say's law-like truism that the selling of X is the buying of A and *vice versa,* which leads us only to the barter of X for A, the "power of exchange" being equally distributed between X and A. In other words, in Arthur's expression of value is already presupposed an equal magnitude of value in X and A, which should mean that the price-mechanism has already worked its way through, *measuring* commodity-values in the market, and, in the process, equating the demand for, and the supply of, all commodities including X and A. How can that sort of thing happen *without physical money already present and fully active in the market?* No sound economic theory should be short-circuited by such a *deus ex machina,* dialectical or otherwise, as "force and solicitation". I am thus obliged to conclude that, notwithstanding the discretion whereby he postponed reference to the substance of value until later, Arthur falls into the same trap as Marx, and *uses money (and what money does in the market) before he has logically derived it.*

Further on Arthur's "Dialectical Understanding" of the form of value

Now let us return to "total" value-form, (3), in which (a^x of X) is equated in *value* not only to (a_x of A) but also to (b_x of B), (c_x of C), etc., that is to say, to some quantity of *all* existing commodities. This cannot be said to be an expression of the value of X by its seller in terms of the other commodities. For, if it were, the X-owner would normally be stating (if subjectively) *different* quantities of X, as (b^x of X), (c^x of X), etc., for (b_x of B), (c_x of C), etc., that are given to him. It seems as though (3) rather indicates the position of the X-owner who views his/her (a^x of X) to have the same "power of exchange" as the indicated quantities (b_x of B), (c_x of C), etc., of the other commodities. Such "equivalence" makes sense, however, only when the magnitudes of value of all commodities are already known in the market, a situation which can emerge only *after* physical money has already evolved and has functioned as the measure of value. It is as if 20 yards of linen were sold for, say, $10, in the first instance, before the X-owner rushes to the market to see how much of the other commodities he/she can reasonably purchase for that sum of money. As he/she lists up the $10's worth of each of them in appropriate quantities as "equivalents" of (or having the same "power of exchange" as) the 20 yards of linen, the dialectical prestidigitator skillfully suppresses this fact by hiding the $10 from the spectators' view, in order to suddenly pull them out again into the open, upon the miraculous *reversal* of (3), with a bogus cry of *eureka* to the amazement of all present! But, the "unitary equivalent" or "unitary essence" which is now so ceremoniously "discovered" is not different from the $10 long ago smuggled into (3) without our knowledge.

   The reversal of the total into the general value-form was performed very simply by Marx with his famous "If, then, we reverse the series ...," with no further ado. This apparently does not satisfy Arthur, since he does not believe that it is "a question (as Marx unfortunately implies that it is) of different owners offering competing determinations of value", such that the expression of value of X in A, as "(a^x of X) for (a_x of A)", where X is active and A passive, *and* the expression of the value of A in X, as "(a_x of A) for (a^x of X)", where A is active and X passive, can "coexist within a consistently framed universe of value". He wants to *reverse* the value expression of X in A, while retaining X on the active pole always, never letting it pass to the passive pole. This problem he proposes to solve by allowing X "determine itself to the position of unitary equivalent by a process of the negation of the negation (which differs from flat contradiction)". First, when the value of X is expressed in A, it becomes not-X. But when the value of A (not-X) is expressed back in X by the reversal, that becomes not-A, which is equal to not-not-X, or simply X. But this last X "now *contains* in sublated form the opposition of relative and equivalent forms within itself, *actively* determining itself to the position of value in autonomous form, attracting the other commodities to it accordingly"[26] I must confess to having profound difficulty in following the progress of this speculative dialectic *in economic terms*. In what way is money *derived* here? All I see is the assertion of an incorrect thesis that *any commodity* (linen or non-linen) can become money with equal right.

For the argument only says this: If linen is regarded as just an ordinary commodity, it must express its value in the use-value of another commodity. But if linen is regarded as money, its use-value has already become the common value-reflector of all commodities, so all other commodities express their value in it, while linen need no longer do so in any other commodity. While this statement is in itself correct, it becomes meaningful only *after the money commodity (the general equivalent) has been derived as distinct from ordinary commodities*. But no explanation is provided as to the (dialectical) process whereby the commodity-economy necessarily singles out (and excludes) *one and only one commodity from all the rest to let it function as money*. This logical requirement must indeed be considered quite apart from "the selection of an appropriate empirical instantiation of money".[27] But precisely that logical requirement is missing in both Marx and Arthur. Instead of tracing the origin of money, they somehow obtain ready-made money and use it to construct the spurious value-form, (3), pretending it to be "reversible". In this fashion, they hope to evade the legitimate query as to *where* they first got that ready-made money. Of course, they do not know, nor do they want to know. If, however, the magnitude of value is already known, whether in labour or in some other "unitary essence", it means that it has been *measured,* which further means that *(physical) money is already present,* and need not be derived anew. Value-form theory has its meaning in identifying the necessity of money, in the first instance, *ideally* in the "head" of the commodity-seller. It is the selling of the commodity that gives birth to money, if ideally in the head of the seller in the first instance. For, the commodity can be *sold*, in the real sense of the term, only when sold for *money, as the general equivalent,* the discovery of which is the sole aim of the theory of value-forms. Only after that can the question of *physical* money "in the hands of the buyer" be introduced legitimately.

The general (or unitary) equivalent cannot be obtained from the meaningless *reversal* of the total value-form. It must, instead, be derived from a deliberate dialectic applied to the Unoist "set of sets" made up of the expanded value-forms of *all* commodity-sellers, (1'). For there, some commodities are bound to recur more frequently than others. Among them the ones that are *less perishable, less urgently needed for immediate consumption, less costly to hold over time and more readily saleable* are more likely to be selected as the general equivalent. For, in the general equivalent, the material-sensuous use-value should be sufficiently *attenuated* to become secondary to the commodity-economic use-value of the commodity. This tendency will assert itself in the actual practice of selling commodities, i.e., in the capitalist search for the socially most appropriate, single commodity to serve as the exclusive means of purchase.

Once a single commodity becomes *the* general equivalent, all commodity-owners will wish to acquire as great a quantity of it as possible in exchange for the whole stock of their commodity, and, at that point, the owner of the general equivalent can purchase any other commodity without any quantitative and qualitative restrictions. The general equivalent has now become money, the *exclusive* means of purchase. All commodities now appear in the market with their *supply prices* in money terms tagged. A universal market for commodity-exchanges develops then, with ordinary commodity-owners (with their value-expressions) *on the supply side,* and the money-owners (with their purchase-plan) *on the demand side.*[28] (The value-expression of commodity-owners and the purchase-plan of money-owners must not be confused, even though the same person may sometimes act as a commodity-seller and at other times as a commodity-buyer.) All commodities are thus *repetitively* bought and sold in the market, as supply-prices tend to be equated with demand-prices. This is the process of the *measurement of value,* which does not apply to so-called "simple" commodities (or commodities by chance), but, in principle, only to "capitalistically-produced" (genuine) commodities. Many articles are, in fact, bought and sold at arbitrary prices, but the prices of capitalistically-produced commodities tend, in the end, to settle to *normal prices.* These normal prices (and only they) *measure* commodity-values at definite magnitudes. They are "containers" as it were into which economic substance may flow. Thus, value-forms will in the end be filled with value-substance.

Enough has been said to demonstrate that Arthur's effort to develop a value-form theory à la Marx, without reference to the substance of value was a non-starter. For, like Marx, he suffered from the illusion of having logically derived money from the commodity, though, in fact, he (as Marx) surreptitiously assumed money's presence in the beginning. In consequence, all he (like Marx) could do was to derive the logically incorrect conclusion that *all* commodities (presumably even ice-cream) can become money.[29] The crucially important thesis that one and only one suitable commodity will be excluded from the rest to become money remains for all intents and purposes undemonstrated. Arthur's value-form theory thus remains in the same state of imperfection as Marx's.

Conclusion

Having said all the above, I am conscious of the fact that I have taken an unfair advantage over Arthur for having direct access to Uno's writings in Japanese (which he has not), especially to the article quoted above, in which Uno cogently demonstrates the inadequacies of Marx's value-form theory (which also severely constrained his treatment of the measure-of-value function of money). Had a translated version of that article been available to Arthur, he could have reasoned differently, and may even have taken an approach closer to Uno's, so that in my Arthur-critique I would not have had to reproduce as much of the tenor of Uno's Marx-critique. For the thrust of this paper (in the last half) is essentially the same as Uno's of fifty years ago.

I am grateful to Christopher Arthur for having given me this opportunity to highlight, once again in English, the virtue of the Unoist approach to economics, which is undoubtedly informed by the Hegelian dialectic and not merely by formal (i.e., tautological) logic.[30] It is for that reason that, despite many disagreements, I have always held in high esteem Arthur's unchallenged scholarship in Hegel studies, which is potentially a most valuable asset in any attempt to arrive at an adequate grasp of Marxian economics. It is, however, important *not* to unduly "philosophize" or "hegelize" economic theory, for the latter has its own logic which must be respected. Uno, unlike Lenin, never counseled his students to use Hegel as a "tool" to better understand economics. He, on the contrary, intimated that Hegel's logic would become clearer and more intelligible, if one learned the economics of *Capital* thoroughly. By this he meant that the materialist dialectic must be discovered within economic theory (or the dialectic of capital), not the other way round.[31]

Notes and References

[1] Arthur, C. J., "Money and Exchange", in *Capital & Class*, #90, (Autumn 2006).

[2] Marx, Karl, *Capital I* (New York: International Publishers, 1987), pp. 43-96.

[3] By the consumer being "active" I mean that he/she, like the neoclassical one, possesses an explicit system of preference, such as an "individual" utility function, in deciding his/her consumption-plan, i.e., in specifying how much of what to consume.

[4] Sekine, Thomas T., *An Outline of the Dialectic of Capital,* vol. I (London: Macmillan, 1997), pp. 34-49.

[5] "A fully commodified system of production" (Arthur, C. J., "Money and Exchange", in *Capital & Class*, #90, Autumn 2006, p. 8). I take that to mean the fully developed form of what Marx called "the capitalist mode of production", and what the Unoists call "capitalist society" or simply "capitalism". See also Bell, John and Sekine, Thomas T., "The Disintegration of Capitalism: A Phase of Ex-Capitalist Transition", in Albritton, Robert, *et al.* (ed.), *Phases of Capitalist Development* (Basingstoke: Palgrave, 2001), pp. 37-55.

[6] Many years ago, when I addressed a sophomoric question to Uno over his version of value-form theory, he responded, with a genial smile, saying, "Dear Sekine, I bet you never sold a merchandise in your life, did you?", then he added, "For my part, I spent my childhood often helping my uncle sell books in his store". The point of the lesson was clear to me: Do not try to understand the dialectic of capital (including the derivation of money) with a samurai spirit (nor, if I may add, with the spirit of a monk). One has to become (if mentally) a capitalist seller of the commodity to appreciate the meaning of its "pricing".

[7] Suppose that an artist is painting a portrait of the Queen. His first stroke of brush on the canvas has to do with *her* silhouette, not with that of a man. But, someone who sees only the canvas, say, from out of the window, not realizing that the Queen is sitting in the room to have her portrait drawn, is (formally-logically) entitled to guess that the painter is working on the portrait of a man. But the dialectician, who is not a casual observer and hence privy to "the insider's information", knows better.

[8] This is what Arthur *kindly* demonstrates in section II of his paper: "The Actuality of Exchange". He, however, does not act there for us as a devil's advocate, but out of his own conviction that commodity-owners' motives are dominated by use-values, and that they are, therefore, bound to be making *buying* (instead of *selling*) proposals in the market.

[9] Herodotus, *The Persian Wars,* Book IV (New York: Modern Library, 1942), p. 196.

[10] Tamanoi, Yoshiro, "The Origin of Commodity Exchange", in *Collected Works* [in Japanese], volume IV, Tokyo (1990), pp. 120-164.

[11] Radford, R. A., "The Economic Organisation of a POW Camp", in *Economica* (1945).

[12] Marx, Karl, *Capital I*, p. 91.

[13] Radford, R. A., "The Economic Organisation of a POW Camp", p. 191.

[14] Arthur ("Money and Exchange", p. 28) makes an incomprehensible claim such as follows: "This set of sets offends against the basic principle that a commodity cannot appear in both relative and equivalent form; here each commodity is supposed to appear once in 'relative' form and an indefinite number of times in 'equivalent' form. This is a contradiction." (Arthur, "Money and Exchange", p 9). But if that were indeed the case, any commodity which is once desired as equivalent by the linen-owner would never again be permitted to be offered for sale, or express its value in the market, an impossibility. What is excluded is for the seller of X to also desire to buy X (for all X = A, B, C, ..., N). There is clearly no reason why N expanded value-forms cannot exist side by side.

[15] Radford, R. A., "The Economic Organisation of a POW Camp", p. 191.

[16] Menger, Karl ("On the Origin of Money", reprinted in Ross M. Starr (ed), in *General Equilibrium Models of Monetary Economics*, Academic Press, 1989, pp. 68-82) has quite correctly emphasized the fact that, in addition to goods in which the seller is directly interested, he intends to acquire a commodity "which is more saleable than his own" (p. 76), even if he is not himself directly interested in it, and that this is in his economic interest. One commodity is more readily "saleable" than another, in the sense of being relatively easier to dispose of, as Menger says. But when a particular commodity (in addition to satisfying a few other requirements) becomes "absolutely" saleable, we may say that "it is no longer sold" (since always accepted), having become money or the exclusive means of purchase. Menger's view makes eminent economic sense, and is perfectly compatible with ours.

[17] Marx then continues: "Nomad races are the first to develop the money-form, because all their worldly goods consist of moveable objects and are therefore directly alienable; and because their mode of life, by continually bringing them into contact with foreign communities, solicits the exchange of products" (Marx, Karl, *Capital I*, New York: International Publishers, 1987, p. 92).

[18] Even if gold is finally selected as the universal equivalent, the demand for its various non-monetary uses does not disappear. It only becomes *secondary* to the monetary use. There is no commodity "that is *special as not-use-value*" (Arthur, "Money and Exchange", p. 23).

[19] Arthur, "Money and Exchange", pp. 9-10.

[20] Arthur, "Money and Exchange", pp. 11-18.

[21] For, he says, "Since the purpose is to specify [?] the value of the '20 yards of linen', the amount of the equivalent has nothing to do with satisfying 'desire' because that is oriented to use-value." (Arthur, "Money and Exchange", p 13).

[22] The labour theory of value, for instance, claims that productive labour in capitalist society will be optimally allocated to all branches of production in accordance with the structure of social demand, *when the price-mechanism of the capitalist market works effectively* so that the latter approaches equilibrium.

23 Of the many writings of Kôzô Uno on the subject, this piece (Uno, Kôzô, "Kachikeitai-ron to Kachijittai-ron [Theory of Value Forms and of Value Substance]", in *Keizaigaku-Hôhôron* [*Methods of Economics*], The University of Tokyo Press, 1962), to my knowledge, was the latest and the most accomplished version.

24 Arthur, "Money and Exchange", p. 12.

25 Arthur, "Money and Exchange", p. 15.

26 All citations in this paragraph are from Arthur, "Money and Exchange", pp. 15-16.

27 Arthur, "Money and Exchange", p. 17.

28 Unlike the classical and neoclassical approach, Marxian economics sharply distinguishes between the seller (supplier) and the buyer (demander) of the commodity. The commodity-owner is always found on the supply side. Only when he/she has sold the commodity and become a money-owner can he/she also stand on the demand side.

29 "As we have seen, the 'static' analysis of the first part had too many candidates for money, because logically any commodity could serve; but the 'dynamic' analysis of the second could not find any universal commodity to be money, because none is empirically always exchangeable." (Arthur, "Money and Exchange", p. 32). Thus, according to his own admission, he has failed to derive money, in his 'static analysis' of Part I, by the logically meaningless *reversal* of the total into the general value-form, and in his 'dynamic analysis' of Part II as well, by postulating a neoclassical buyer of use-values instead of the Marxian seller of the commodity.

30 In just the same way as Hegel's "logic coincides with metaphysics" (Wallace, William, *Hegel's Logic*, Oxford: Oxford UP, 1975, p. 36), the materialist dialectic should coincide with economic theory (Sekine, "The Dialectic of Capital, an Unoist Interpretation", in this volume and "The Dialectic, or Logic that Coincides with Economics", in this volume).

31 I am grateful to Christopher Arthur for reading a penultimate version of this paper and making detailed comments on it which were of great help to me. I have, however, not materially altered the general tenor of my argument here, taking advantage of our longstanding mutual pact to "agree to disagree" on matters pertaining to the dialectic and Marxian economic theory. I am also grateful to a referee of this paper, whose pertinent remarks enabled me to tighten my argument at several places.

General Equilibrium and the Dialectic of Capital

Because of its emphasis on "pure" theory and "general equilibrium", the dialectic of capital[1] is frequently misunderstood to be another "neoclassical" interpretation of Marx's economics. That is surely not the case. Yet it is true that the dialectic has adopted some analytical tools (techniques of analysis) from the neoclassical, and especially Walrasian, school. This article thus intends to show, in the first instance, the precise sense in which the dialectic of capital differs from neoclassical-Walrasian economics. On the other hand, the dialectic of capital differs as well, in a very significant manner, from conventional approaches to Marx's economics. That then is the second issue discussed in this article. I also wish to touch on some recent developments in Marxist economics and evaluate them from the point of view of the dialectic of capital. That constitutes the third topic of this article.

The dialectic of capital, or Unoist economic theory, is fundamentally inspired by Marx's works, especially the three volumes of *Capital*, but it does not pretend to offer an authentic doctrinal interpretation of Marx's texts. In other words, it claims no monopoly of a correct, faithful or true (whatever that might mean) interpretation of Marx's writings. The dialectic of capital has appropriated Marx's thought in its own way, and, in so doing, has departed (or diverged) from it to some considerable extent. I regard that to be inevitable inasmuch as it aims at more than simply regurgitating the words of the grand master. It is, therefore, willing to defend itself on its own ground, but not in light of passages quoted from Marx. In this sense, I would describe the dialectic of capital as being "Marxian" rather than "Marxist".

While not willing to be involved in the hermeneutics of the scripture, I certainly do not fail to appreciate doctrinal studies on Marx undertaken in the context of the history of economic thought. Nor do I fail to value the efforts of Marxists who search for some novel insight or inspiration by re-reading the original text. These are certainly worthy and commendable efforts for which I do not wish to lack respect. However, the dialectic of capital is not a study in the history of economic thought, nor is it a search for the revitalisation of Marxism as a political ideology. What the dialectic of capital seeks is a "correct" (or "true") economic theory, and that alone.

The dialectic of capital hopes to inherit from Marx his spirit of the critique of political economy, i.e., his critique of bourgeois (modern, liberal and capitalist) social science, of which economics constitutes the core. Since social science is a product of the modern, capitalist age, it is thoroughly imbued with its presuppositions, so much so that few writers in the field are really immune from bourgeois-liberal biases. To this rule Marx is an outstanding exception (even though he too may at times have lapsed into a "modernistic" glorification of industry and science). The dialectic takes this intellectual heritage from Marx very seriously and wishes to extend it to the context of the present age.

It is, however, by no means an easy task to disengage social science from its bourgeois-liberal biases. An unflinching loyalty to Marx's political ideology is certainly not enough for the task. A much more cool-headed inquiry, together with a great deal of soul-searching, will be necessary, if we wish to make significant progress in the right direction.

II

We must first of all grow out of the commonly-held but erroneous view that social science, as "science", shares the same method of inquiry with natural science. For no critique of political economy and of capitalism itself can be consistent with a natural-scientific approach to social science. Although I have elaborated on this matter elsewhere, it would be useful to recapitulate the gist of the argument here in view of its fundamental importance.[2]

In natural science we essentially seek "predictive" knowledge.[3] That is to say, by studying various aspects of nature from the outside, we try to discover certain regularities in what nature does in specific contexts. For that would enable us to "predict" what nature might do next in the particular context in which we take interest. For instance, a close study of earthquakes may enable us to predict when and where another one of a certain intensity may strike. To the extent that the prediction is accurate, such knowledge will benefit us in allowing us to take advance measures to minimise the harm that might otherwise befall us. But we can never negotiate with nature so as to either abolish that earthquake itself or to change its time, place and intensity. For nature has already decided to wreak havoc without previously consulting us and is unwilling to concede to us later by changing its course. That is why we must "conform" to nature and "piggyback" on its whims, rather than endeavouring to reform it or to repudiate its will. The recent outburst of ecological disasters is testimony enough to the inadvisability of tampering with nature's plans. Society, by contrast, is that which we ourselves create. It is certainly not given to us irrevocably from the outside as nature is, and we ought not to be content to discover some of its predictable regularities, the knowledge of which might enable us to conform to it wisely. What we learn from social science is nothing other than a knowledge of ourselves as social beings. From social science we do not derive a "predictive" knowledge of that which lies outside ourselves, but rather a "post-dictive" (Hegel would say "grey") knowledge of what we have been doing, and hence of who we are. It must thus be perfectly clear that social science seeks an entirely different type of knowledge from natural science. It must also be clear that economic theory as part of social science does not offer a natural-scientific hypothesis to be empirically tested for its validity or verification.

Indeed, we must once and for all set aside positivist-empiricist presuppositions by which our mind is so often clouded, if we wish to understand the nature of the dialectic of capital. Nevertheless, there is a deeply entrenched, conviction that true science is natural science, and that social science must imitate the method of the latter if it aspires to be truly "scientific". Such a conviction is shared not only by the positivists but also by a large number of Marxists ("dialectical-materialists" or otherwise). The latter are often unaware of the fact that they are then, in effect, supporting a doctrine of "the divine right of kings"[4] as the logical consequence of such a naïve misconception. For in all societies there is a class of privileged individuals whose interest is well served by the existing order. It is, of course, in their interest to assert that the existing social order is as immutable as the natural order or is ordained irrevocably by divine wisdom. In capitalist society the bourgeois-liberal tradition of social science has always claimed that all societies are in essence capitalist societies, and that human beings can never transcend them. We shall presently see how this false claim manifests itself in economics.

III

Economic theory is nothing other than "a definition of capitalism by capital itself". Economics evolved as a systematic body of knowledge only in modern times; that is to say, with the birth and development of capitalism. Indeed, it was in order to account for the nature of a capitalist society that the knowledge of economics was sought after. Thus, Marx wished to "lay bare the economic law of motion of modern society". But the "law of motion of modern society" which, he believed, had to be exposed, is just another name for the inner programme (logic) of capitalism, i.e., the "software" that makes capitalism what it is. Thus, in claiming that economic theory is nothing other than a definition or specification (*Bestimmung*) of capitalism, I am in no sense departing from the time-old tradition of economic studies. Following Uno, however, I have added the phrase "by capital itself", since this point, despite its extreme importance, has not been widely appreciated and has often been neglected. The point is that economic theory in the Marxian tradition is not a subjective "model" or an "ideal type" which we, as human observers, may arbitrarily construct to represent aspects of our market-based economic life.

By "capital" I here mean human "economic motives" extended and made infinite. The economic motives whereby we seek to maximise gains and minimise losses are present in all human beings, yet they always operate within limits, interwoven with other human motives, as K. Polanyi has especially emphasised.[5] When these economic motives alone are extracted and made infinite and absolute, we get "capital" the personification of which is "the economic man". This definition of capital, contrary to frequent misunderstanding, does not make capital an "idealist" object. It only means that capital is the concept (i.e., the idealisation) of a material (real) fact. No one denies the fact that we all have economic motives; for, if in doubt, we only have to ask ourselves to confirm its presence. Nor would anyone deny that theory consists of concepts and not with crude facts.

Because capital is thus endowed with the property of being infinite, it can act as the subject of a dialectic. For a dialectic is a logical self-synthesis of that which is infinite. On the nature of the dialectic, as I understand it, I have written elsewhere at some length. For example, I have claimed that the dialectic of capital "coincides with" economic theory, in exactly the same sense as Hegel claimed that his dialectic coincided with metaphysics. I have also claimed that capital, as defined above, is both subjective and objective. It is objective because it transcends us, finite human beings, and operates unrestricted by our human preoccupations; yet it is also subjective because we know it from the inside, i.e., we know exactly how it behaves, it being originally "we" ourselves as human beings, only divested of our limitations. Capital thus cannot lie to us or deceive us.[6]

The reason why "capitalism" constitutes the direct object of study of economics is that capitalist society operates its "use-value space" (i.e., the real-economic life of society involving concrete use-values of all sorts) almost entirely by the abstract-general principle of commodity exchanges (i.e., the "market principle" of capital by which one pursues abstract-general, mercantile value rather than concrete-useful wealth). The use-value space which forms the material foundation of any society is as old as human existence. But, due to its technical diversity, it does not admit direct logical analysis. Only when it is "subsumed" under the abstract-general principle of the commodity-economy does it become possible to disentangle what is "economic" from what is not. Thus, it is only in the age of capitalism when the operation of the market extended itself to cover an overwhelming proportion of our economic life (use-value space) that the science of economics began finally to take shape.

Yet the subsumption of society's use-value space under the market principle of capital is never complete or absolute even under capitalism. There always remains an incongruity, cleavage, tension, conflict, gap, etc., between the two aspects of the capitalist economy: the formal (which belongs to the market principle of capital) and the substantive (which belongs to the human world of use-values). It is this fact that the dialectic of capital, following Marx, calls the "contradiction between value and use-values", and takes as a matter of prime methodological importance. Indeed, the dialectic consists of nothing other than logically overcoming, and synthesising, this contradiction. For the existence of capitalism, the object of its study, depends on a successful synthesis of these two "contradictory" sides (or, in a more common language, on a chance reconciliation of these two basically incongruous aspects) of the capitalist economy.[7] Here lies the most fundamental difference of the dialectic of capital from bourgeois positivist-empiricist approach to economics.

What characterises bourgeois economics, in contrast, is that it does not (want to) recognise the gap between the substantive economic life which exists in all societies and its specifically commodity-economic organisation under capitalism. It, therefore, collapses the two senses of the word "economic" (real-economic and commodity-economic) together, and refuses to distinguish between them. Whence follows the "economistic postulate" that the "market", which derives from the permanent human "propensity to barter, truck and exchange", exists, if implicitly, in all societies.[8] This amounts to the same thing as to say that all societies are in essence "capitalist". It denies the historical transience of capitalism and makes it appear as permanent as the natural order.

From this basic misconception, and fundamentally from that alone, follow the errors of bourgeois economics and "modernistic" social science. From the point of view of the dialectic of capital, any economics which succumbs to this misconception, regardless of its ideological protestation, suffers from "bourgeois-liberal" biases and is, hence, irrevocably misguided. I would stress here that such a misconception is inherent in all natural-scientific approaches to economics, whether empiricopositivist or dialectical-materialist. From the presupposition that capitalism is as immutable as nature follows the reactionary conclusion that "we", as human beings, can never be free from capitalism. On the other hand, the "revolutionary" self-arrogation of the superhuman power to "change nature", by carrying out a trigger-happy Armageddon for the salvation of this world, also parallels the blind faith in science and technology in the age of ecological disaster.

IV

The above, however, does not suggest a wholesale rejection of bourgeois economics. For what divides the dialectic of capital from bourgeois, or bourgeois-inspired, economics is only that fundamental difference just mentioned. Other differences are either minor and superficial, or derivative of the fundamental one. Bourgeois economics too has studied the capitalist economy and achieved, within its limitations, many valuable insights into it, especially into its practical working. It is foolhardy to reject all of them indiscriminately as ideologically tainted. That would be contrary to Marx's own example. Not only did he give full credit to the works of classical political economists, but he also occasionally took observations of a minor author such as Samuel Bailey seriously, whenever they appeared to contain a grain of truth. What is important in trying to learn from another school without making an unwarranted concession to it is to have a firm conception of what constitutes the basic, methodological difference between its approach and ours.

Due to an inadequate comprehension of the nature of capitalism and hence of economics, many Marxists have launched irrelevant and pointless "critiques" of the bourgeois approach, and have in the process erected monstrous versions of "Marxist" economics. Frequently, it is asserted that Marx's cabalistic teaching, yet to be fully explored, is potentially capable of a grand dynamics in the light of which the destiny of the human race is to be scientifically exposed (or prophesised), to the shame and discomfiture of bourgeois social science, which can paint only a static and myopic picture of the capitalist world. Here, I wish to warn against the groundless incantation of some magic power which Marx's economics does not, in fact, possess.

One of the commonest claims that Marxists make is that economics should stress the instability and not the equilibrium of the capitalist economy because the latter is a "contradictory" system doomed to automatic breakdown. According to such a claim, "equilibrium" is nothing more than a false vision of capitalism, complacently entertained by the bourgeoisie, and should have no place in Marxist economic analysis. Such a view, to my mind, reveals a complete misapprehension not only of the dialectic but also of economic theory as such. It is true that capitalism is a "contradictory" system in the above-explained sense that it combines the real-economic and the commodity-economic, the mutual accommodation of which is not always guaranteed in history. This, however, does not justify the thesis that capitalism as a system is always fraught with uncontrollable instabilities and is destined to break down at any moment. The purpose of economic theory is not to concoct a scenario of magnificent dynamics, in the light of which we may "prophesise", in Nostradamus-style, the future of human civilisation. It is to provide us with an objective definition of capitalism. But that cannot be obtained unless the use-value space is controlled or "neutralised"; that is to say, rendered in thought more amenable to the logic of capital than it actually is.

In "pure" economic theory, therefore, use-values are no more than distinct objects of use or consumption (x_1, x_2, ..., x_n) which are produced with a different technology in a different industry, such that "iron" and "coal" are distinct from each other in just the same way as "cotton" is from "silk". Capital can readily produce all these use-values as commodities provided that labour-power is readily available to it. Labour-power, which capital cannot itself produce, must nevertheless appear in theory as the only "simple" commodity. This is like assuming an ideal, frictionless space in which the logic of capital can unfold without any obstruction or hindrance, if and when labour-power is under its control. Capital then tends to produce all commodities in accordance with the pattern of social demand and, thus, to approach a state of general equilibrium. A general equilibrium emerges in this context as a teleological end of capital, and, as such, it forms an integral part of the definition of capitalism by capital itself. It is by no means a chance invention by Walras or any other individual economist, bourgeois or non-bourgeois. Nor can it be arbitrarily dismissed or abolished by us to suit our whimsical likes and dislikes.

It is, of course, Walras who gave general equilibrium theory its first adequate mathematical formulation. It was then studied primarily by neoclassical economists rather than Marxists. But the concept of general equilibrium itself is present in the doctrines of the classical school and of Marx himself.[9] The law of value, after all, can never be adequately accounted for except in the light of a general equilibrium of the capitalist economy, in which resources are presumed optimally allocated to all branches of production. In the dialectic of capital, a state of general equilibrium exists when no commodity is either overproduced or underproduced relative to the existing pattern of social demand, i.e., when all commodities are capitalistically produced in their socially necessary (i.e., equilibrium) quantities. In such a state, capital allocates the productive resources available to society "optimally" to all branches of production, in which a uniform rate of profit prevails. In such a state all commodities will be exchanged one for another at their respective production-prices, while embodying no more or less than the socially necessary labour for their production as value.

Needless to say, the general equilibrium just described is a notional, rather than a factual, state. That is to say, it is a state towards which the actual capitalist economy tends theoretically, i.e., when ideal conditions are presupposed as in theory, and not a state which the economy will actually attain and which we can then empirically verify as a fact. It is the "teleological end" of capital in the sense that the latter insists on reaching it, whether "we" want it to or not, if the use-value space given to it is ideal and if labour-power as a commodity remains under capital's control. In other words, a state of general equilibrium is an integral part of the definition of capitalism by capital itself. That, of course, does not by any means imply that general equilibrium is only a theoretical fiction. It is indeed vitally important to determine whether the tendency towards it actually exists or not. For, if our empirical observation of the economy suggests such a tendency to be absent, that simply means that the economy, which fails to embody the definition of capitalism, cannot be a capitalist one. It does not mean that the theory is wrong or outmoded. For economic theory is a referent in the light of which reality is to be judged. Unlike a natural-scientific theory, the objective definition of capitalism is not meant to be revised every time "reality" reveals its new facets so as to adapt to it.[10]

V

Thus, the thesis that a capitalist economy tends towards a state of general equilibrium is fully justified, provided that labour-power is already near a state of equilibrium and behaves as any other commodity. But labour-power is a special commodity which capital cannot directly produce even within an ideal, "frictionless" use-value space. Thus, if by any chance the market for labour-power gets out of control, the competition among capitals cannot by itself remedy the situation. It is at this point that a special macro-mechanism is called upon in order to ensure the continued existence of capitalism. The so-called law of relative surplus population is there to fulfil that function.

According to the dialectic of capital, the actual process of capital accumulation must undergo cycles, as it alternates between the phases of "widening" and "deepening". When capital accumulates itself under a given technology (in the so-called phase of "widening"), it unilaterally absorbs the existing supply of labour-power until its price rises (real wages rise) to such an extent that further accumulation of capital becomes unprofitable and, hence, meaningless. Once this state of "the excess of capital" is reached, capital is forced to adopt innovations which then generate a relative surplus population (in the so-called phase of "deepening"). The relative surplus population thus made available enables capital to continue further accumulation under a new generation of technology. The path of capital accumulation alternates between the two phases because of the presence of fixed capital. Fixed capital embodies the prevailing technology and can be renewed only as it nears the end of its durable life. The two phases of capital accumulation roughly correspond with the phases of prosperity and depression in business cycles, which are empirically observable in the capitalist market. In the nineteenth century, the typical Juglar cycles were periodically punctuated by "decennial crises", reflecting the fact that plants and equipment then typically lasted for about ten years.[11]

Economic theory consists of two parts, the micro-equilibrium part and the macro-dynamic part, and each comes from the nature of capitalism itself. Marx's *Capital* contains elements of both. When Marxists talked vaguely of "value and crises", they were referring to these two aspects of the definition of capitalism, whether they were fully aware of that or not. In contrast, classical and neoclassical economists had no macro-dynamic "theory" to speak of until they were confronted by Keynes, as they had left the "empirical" study of business cycles to historians and statisticians. In any case, the two parts of economic theory have no relation with the division of physics into statics and dynamics or into its micro and macro components. In economics, one studies micro-equilibrium theory *insofar as the working of the labour market can be deemed broadly under the control of capital*, and one studies macro-dynamic theory when that cannot be taken for granted. Indeed, capitalism exhibits both of these aspects. It undergoes business cycles for the reasons already mentioned, but, in the so-called sub-phase of "average activity" during its prosperity phase, a purely capitalist society approximates the condition of general equilibrium, in which an average profit prevails in more or less all branches of production.

In contrast to the clear methodology of the dialectic of capital just outlined, the so-called neoclassical synthesis, despite its pretentious proclamations, does not in fact "synthesise" the micro and the macro component of economic theory at all. Micro-theory remains *a priori* (deductive) and macro-theory *a posteriori* (inductive), and no explanation is offered as to why that must be the case. In the neoclassical theory of the market, the demand and supply of labour-power are explained respectively by its marginal productivity and the marginal disutility of labour because labour-power is not viewed in any sense as a special commodity. It is, therefore, impossible for the theory to even perceive the need for a "macro-foundation of micro theory". Instead, it vainly seeks a "micro-foundation of macro theory", only to be frustrated by the undeniable fact that the collective marginal propensity to consume can never be derived from the utility maximisation of the individual. All this, however, is only to be expected inasmuch as bourgeois economists do not comprehend the true nature and scope of economic theory. Instead of letting capital itself define capitalism objectively, they merely construct subjective and arbitrary models of the market economy to suit their ideological purposes. They accept, as an article of faith, the perfectibility of the market, and add natural-scientific embellishments to their analyses in order to make them appear objective. But the failure to truly combine the micro and the macro components of their theory testifies to the deep-rooted methodological confusion which their economics continues to suffer.

What is to be emphasised here is that the only instability that can be properly treated within the scope of economic theory is the periodic eruption of the "decennial crises". A crisis signifies that the market for labour-power has gotten out of control, as the "widening" phase of capital accumulation reaches its limit. It then throws the reproduction-process of society into disorder. This, however, does not imply the end of capitalism, but, only a switch-over from "widening" phase of capital accumulation to the "deepening" phase. This point must be stressed, for Marxists have traditionally misunderstood it. A crisis can lead to a revolution for contingent reasons but not as a necessary consequence of the operation of the logic of capital. To a great extent, Marx himself, as a political ideologue, has sown the seed of this misunderstanding. But capitalism has never, in fact, been as fragile as revolutionary rhetoric often makes it out to be. That is another reason why economic theory must be taken seriously.

By this time, I hope, the contrast between the dialectic of capital and bourgeois economics, represented by the neoclassical school, has become clearer. According to the dialectic, even in the "pure" space in which capital is supposed to have full control over all producible use-values, labour-power can still get out of hand and can give rise to a so-called "fundamental disequilibrium" in the system. When this occurs, the market logic of capital is powerless to remedy it; *an element of the use-value space itself (technology) must change* in order to ensure the system's survival. This is the reminder of the imperfect subsumption of the use-value space under the logic of capital, i.e., the reminder of the historical transience of capitalism. It is this thought that is typically absent in bourgeois economics, which regards the conversion of labour-power into a commodity as unproblematic, and which, therefore, believes capitalism to be a permanent system.

VI

This point is further related to the much misunderstood concept of value. It must be clearly understood, in the first instance, that "value" is a crucial concept for the Marxian approach to economics (i.e., for the dialectic of capital), but that it is quite irrelevant to bourgeois-liberal (including Sraffian) economics. The latter does not need a concept of value as distinct from that of price, even though it took some time before its practitioners realised this fact. The reason why it is irrelevant to bourgeois economics is that, in keeping with its liberal creed, it recognises no economic life outside the market; that is to say, no economic life other than that which is capitalist. The Marxian approach, by contrast, cannot dispense with the concept of value, as distinct from that of prices, precisely because it regards capitalism as an historically transient, and not a permanent, social formation. Value is the concept that relates the commodity-economic (i.e., that which takes place inside the market) with the real-economic (i.e., that which occurs outside it). It links specifically capitalist commodity production with the production of use-values in general, which occurs in all societies. If the market and substantive economic life were always inextricably linked to each other, there would arise no question of relating them. Value would indeed become wholly "irrelevant", as has been recently broadcast by the Sraffians.

The form of value is the money price of the commodity bought and sold individually in the capitalist market, but the substance of value is the real cost that society bears in producing it in terms of the expenditure of productive labour. All societies incur the cost of producing a use-value in terms of the labour spent (the only original factor of production which is used up in the process, and which is not specific to the production of any particular use-value). We cannot simply say that value is the same thing as price (or exchange value), nor can we say that it is just abstract labour embodied in a commodity. Value is that which expresses itself as a price in the sphere of circulation and that which consists of abstract (in the sense of "socially-necessary") labour in the sphere of production. It thus mediates between that which is specifically "commodity-economic" (the form of exchanges) and that which is "supra-historic" and common to all societies (the substance of use-value production), residing, as it does, in the intersection of the two.

Even in bourgeois economics it is well understood that the equilibrium price of a commodity implies that society's resources have been optimally allocated to its production. Bourgeois economics, however, interprets the allocation of "resources" in society as a strictly techno-physical issue with no "social" dimension. The two original factors of production into which "resources" are ultimately resolved are believed to be labour and land, both understood in their concrete-useful variations (meaning that weaving labour, for instance, is counted as a different type of labour from coal-mining labour). Whence follows the questionable theory of distribution in terms of marginal productivities. In the Marxian approach, by contrast, the allocation of resources is primarily a matter of the social organisation of production, to which Marx frequently referred to as the "social division of labour". The equilibrium prices determined in the capitalist market must, in other words, reflect society's optimal division of labour, i.e., an optimal allocation of productive labour for the provision of the use-values that society needs and wants. This trans-historic need of human society is operated by capital, i.e., regulated by the market in capitalist society. Even the commodity which is regularly traded in the capitalist market for profit is a use-value, and, hence, must be a product of the social division of labour.

It is, thus, consistent with the nature of Marxian economic theory (or the dialectic of capital) to claim that "value" is by far the most fundamental of its concepts. If all societies were capitalist, we would not need it; if no society were capitalist, we would not need it either. To understand "value" is to understand the *differentia specifica* of capitalism as an historically transient society. But, precisely for that reason, the history of economic thought shows that this enigmatic concept of value has always been a source of maximum confusion.

According to Marx, Adam Smith discovered the concept of labour in general. Smith understood "labour in general, that is the entire social aspect of labour as it appears in the division of labour" to be "the sole source of material wealth or of use-values".[12] This discovery of abstract labour no doubt gave classical economics a powerful ideological weapon in the critique of mercantilism. (In its early days, liberalism was a progressive ideology, which combatted the outdated canons of the mercantilist *ancien régime*.) It is, however, also true that the classical school erred from the outset in trying to explain the relative prices of commodities by the amounts of labour embodied in them. Classical economists propounded the labour theory of *prices*, rather than that of value, and got increasingly confused as time went by, until the Ricardian school disintegrated, in the end, owing to its inability to account for the so-called "transformation problem", i.e., to reconcile the apparent contradiction between the labour theory of value and the law of average profit.

After the "marginal revolution" neoclassical economics was charged with the task of filling in the vacuum left by the disintegration of the classical school. It responded to the call by replacing the labour theory of value, an objective theory, with the marginal utility theory of value, a subjective theory. But it abided by that subjective value theory only for the first forty years, during which period the prominent representatives of the neoclassical school made a number of significant contributions to economic analysis in their own ways. Interestingly, many of them were far from apologists of capitalism, if not self-professed "socialists" like Walras, Wieser and Wicksell. An important change occurred during the 1920s, however, when "measurable utility" was abandoned for "indifference" and "real cost" for "opportunity cost". At this point, the liberals jettisoned their pride of being anti-establishment ideologues, and turned into professional apologists of capitalism. In their hands, the concept of value has long since been replaced by that of "trade-offs", which implies that "value" as distinct from "price" no longer retains any theoretical meaning, the commodity-economic and the real-economic having been irrevocably merged and blended together.

VII

Neoclassical economists are to be credited rather than criticised for their formulation of general equilibrium, but their error lies in deriving it from the false principle of substitution (utility maximisation of the consumer). The general equilibrium in the capitalist market results from the mercantile behaviour of "buying cheap and selling dear" any commodity, i.e., from the indifferent act of "arbitrage" on the part of the capitalist, and not from the consumer's act of substituting one use-value for another. A merchant, which the capitalist most certainly is, shifts any commodity from where the demand for it is low to where the demand for it is high by the capitalist act of arbitrage, so that the available commodities in the market are reshuffled and shifted to where they are most needed by society. If production is also involved, capital sees to it that the most needed and wanted commodities are produced first, allocating society's productive resources optimally to all industries. In other words, a general equilibrium of the capitalist market is achieved by the mercantile act of arbitrage. The reason is that the capitalist market trades commodities by the medium of money rather than exchanging use-values directly.

The consumer's act of substitution whereby he intends to achieve a maximum level of satisfaction by allocating resources in such a way as to ensure equi-marginal utilities for himself is wholly irrelevant. Such an act applies only to an exchange of use-values; it does not apply to an exchange of commodities (or value-objects). When John and Mary exchange their toys in a children's playroom, they do indeed worry about such thing as how much "play-time with toy-A" one has to sacrifice in order to gain one unit of "play-time with toy-B" from the other. They negotiate with each other face to face until their "offer curves" nicely intersect. They are, in other words, "sharing" rather than "trading", i.e., exchanging use-values rather than exchanging commodities. The capitalist market, in which commodities are exchanged, is an impersonal one. No capitalist trader buys and sells commodities so as to maximise his individual satisfaction, i.e., so as to equate his marginal utilities per dollar spent of the use-values involved. He buys and sells commodities as an arbitrageur or speculator, i.e., in pursuit of mercantile (i.e., abstract-general) wealth, being completely indifferent to the specific characters of the use-values involved. It is quite the same with the capitalist producer of commodities. He produces any one of them which fetches him the most profit for his capital outlay, because he is completely indifferent to specific use-values. An equal rate of profit tends to prevail in all industries, if the market is competitive. An optimum allocation of resources is not the direct result of the individual act of substitution on the part of the capitalist producer, trying to achieve equi-marginal returns in all branches of his diversified activities.

One of the most dubious accomplishments of neoclassical economics was to surreptitiously replace the idea of arbitrage with that of substitution. Nowhere is this trick more evident than in the history of the so-called price-specie-flow mechanism. When Hume, who obviously had no idea of substitution, gave it a first classical exposition, his explanation was as follows: An inflow of gold into a nation, due to a balance of trade surplus, raises the prices of all commodities in that nation, while the outflow of gold due to a balance of trade deficit will produce the reverse effect. Since everyone buys any commodity cheap and sells it dear, the balance of trade will soon be restored as the price of each commodity becomes level throughout the world. It is clear that the act of arbitrage was counted on in this case to produce the result. But by the time Mill's theory of "international values" was reinterpreted by Marshall *et alii* in terms of "offer curves", the idea of arbitrage had been suppressed and had been replaced with that of substitution: The flow of gold from one country to another gives rise to changes in relative prices between the export goods of those countries, to which the purchase plans of utility maximising consumers adapt. Thus, when Keynes controverted with continental European economists over the so-called "transfer mechanism" of the German reparations after the First World War, his argument was entirely based on substitution. The Europeans were understandably incredulous in the face of the altered mechanism of international transfer so crudely divorced from actual monetary and capitalist behaviours in the market. They thus offered an alternative explanation in terms of the purchasing-power shift or *Kaufkraftverschiebung* only to be rebuffed by the then neoclassical orthodoxy of Anglo-America.[13]

It is indeed a sheer folly to try to explain such a thing as the mechanism of international adjustment only in "real terms", i.e., only by the principle of substitution, ignoring money and capital altogether. But that is precisely in the spirit of neoclassical economics, which postulates a complete merger or fusion of the use-value space and the market, without recognising any stress or incongruity between them. It is well known that Walras struggled very hard with money and capital after his theories of exchange and production were completed, but he was not nearly as successful with these matters as he was with the moneyless world of the *numéraire*. That is to say, his theory of general equilibrium represents, in essence, an imaginary system of generalised barters, and not a system of capitalist commodity exchanges.

Another striking limitation of neoclassical general equilibrium is evidenced by the proposition called Walras' law, which says that the excess demand for all commodities must add up to zero. This law can actually be derived from the summation of the budget constraints of all individual consumers, who spend all of their incomes on consumption and make no savings. Such a law is necessary to solve the price-equations of the system, but it also commits the Walrasian general equilibrium to a stationary state. For, without savings, no accumulation of capital is possible. That is a very high price to pay for a general equilibrium theory, given that no capitalist economy in fact remains stationary. Yet, this limitation is inherent in a general equilibrium theory of the consumer economy, governed by the principle of substitution, which the Walrasian system essentially is. In order to move beyond an economy of consumers, neoclassical economics has more recently shifted its focus to "linear production models" characterised by "non-substitution". These models, now going to the other extreme, ignore consumers' tastes and utility maximisation completely and represent, in a purely "technocratic" fashion, an economy of producers. Before commenting on this approach, however, I wish to outline some of the salient characteristics of the general equilibrium theory according to the dialectic of capital.

VIII

The simplest representation of a general equilibrium in the capitalist market contains only three commodities: the capital good (or the means of production), the wage-good (or the article of consumption for productive workers), and the luxury good (the consumption good for capitalists and their associates). Let X, Y, Z be the output levels of these three products, respectively. Let X_x, X_y, X_z, be the amounts of the means of production currently consumed, and L_x, L_y, L_z be the number of hours of direct labour currently employed, for the production of each of the three commodities. All these numbers, we suppose, are known and are positive (> 0). Let p_x, p_y, p_z be the prices of the three goods, and w and r be the wage-rate per hour and the general rate of profit, respectively. Then we have the following price-determining system:

$$(p_x X_x + w L_x) \, (1 + r) \quad = \quad p_x X \ , \tag{1}$$
$$(p_x X_y + w L_y) \, (1 + r) \quad = \quad p_y Y \ , \tag{2}$$
$$(p_x X_z + w L_z) \, (1 + r) \quad = \quad p_z Z \ , \tag{3}$$
$$p_y Y \equiv (L_x + L_y + L_z). \tag{4}$$

The first three, (1) (2) (3), are the price-equations, and the last identity, (4), is what I call the "fundamental constraint of the capitalist market". It says that the wages-bill currently paid out is entirely spent on the currently produced wage-goods, so that the workers do not, in principle, save. It plays here the same role as Walras' law does in the neoclassical system, and imposes the most fundamental condition of the viability of capitalism. Walras' law is, in fact, no more than a watered-down version of this relation, without which capitalism would not hang together.[14] [15]
  The core of this price system is represented by the following two equations:

$$(p_x X_x + w L_x) \, (1 + r) \quad = \quad p_x X \ , \tag{1}$$
$$(p_x X_y + w L_y) \, (1 + r) \quad = \quad w L \ , \tag{5}$$

where, for simplicity, I write: $L \equiv L_x + L_y + L_z$. The first, (1), is the price equation of the capital-good sector reproduced, and the second, (5), is the price equation of the wage-good sector, (2), combined with the fundamental constraint, (4). These two equations, (1) and (5), determine the price of the capital good, p_x / w, and the general rate of profit, r, simultaneously. When these are known, the other prices, p_y/w and p_z/w, can be derived from the second and the third price-equation, (2) and (3). The solution of the core system can be graphically illustrated as follows. Re-writing (1) and (5) as

$$p_x/w \quad = \quad L_x / \{X (1 + r)^{-1} - X_x\} \quad , \tag{1'}$$
$$p_x/w \quad = \quad \{L (1 + r)^{-1} - L_y\} / X_y \quad , \tag{5'}$$

we find that (1') is a monotone increasing curve, on which $p_x/w > 0$ when $-1 < r < (X - X_x)/X_x$. It approaches $+\infty$ as r approaches $(X - X_x)/X_x$ and assumes the price of $p_x/w = L_x/(X - X_x)$ when $r = 0$. As for (5'), it is a monotone decreasing curve with an asymptote $r = -1$. It takes the price of $p_x/w = (L_x + L_z)/X_y$ when $r = 0$, and the price of $p_x/w = 0$ when $r = (L_x + L_z)/L_y$. These two curves intersect in the positive quadrant if and only if

$$(L_x + L_z) / X_y \quad > \quad L_x / (X - X_x) \quad , \tag{6}$$

as is illustrated by the graph below (Figure 1). But it can be easily shown that (6) is equivalent to the fact that the rate of surplus value is positive $e > 0$.[16] Thus, the existence of a general equilibrium in the capitalist market is ensured by nothing other than the positivity of the rate of surplus value.

The present system is defined only in a small neighbourhood of the equilibrium, so that the numbers representing physical quantities as in:

$$\begin{cases} (X_x, L_x) \rightarrow X \ , \\ (X_y, L_y) \rightarrow Y \ , \\ (X_z, L_z) \rightarrow Z \ , \end{cases} \tag{7}$$

are supposed to hold only at or near the equilibrium activity levels. It implies a technology in use when the allocation of resources is close enough to being optimal. Although this technology can always be linearly approximated (i.e., expressed in the per-unit-of-output form) near equilibrium, the system does not by itself pretend that the same should hold everywhere, i.e., even far away from equilibrium. Since, within the scope of definition of this system, both of the above curves, (1') and (5'), are monotone, the equilibrium identified by their intersection is bound to be unique. The uniqueness may, of course, not hold in a more globally defined system.

Figure 1

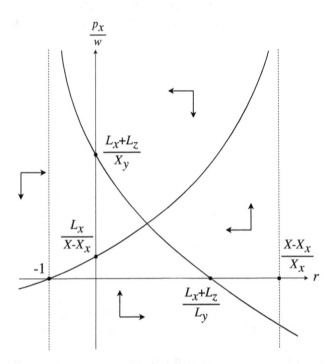

Next, let us examine the stability of this equilibrium. The first curve, (1'), represents the combinations of p_x/w and r which maintain the market for the capital good in equilibrium. The rate of profit cannot be determined in this market alone, so that it must be viewed there as a parameter in the light of which to decide on the price of the capital good. Thus, at any point above the (1')-curve, a force downward to the curve must be at work; and at any point below the curve, a reverse force upward to the curve must be at work. As for the (5')-curve, it represents the combinations of the same two variables so as to maintain equilibrium between the wages-bill paid out currently and the current supply of the wage-good. In this case, the price of the capital good, which is determined elsewhere, must be a parameter, and the burden of adjustment falls on the rate of profit. Thus, at any point to the left of the curve, the rate of profit is deemed too low (the price of the wage-good, p_y/w, is too hish) so that there will be unsatisfied demand for the wage-good. Consequently, a force is generated to raise the rate of profit. At any point to the right of the (5')-curve, the reverse force will work to bring down the rate of profit.

Whether the equilibrium defined by the intersection of the two curves is dynamically stable or not depends on the relative slopes of the curves and the vectors of the adjustment forces existing in each of the quadripartite areas demarked by the curves. Under very ordinary conditions, we can expect the equilibrium to be dynamically stable. By "ordinary conditions" I, of course, mean such conditions as can be ordinarily expected to hold in a capitalist market, which is based on the principle of arbitrage. The present theory has nothing to do with the neoclassical system of generalised barter in which the consumers are busy substituting one use-value for another. Nor does it concern itself with such a neoclassical consideration as "false (non-*tâtonnement*) trading" which might interfere with the stabilising force of the market.[17]

Since the present system is defined in regard only to a small neighbourhood of the equilibrium and does not intend to account for a vastly off-equilibrium situation, it is otiose to concern ourselves with global, rather than local, stability. As already remarked, the scope of application of micro-equilibrium analysis is more or less limited to the sub-phase of "average activity" during business cycles. For only then can the market for labour-power be deemed close enough to equilibrium. At any other time, the capitalist economy is far from achieving an equalisation of profit-rates in all branches of production, reflecting the fact that the labour market is out of equilibrium. Under the circumstances, the law of value, working through the motion of prices, i.e., supported by the micro behaviour of individual capitals in intersectoral competition, remains wholly powerless to lead the economy to a general equilibrium. In the meantime, it is the working of the law of population which shelters the capitalist system from disintegration. This process must be studied in the perspective of macro-dynamics, not in the light of the micro behaviour of capitalist industries towards equilibrium. Indeed, when the survival of capitalism itself is in question, the time is not yet to ascertain the teleology of capital.

IX

The earliest and the simplest of the linear production models is the Leontief system, which is also said to have been originally inspired by Walras. It has the form $AX + Y = X$, where $A = [a_{ij}]$ is an $n \times n$ square matrix of technical coefficients, X is a column vector of activity levels, and Y is a column vector of final demands. It can be solved as $X = Y(I - A)^{-1}$ given Y, so that, once the vector of final demands is given, the activity levels are determined strictly in technical terms. If Y reflects an autonomously-shaped pattern of social demand, this system may still represent an aspect of the capitalist economy. However, it can also and more easily represent a choice which the central planning authority of a command economy may dictate, in which event the system would have little bearing on capitalism. The price side, defined as a "dual" to the above system, is written $PA/wL = P$, where P is a row vector of prices, w a scalar indicating a wage-rate, and L a row vector of labour coefficients. This can be solved as $P/w = L(I - A)^{-1}$, given L. As in Walras' case, pure economic profits disappear at equilibrium, and the managerial labour of the capitalists receives wages in much the same way as the productive labour of the workers does. Because of the fact that l is autonomously given, people once talked of Leontief's labour theory of value, but only a generation later it was replaced by $PB (\equiv L)$ where B is a matrix of "labour-feeding" coefficients.[18] In other words, "labour" has now become an intermediate commodity presumed to be producible with an appropriate bundle of wage-goods.

This method, which I have elsewhere called the "fodder method"[19] has been very widely used. It is adopted not only in the mathematical rendition of Marx's price-and-value theory by von Bortkiewicz but also in the maximal growth model of von Neumann. When all "original" factors of production are suppressed, it becomes easier to generalise the concept of production into a strictly technical transformation of a bundle of commodities X into another X, in a manner analogous to the market transformation of a basket of goods into another by exchanges. Though some apologetic remarks are still heard in regard to the suppression of land, the reduction of labour into an intermediate good seems to be accepted with few qualms. The dialectic of capital has no theoretical affinity with such a crudely mechanistic view of human society. Yet on a purely technical level, it has an artifice to learn from the "linear production models".

The strength of the linear production models lies in the treatment of many capital goods (intermediate goods). In the previous section, I presented a general equilibrium of the capitalist market, according to the dialectic of capital in its simplest form, involving only one capital good. But that is, of course, a radical simplification. In reality, a number of capital goods are employed in diverse proportions in different branches of production. When that is the case, we must be able to produce a composite capital good which Sraffa calls "the standard commodity". This amounts to a basket of capital goods such that the output-basket contains these goods in the same proportion as they are used as inputs for its production. If capital goods always appear in the same proportion whether as inputs or as outputs, like an alloy containing different metals in fixed proportions, they are as good as being a single capital good.

This, however, is not usually the case. But, even if many capital goods are used in different proportions in different industries, it is possible to construct a "standard capital good", in reference to which many basic theorems can be stated, and Sraffa has shown that procedure.

Let us suppose that there are two means of production, steel and coal, and that their current outputs are, respectively, $x_1 = 183$ and $x_2 = 190$. Suppose also that the 183 units of steel are produced by $x_{11} = 38$ units of steel itself and $x_{12} = 22$ units of coal, and that the 190 units of coal are produced by $x_{21} = 40$ units of steel and $x_{22} = 10$ units of coal itself. We may then tabulate these assumptions as follows:

$$(x_{11}, x_{12}) \rightarrow x_1 , \qquad (38, 22) \rightarrow 183 ,$$
$$(x_{21}, x_{22}) \rightarrow x_2 , \qquad (40, 10) \rightarrow 190 .$$

Sraffa's idea is to find a set of multipliers z_1 and z_2, such that, if these are applied to the above two production-processes, we can get the following result:

$$183 z_1 / (38 z_1 + 40 z_2) = 190 z_2 / (22 z_1 + 10 z_2) .$$

This problem can be easily solved as follows.[20] Let

$$S = \begin{bmatrix} 38 / 183 & 22 / 190 \\ 40 / 183 & 10 / 190 \end{bmatrix} .$$

Then any eigenvector belonging to the Frobenius root of this matrix will contain the required multipliers as its elements. Since $Z = (z_1, z_2)' = (1, 0.455)'$ is an eigenvector belonging to the Frobenius root $\mu = 0.3071$ of S such that $(\mu I - S) Z = 0$, it can be used to derive the following relations:

$$(z_1 x_1, z_2 x_2) = (183, 86.45) = (56.2, 26.55) / 0.3071 =$$
$$(z_1 38 + z_2 40, z_1 22 + z_2 10) / \mu .$$

and it can be readily confirmed that $183 : 86.45 = 56.2 : 26.55 = 2.12 : 1$. In other words, the standard basket contains the two capital goods always in the ratio of $2.12 : 1$, whether as output or as input. Sometimes it is convenient to express the output of the standard capital good as a number x rather than as a vector (z_1x_1, z_2x_2). Since this is purely a matter of convention, any arbitrary function f can be contrived to map such a vector into a scalar, so that, for example,

$$x = z_1x_1 + z_2x_2 , \quad z_1 = 1$$

is as good as any. In the present case, we shall say that 269.45 units of the standard capital good has been produced, since $x = 183 + 86.45 = 269.45$.

It is important that a standard capital good could always be constructed in case the system contains more than one capital good, since it will serve as a referent in many traditional Marxian theorems. For example, the law of average profit is usually stated in the following terms:

$$p_i \lessgtr q_i \quad \text{if and only if} \quad k_i \lessgtr k, \quad \text{for all } i$$

where p_i is the production-price, and q_i the value-proportional price (so defined as to equate the aggregate output in production-prices to that in value-proportional prices), of the output of the i-th sector, and k_i and k are, respectively, the value composition of capital of the i-th sector and the social average value composition of capital. But, strictly speaking, this well-known statement applies only in a system which does not contain any more than one single capital good. If there are more in use, the statement of the law should be:

$$p_i \lessgtr q_i \quad \text{if and only if} \quad k_i \lessgtr k, \quad \text{for all } i,$$
$$\text{as } u \to 1 \quad \text{and} \quad u_i \to 1.$$

If the first two commodities are capital goods, the definitions of u and u_i's will be the following:

$$Av_i \ (p_1/q_1, p_2/q_2,) = u_i \ (p_x/q_x,) ,$$
$$Av_{all} \ (p_1/q_1, p_2/q_2,) = u \ (p_x/q_x,)$$

where the operator Av_i says: "take the average of the following price-to-value ratios with the weights in value of the capital goods as they are employed in the i-th sector", and the operator Av_{all} says: "take the average of the following price-to-value ratios according to the weights in value of the capital goods as they are employed in the whole economy", and where p_x, and q_x are, respectively, the production-price and the value-proportional price of the standard capital good.

Clearly, many well known Marxian theorems can be stated more rigorously than hitherto by the use of the standard capital good as a referent. But the useful service which the linear production models, including Sraffa's innovation, render to the dialectic of capital is limited to this strictly technical refinement. Sraffa's work makes no other contribution to Marxian economics. Although Neo-Ricardianism and neoclassical economics are different in certain respects, they are both fundamentally "bourgeois-liberal" in the strict sense specified above. One should have no illusion about it. "Sraffian Marxism", like "bourgeois Marxism", is a blatant oxymoron. Indeed, the main thrust of Sraffianism has been to discard the labour theory of value as "irrelevant", and, thus, to render Marxian economics empty and meaningless, i.e., to reduce it to another variation of bourgeois economics.

Yet Sraffa seems to have exerted a stupendous influence over a large number of Anglo-Marxists. For a long time since the late 1970s, they seem to have been trapped under the mesmerising spell of Sraffa perhaps because of the misleading title of his book, *The Production of Commodities by Means of Commodities*, even though Sraffa's "commodity" patently has little affinity with Marx's. They may have wishfully thought that Sraffa had provided them with a powerful enough tool with which to exorcise the more petrifying terror of neoclassical economics. In any case, they quickly converted themselves into Sraffianism, and willingly collaborated towards the undoing of Marxian economics, whilst the impenitent "fundamentalists" (sometimes also scorned as "obscurantists") lapsed into grumpy silence. It is only in recent years that signs have appeared to suggest an anti-Sraffian regrouping on the part of the latter. But the injury has been so stunning that it will be some more time before it adequately heals.

X

Recently, a group of economists led by A. Freeman and G. Carchedi have published a new book,[21] resolved to free Marx's theory from the deleterious influence of Sraffianism, and to restore the labour theory of value to its rightful place. They all believe that the "dualist" approach, adopted early by von Bortkiewicz *et alii* and adhered to ever since by the majority of the economists, which contrasts the two separate equilibrium systems, one in price and the other in value, has led to the inadvised Sraffian dismissal of the labour theory of value, which they continue to regard as absolutely indispensable. They reject the usual understanding that Marx failed to complete the transformation of values into prices because he left the values of the inputs untransformed. They vigorously defend Marx by claiming that his reasoning, based on what they call the "single (value-price) system" approach, was flawless without the transformation of input values into prices. For this approach, according to them, takes the constant and variable capital advanced by industries and firms as historically given and as already representing the replacement *price*, not value, of the means of production and labour-power, and determines the output values and prices on the basis of whether each sector or firm receives the surplus value it has actually produced or only the share of the aggregate social surplus value proportional to the total capital which it has advanced. In that case, *they* claim, Marx's so-called double equalities (total value = total price *and* total surplus value = total profit) do not fail to hold.

All authors seem to be agreed up to this point, an I myself cannot object to their definitional stage-setting. If, in their well-meaning effort to defend Marx's transformation exercises, they wish to redefine the concepts of value and prices so as to achieve that single end, they may have been successful. But the problem arises afterwards, i.e., when we must decide on what to do with the newly interpreted value and prices. Not every author seems to be agreed on the precise nature of the single-system approach. Some declare their partial association with the so-called "new approach" propounded earlier by Messrs. D. Foley and G. Duménil, but others do not. There are thus considerable uncertainties, which is suggestive of how open-ended many of the contributions to this volume are. My purpose here is, of course, not to offer a systematic review of the book but rather to make a few passing comments on the new enterprise, which the book seems to represent, from the point of view of the dialectic of capital.

In one of the most perceptive essays in the volume, Alfredo Saad-Filho evaluates the New Approach to the transformation problem as a "potential contribution for a non-equilibrium interpretation of Marx's theory of value".[22] Evidently, he is one with all other authors of the book in banking on a non-equilibrium economics. What is most interesting and revealing in this article is that he follows Marx in distinguishing two "qualitatively distinct kinds of competition", one "between capitals of the same branch" (intrasectoral competition) and the other "between capitals of different branches" (intersectoral competition). Although the latter leads to the equalisation of profit-rates in the system, the former, which he seems to consider to be the more important, leads to the divergence of individual profit rates.[23] This is quite true and important.

As a matter of fact, I have indicated above, precisely for that reason, that the scope of application of equilibrium analysis should be limited to the sub-phase of "average activity" in business cycles. The point is that the intersectoral competition of capitals is meaningless, when the labour market remains far away from equilibrium. In the phase of depression, following an industrial crisis, when commodity prices are held rigid at a low level, competition among capitals intensifies. But this is not one of the *inter*sectoral type; it is more frequently *intra*sectoral competition, which induces the adoption of new techniques. Thus, when the labour market is out of equilibrium in the depression phase of a business cycle, the market for commodities has not yet acquired firmly given technical parameters to operate by. Under those circumstances, if competition among capitals occurred intersectorally, it would not tend to equalise profit-rates, nor would it point towards a general equilibrium.

It is, of course, perfectly legitimate to emphasise the macro-dynamic component of Marx's economic theory. As remarked above, neoclassical economics hardly paid attention to the macro-dynamics of the capitalist economy, prior to being challenged by Keynes. Marxian theory, by contrast, has always emphasised that aspect. Thus, the law of relative surplus population enforces itself through the actual process of capital accumulation, in which the phases of widening and deepening alternate. This alternation appears in the capitalist market as the sequence of prosperity and depression in business cycles. The prosperity phase is further divided into the three sub-phases of recovery, average activity and precipitancy. If the Juglar cylce normally runs over the span of about ten years, the sub-phase of average activity will last for a year or two at most. That, it would appear, is far too short and negligible a period of time to "privilege" in the whole operation of the capitalist economy, especially from an empiricist point of view. Since capitalism is most of the time out of equilibrium and does not always necessarily point towards it, why should one attach such a disproportionate emphasis to the idealist state of equilibrium? There seems to be a consensus in the negative on this point among the authors of the book. The dialectic of capital, however, is not an empiricist theory. Consequently, it takes a different view on this issue, as I have already pointed out.

Basically two questions are raised here: (1) Is the micro analysis of general equilibrium a magnification out of all proportion of what should more soberly be considered negligible in economic theory? (2) What is the status of the theory of value in non-equilibrium? In the remainder of this paper I wish to discuss these two issues in turn.

Figure 2

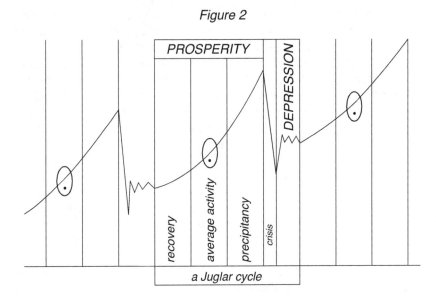

a Juglar cycle

The answer to the *first question* hinges on the nature of the economic theory which one seeks. If one seeks a natural-scientific theory of capitalism, viewed as an external object, by applying an empiricist-positivist method, it surely does not make much sense to insist on the "privileging" of the short sub-phase of average activity, during which one may presume that the capitalist economy tends towards a general equilibrium. I have, however, elaborated above on the reasons why the dialectic of capital refuses to accept such a method. The dialectic claims that pure economic theory consists of a definition of capitalism by capital itself. To obtain such a theory one asks capital what it would do if it were given an ideal use-value space. One only has to passively record or "copy" the answers given to one until no further clarification is needed. That is how a pure theory of capitalism is obtained. But even if an ideal use-value space is presupposed in which capital can easily produce all material use-values as commodities, there still remains labour-power, the only "simple" commodity which capital cannot produce and which the logic of capital alone cannot fully control.

Thus, in the actual process of capital accumulation, there is sometimes an excess supply of labour-power; sometimes an excess demand for it. The only time in which the demand for and the supply of labour-power can be deemed more or less in equilibrium is during the brief period of average activity. If so, it is only in this brief period that capital reveals the fullest extent of its logic and asserts its teleology. In other words, capital itself exposes to us a state of general equilibrium as its destination, when all conditions (including the labour market) are right. Since the dialectic "copies" capital in striving to reach this destination, instead of ignoring this signpost, it can provide an objective theory of capitalism, instead of a mere model or an ideal type arbitrarily constructed to suit "our" subjective need. That objective theory demonstrates the fact that, if the capitalist economy ever reaches a state of general equilibrium, it will also realise an optimal allocation of the productive labour (resources) of society, so that all use-values will be produced as value (i.e., as commodities) with nothing more or less than the socially necessary labour. This constitutes the *raison d'être* of capitalism. For, if capitalism did not *tend to* realise an optimal allocation of resources, *even when all conditions are right,* its claim to be an historical society would not be justified. An economic theory of capitalism must, therefore, always demonstrate that, in its cyclical process of accumulation, capital never fails to pass through a period of average activity during which it points to a general equilibrium.

Thus, given a set of technical parameters, the path of capital accumulation always comes close enough to, or within potential reach of, a corresponding state of general equilibrium. This state, which then defines the value-relation of the system, must be considered as the referent even when the system is out of equilibrium. Here, I am addressing the *second question* raised above concerning the status of value theory in non-equilibrium. Given the technical parameters of the market, values and production-prices of certain magnitudes are determined by the logic of capital, provided that the labour market is already in equilibrium. If the capitalist economy is out of equilibrium, the market prices of commodities deviate from their production-prices, as these commodities are not being produced in socially necessary (equilibrium) quantities, and, hence, not with socially necessary labour. Even in such a case, the market prices must be compared with what the production-prices, which reflect values, would be.

For instance, in the depression phase, the prices of commodities tend to be held rigid at a low level, which generates conditions favourable for innovation. Such a situation may be analysed as follows.[24] Consider a commodity produced with an organic composition of capital which agrees with the social average. Suppose that its value or production-price would be 5 hours of labour per unit, if the reproduction-process were in equilibrium, but that the current money price effectively acknowledges only 4.2 hours of labour, even when the commodity is supplied in the quantity which meets the current social demand for it. If the cost-price is 4 hours per unit, the capitalists who produce the commodity make the profit of

5%, assuming, for simplicity, fixed capital to be absent. If, in other industries, profit-rates are not higher, these capitalists will keep producing the commodity, which requires 5 hours of labour to produce and may continue to sell it for only the worth of 4.2 hours of labour. This contradicts the law of value; for 0.8 hours of surplus labour, actually performed, in the production of every unit of this commodity systematically fails to become surplus value. The only possible solution is to introduce a technical change, such as to actually reduce the value or production-price of this commodity from 5 to below 4.2 hours of labour per unit. Such an analysis could not be made if value and production-price were defined, as the authors of the book endeavour to do, without any reference to a general equilibrium of the system.

The point at issue again boils down to what one wishes to do with the labour theory of value. In their seminal articles on the "new approach", Messrs. Foley and Duménil both seek a labour theory of value as "an operational tool of quantitative analysis and explanation for the historical development of capitalism"[25] or as "a consistent, logically coherent, necessary theoretical tool".[26] But the usefulness of a "tool", whatever its exact meaning may be, must be demonstrated by its use, not by its advertisement. It has not been clear what they and their followers wish to accomplish by means of the newly interpreted labour theory of value, since none of them have so far shown a significant result of its application (i.e., a significant thesis which cannot be advanced without depending on it), going beyond a trivial proof of Marx's infallibility. The dialectic of capital does not adopt an instrumentalist view of theory. Value, to the dialectic of capital, is an essential component of a pure theory of capitalism, i.e., the definition of capitalism by capital itself, since it links what is specifically capitalist and, hence, historically transient with what is trans-historically general to all societies, i.e., it links the commodity-economic with the real-economic. I have already expanded on this matter in Section VI above. To fulfil its role, the theory of value in the dialectic of capital stipulates that the magnitude of value must be determined by "socially necessary labour", i.e., labour required to produce an *equilibrium* quantity of the commodity. Thus, behind values and production-prices there must always exist a general equilibrium of the capitalist economy.[27]

Notes and References

[1] On the nature and scope of the dialectic of capital, or the Unoist approach to economic theory, see Sekine, Thomas T., *An Outline of the Dialectic of Capital,* two vols. (London: Macmillan; New York: St. Martin's Press, 1997). In the introduction to that book (hereafter referred to as *Introduction*) I tried to highlight some of its epistemological-methodological features. In the present article, I wish to focus on how the dialectic differs from other economic theories. The dialectic of capital differs rather radically from the more conventional approaches not only to economics proper but also to social science more broadly, so that one cannot adequately come to grips with its nature and aim without first leaving aside many conventional presumptions. It turns out that neither the Introduction nor the present article can hope to be fully effective in disabusing the reader of the many false presumptions, even though the two combined will be better than either one of them taken in isolation. Consequently, I humbly request the interested reader to consult the above-quoted book in detail for better comprehension of the dialectic of capital.

[2] In addition to the above-mentioned Introduction, see also: Sekine ("An Essay on Uno's Dialectic of Capital", in this volume; "Introduction to the Dialectic of Capital", in: *The Dialectic of Capital, A Study of the Inner Logic of Capital,* vol. I, Tokyo: Yushindo, 1984, republished by Toshindo in 1986; "Uno's Method of Marxian Economics", in this volume; "The Dialectic of Capital: An Unoist Interpretation", in this volume). My argument in this section, as elsewhere, is based on extensive writings by Uno himself on the methodological contrast between social and natural science. Today's specialists in "scientific methodology" may find the argument of this section to be rather cryptic, dated or even cavalier. But details and sophistications must not obscure the basic outline of the problem, which has not been settled since Uno's time. "Social science, to which the dialectic of capital offers a foundation, must not be regarded as a branch of natural science. Why?" To answer this question, I have here just enough space to disabuse the reader of the very widely-held, common presumption, for instance, that a scientific theory must always be empirically testable, i.e., verifiable in some sense in the light of the "facts".

[3] A predictive knowledge is the one that can stated as "(a, b, c, ...) $\rightarrow$ x", or, "if conditions a, b, c, ... materialise, event x will occur". When the "factual" meanings of the conditions and the result are appropriately specified, it becomes a scientific hypothesis or conjecture subject to empirical testing, whether by way of observation or of experiment, the operational procedure of which must also be previously agreed. When the experiment or observation conducted according to the conventionally agreed procedure produces, or appears to produce, no "counter evidence" (falsification), the statement is accepted as scientific knowledge. Elsewhere, I called it so-far-so-good hypothesis or conjecture: Sekine, "An Essay on Uno's Dialectic of Capital", in this volume, p. 49). In the present context, I use the word "prediction" in this narrow sense and contrast it with "post-diction" in the sense of which will be explained presently.

[4] I refer to this doctrine as the most blatant example of all self-serving justifications of the existing social order. Any other claim that the existing social order cannot be changed and must be accepted on the ground that it is divinely ordained or nature-imposed belongs to the same category. Typically, the contemporary argument for free trade (by the neo-liberals) belongs to this category. For every time empirical facts are brought up against it, they are immediately judged as evidence of human failure to abide more strictly by the "providential" law of the market ("too lazy to compete", etc.), which is by definition above reproach.

[5] In various places in Polanyi, Karl, *The Great Transformation* (Boston: Beacon Press, 1957) and other writings of the same author.

[6] See references quoted in footnote 1 and 2.

[7] Uno's approach to the study of capitalism is unique in that it distinguishes the three levels of inquiry: the level of pure theory, the level of stages-theory and the level of empirical history, the second level mediating between the first and the third. About the three levels of inquiry, see Albritton, Robert, *Japanese Reconstruction of Marxist Theory*, London: Macmillan (1986) and Albritton, *Robert, A Japanese Approach to Stages of Capitalist Development*, London: Macmillan (1991). Since the subsumption of the use-value space by the market logic of capital is imperfect even under capitalism, there remain there "externalities" (or factors which do not conform to the dictates of the market) which must be "internalised" by means of economic policies. Under capitalism, three types of economic policies: mercantilist, liberal and imperialist, internalise these externalities successfully. If the use-value space is such that none of these types of economic policies can achieve the necessary "internalisation" of its externalities, capitalism is not expected to survive. As will be explained below, the use-value space is "idealised or neutralised" at the level of pure theory (the dialectic of capital in the narrow sense), "typical" at the level of stages, and "naked and raw" at the level of history. An actual capitalism consists of the interaction between "(pure) theory", which belongs to capital, and "history" which belong to us, humans.

[8] Smith, Adam, *An Inquiry into the Nature and Causes of the Wealth of Nations* (Oxford: Oxford University Press, vol. I, 1976), p. 25.

[9] Morishima goes so for as to say that "the general equilibrium theory was formulated independently and simultaneously by Walras and Marx." Morishima, Michio, *Marx's Economics, A Dual Theory of Value and Growth* (Cambridge: Cambridge University Press, 1973), p. 1.

[10] This statement may cause some consternation and disbelief to those who continue to hold the conventional view of science and theory. But that is precisely the reason why I belaboured above, especially in section II, the radical difference between Uno's epistemology-methodology and the conventional one. What I wish to ask the still unbelieving reader at this point is to confirm that, in making this statement, I am in no way contradicting my own premises. I am only contradicting (i.e., rejecting) the conventional view of theory and science.

[11] For details of the theory of "the actual process of capital accumulation", please see my previously quoted book, Sekine, *An Outline of the Dialectic of Capital*, vol. I, pp. 220-229.

[12] Marx, Karl, *A Contribution to the Critique of Political Economy* (Moscow: Progress, 1970), p. 59.

[13] Viner, Jacob, *Studies in the Theory of International Trade* (London: George Allen & Unwin, 1955), chapter 6, especially pp. 307-311 and Eichengreen, Barry "Transfer Problem", *The New Palgraue, A Dictionary of Economics*, edited by J. Eatwell, M. Milgate and P. Newman (London: Macmillan, 1988) and literature quoted there.

[14] This kind of price theory is explained more systematically in Sekine, *An Outline of the Dialectic of Capital*, vol. II, pp. 16-42.

[15] For further commentary on Walras' law and the Walrasian approach to general equilibrium, see Sekine, *An Outline of the Dialectic of Capital*, vol. II, pp. 15-16.

[16]Sekine, *An Outline of the Dialectic of Capital*, vol. II, p. 19.

[17] Weeks, John, "Abstract Labour and Commodity Production", *Research in Political Economy, A Research Annal,* vol. 12, Greenwich Connecticut: JAI Press Inc. (1990), p. 13.

[18] Morishima, *Marx's Economics, A Dual Theory of Value and Growth*, p. 54.

[19] Sekine, *An Outline of the Dialectic of Capital*, vol.II, pp. 23-25.

[20] I first dealt with this problem in a more general context in Sekine, Thomas T., *The Dialectic of Capital, A Study of the Inner Logic of Capital*, vol. II, Tokyo: Toshindo (1986), pp. 117-118. However the matrix I used there for illustration, similar to the S below, contained a numerical error.

[21] Freeman, A., and Carchedi, G., *Marx and Non-Equilibrium Economics*, London: Edward Elgar (1996).

[22] Saad-Filho, Alfredo, "The Value of Money, the Value of Labour Power and the Net Product: an Appraisal of the 'New Approach' to the Transformation Problem", Freeman & Carchedi (1996), pp. 116-135., here pp. 116-7.

[23] Ibid., pp. 721-2.

[24] Sekine, *An Outline of the Dialectic of Capital*, vol. II, pp. 66-67.

[25] Foley, Duncan, "The Value of Money, the Value of Labour Power and the Marxian Transformation Problem", *Review of Radical Political Economics*, 14:2 (1982), p. 45.

[26] Duménil, G., "Beyond the Transformation Riddle: A Labor Theory of Value", *Science & Society*, 47:4 (winter 1983), p. 428.

[27] The following persons very kindly read the first draft of this paper and provided me with many helpful suggestions and corrections: Professors Louis Lefeber, John Smithin and Shin-Hiwan Chiang of York University, and members of the Canadian Unoist Study Group including Professors Robert Albritton and John R. Bell, Messrs. Stefanos Kourkoulakos and Rafael Indart. I wish to thank them all most sincerely without implicating them in errors that might still remain.

Marxian Theory of Value, What We Might Learn from It

This paper is in three parts. In the first part, I will state generally the Unoist position on how the labour theory of value in the Marxian tradition should be interpreted. I will emphasize the fact that the micro value theory must be founded on the macro accumulation theory, which means that a state of general equilibrium can be deemed "real", only on the ground that the capitalist economy never fails to undergo the period of "average activity" in regularly recurring business cycles. In the second part, I will briefly explain the methodological framework that underlies this particular treatment of the subject. In doing so, I shall outline the salient features of the Unoist doctrine, or the approach of the dialectic of capital. Finally, in the third part, I discuss some implications of the law of value, as I understand it, with respect to the comprehension and evaluation of the present-day world economy, which I view to be in the process of ex-capitalist transition with some tentative conclusions.

Value theory and general equilibrium

The labour theory of value says that socially necessary labour constitutes the substance of value. "Socially necessary labour" here means labour that is technical required directly and indirectly, to produce the socially necessary quantity of the commodity, and "socially necessary quantity", in turn, means an equilibrium quantity, a quantity that just satisfies an autonomously shaped social demand.[1] When that quantity of the commodity is produced, it uses productive resources available to society *optimally* (or most efficiently), that is to say, neither too much nor too little but just to the right extent. The productive resources, or elements of production, are often trichotomized into labour, land and capital (meaning here capital goods), of which only the first two are the original factors of production. But land, which generically represents all natural conditions of production is essentially a free gift of nature to society, even though, under capitalism, individual capitalists pay rents to landed property for its use. Thus, the only original factor of production which constitutes the *real cost to society* is labour, and only labour, which, to put it more precisely, is the (productive) consumption of human labour-power. Now, if the productive resources of society are optimally allocated, labour, as one of their components, is also optimally allocated. The substance of value thus means, in effect, nothing other than optimally allocated productive labour.

The labour theory of value, thus interpreted, forms *an integral part of the definition of capitalism*, in the sense that, if it (i.e., what it says) did not hold, capitalism would not hang together and could not exist as a concept (*Begriff*), even if it may do so as a mere representation (*Vorstellung*), to use the specifically Hegelian terms. Capitalism exists conceptually if and only if the labour theory of value holds strictly.

This particularly important theory must not be confused with a "labour theory of prices", by which I mean a questionable theory that purports to explain in one way or another, the determination of relative prices of commodities in terms of the labour embodied in them. This theory would be valid, if at all, only under such highly restrictive conditions as when the value composition of capital is assumed equal in all industries and/ or if it is assumed that no surplus labour is performed. It does not hold in a more general context. In fact, the determination of equilibrium prices (or production-prices) simultaneously with a general rate of profit does not depend on the labour theory of value. In other words, the capitalist market determines equilibrium prices and a general rate of profit on its own, as if such things as value and surplus value never existed, i.e., in total ignorance of the aforesaid theoretical concepts. But the labour theory of value, for its part implicitly presupposes the formation of equilibrium prices, which mediate an optimum allocation of productive resources in society. Since value thus presupposes equilibrium prices, *it would be absurd to even speak of value (and hence also of surplus value), when the capitalist market is deemed out of equilibrium.*[2]

The relation between value and prices in Marxian economics has long been misapprehended and has often caused enormous confusion, which moreover has been exacerbated by the long drawn-out controversy surrounding the so-called transformation problem. I wish to state below the position of the Uno School on this issue. That position involves only very simple and straightforward economics, and may, for that reason not please those who would rather wish to thrive in abstruse and contorted arguments. However the truth is simple when exposed. Much unnecessary confusion has arisen, in my view; from two sources.

(1) Because Marx spoke of the law of value before elaborating on the theory of production-prices, one tends to entertain a false impression that the concept of value is already well defined *before* equilibrium prices are

introduced. Those unfamiliar with the method of dialectical exposition (synthetic logic) and who, therefore, think exclusively in terms of an analytical method (formal logic) do not distinguish between levels of abstraction and erroneously believe that a dialectical concept (be it value or price) is fully defined, once and for all, at the point where it is first introduced. That is not the case at all. For instance, in volume I of *Capital*, where the capital-labour relation is at issue, one talks primarily in terms of values. But that does not mean that prices (whether normal or equilibrium) are absent they must be there, albeit implicitly, standing behind values and supporting them. In fact, an equilibrium situation is *presupposed*, even though the mechanism whereby it is actually attained remains as yet unexplained. In volume III, where the capital-capital relations are in focus, equilibrium prices receive detailed attention. Yet values have by no means disappeared. On the contrary, they are quantitatively determined here for the first time together with the formation of prices. Since Böhm-Bawerk the critics of Marx have systematically ignored the difference in the workings of formal and synthetic logic, while a large number of Marxists, trapped in the same mindset, have tried in vain to defend Marx in strictly "analytical" terms, only to meet the mortifying scorn of Samuelson and his Sraffian (neo-Ricardian) collaborators. To correctly relate value and prices in the Marxian context, one should have learned at least the rudiments of the Hegelian dialectic.[3]

(2) Another type of confusion has arisen from the neoclassical usage of the term "value". In the past, neoclassical economists used to talk of "value and distribution", meaning the pricing of commodities (in this case: goods and services) and the pricing of factors of production. This usage survives, for instance, in the title of Debreu's book: *Theory of Value*. It could have been equivalently entitled *Theory of Prices*. For, in neoclassical theory today, there is no longer a concept of value as distinct from that of price,[4] so that it is only a matter of linguistic coquetry in that paradigm to talk of value rather than of price. The reason why neoclassical economics has suppressed value in favour of price is quite simple. It recognizes no society other than capitalist society, thereby reducing all human relations in effect to exchange relations in the market, i.e., to a system of trade-offs. In that case it is neither necessary, nor even possible, to ground prices on anything that lies outside of the market. This explains why the concept of real cost had to be replaced by that of alternative cost, and measurable utility abandoned in favour of indifference.

Clearly, Marxian economics cannot follow the same path and "eternalize" capitalist society. Unlike the bourgeois ideologues we do recognize societies other than capitalist ones. That is the reason why we need to ground prices on something outside the market, something that is supra-historic, i.e., on the real cost that any society must bear. The concept of value, which resides at the intersection of the market and use-value production in general, enables this crucial operation. Value, of course, means indifference to use-values and represents the abstract-general (or mercantile) side of wealth rather than its concrete-useful (i.e., real) side. Value must therefore express itself in the form of a "price", i.e., in the quantity of another use-value desired, while its substance is made up of "labour" which could have produced any wealth in this society as well as in other societies. "Value" thus relates prices, the market-specific (capitalist) variables, with labour that is supra-historically applicable to the production of any use-value. By understanding the significance of value in this way, we can easily spot the misguided nature of the thesis that values are "redundant".

Samuelson and Steedman have claimed that values are of no use, since equilibrium prices can be determined without depending on values.[5] Faced with this challenge, many Marxists have tried to demonstrate, absolutely to no avail that equilibrium prices could not be determined without depending on values. *That is not only an exercise in futility but it also diverts our attention from the real problem.* When equilibrium prices are determined, values are also (simultaneously) determined willy-nilly, as their shadows,[6] so to speak. Even in neoclassical theory, the determination of equilibrium prices implies that, at the same time productive labour is allocated optimally to all branches of production, and no one thinks of dismissing this fact, as "redundant". The point, however, is that neoclassical economists do not want to give a special name, such as value, to "optimally allocated labour", because they are unwilling to recognize in it the *real* cost to society. But that is just another way of saying that they (want to) see nothing beyond and outside the market. The redundancy charge is, in other words, nothing other than an ideological confession of their faith in the all-encompassing nature of the market, into which they have dissolved human society. This may indeed be the hallmark of their bourgeois identity, but we (as followers of Marx) should part company with them at precisely this juncture for obvious reasons. That is all there is to it.

　　Instead of being so irrevocably terrified and traumatized by the self-righteous and peremptory stance that Marxo-Sraffians assumed, Marxian economists should at once have recognized the bourgeois foundation upon which the redundancy thesis rested, and should have rejected it without hesitation. At the, same time, they should have taken that god-sent opportunity to review and reconfirm their own comprehension of the significance of Marxian, as opposed to bourgeois, economics. Yet subsequent developments in Marxian value theory have been thoroughly disappointing. *I regret especially the ideological rejection of an equilibrium approach to value theory.*[7] Marx's theory of surplus value which defines the fundamental capital-labour relation in volume I of *Capital* holds true only in an equilibrium situation. We can talk neither of value nor of surplus value rigorously, when the economy is out of equilibrium. One can talk of market prices hovering around equilibrium prices, but not of "market value" in the same sense. What is known as "market value" in Marxian economics means "market-determining value" when different techniques are employed in the same branch of production and not the quantity of labour that may be *actually* spent to produce a commodity in non-equilibrium quantities.[8]

This does not mean that the capitalist economy is always, or most often in equilibrium. On the contrary, a state of 'general' equilibrium in the capitalist economy *tends to* be approached only in the phase of *average activity* in the course of a business cycle.[9] In fact, it may never be actually reached. Yet, in the absence of this tendency, capitalism itself cannot be defined. This is in the nature of things, and it must not be confused with the bourgeois faith in capitalism. Capital does tend towards a state of general equilibrium, conditions permitting; and we indeed allow such conditions to prevail in theory in order to enable capital itself to reveal and define capitalism. Some authors go so far as to suggest that general equilibrium is a bourgeois fantasy invented by Walras and that Marxian economics should have nothing to do with it.[10] That, in my view, is an egregious error. Bourgeois (or neoclassical) economics is not to be criticized for elaborating the concept of equilibrium, but for *universalizing it without questioning its ontological base.*[11] It clearly does not apply to just any economy, nor even to any market economy. *The concept of general equilibrium applies specifically to a capitalist economy* in the sense that, if the tendency towards a general equilibrium could not be identified at any moment of its dynamics, such an economy could not be regarded as "capitalist" in any meaningful sense.[12]

The capitalist economy may be deemed to approach a state of general equilibrium during the period of average activity in a regularly recurring capitalist business cycle. For, in that period alone, given the prevailing technological conditions, the demand for and the supply of labour-power come close enough to be in balance (so that one may meaningfully talk of the value of labour-power), and average profits tend to be earned in all sectors of production (so that one may reasonably talk of the values of commodities).[13] At that point, and there alone, it is possible and meaningful to idealize the operation of the capitalist economy as if it tends towards a state of general equilibrium. It is important to understand this crucial connection. For this means that, in Marxian economics, the foundation of micro value theory is to be provided by a macro accumulation theory, rather than the reverse as is often attempted (erroneously and never successfully) in bourgeois economics.

The process of capital accumulation alternates between the "widening" phase during which the organic composition of capital remains unchanged and the "deepening" phase during which it rises.[14] This fact reflects itself concretely in the alternation of prosperity and depression phases in the course of business cycles. During the prosperity phase (or the "widening" process of capital accumulation), as the economy expands under a technology which is more or less given, the labour market must become increasingly tighter, causing a profit squeeze and pushing the accumulation of capital to its limits, until an industrial crisis erupts. The ensuing phase of business depression, characterized by the rigidity of prices at low levels, cannot be overcome until technical innovation occurs "in a cluster", enabling a reduction of costs under the prevailing system of depressed prices. (This phase corresponds to the "deepening" process of capital accumulation.) As new techniques are adopted, the prosperity phase returns, first as the sub-phase of recovery (during which the pace of renovation still differs from one industry to another), then as the sub-phase of average activity (when virtually all industries can expand in unison). But this close-to-ideal situation too sooner or later falls into disarray, as the economy plunges into the last sub-phase of precipitancy (or overheating), distilling the crisis.

The cyclical process of capital accumulation, associated with the Juglar cycles and the decennial crises of which Marx spoke, are but manifestations of the law of relative surplus population peculiar to capitalism. The working of this law sees to it that capital is adequately supplied with the population of labour-power needed for its continued accumulation. It is by virtue of this law, which implies that capital has developed its own "technology and labour-power policy", that the viability of capitalism is secured. This law also guarantees that the actual process of capital accumulation never fails to reproduce the *period of average activity* in which the demand for and the supply of labour-power is more or less in equilibrium, and in which all commodities are produced also in more or less the socially necessary quantities. One can think of a general equilibrium of the capitalist economy because such a state is actually approximated not because it can be arbitrarily imagined. The fact that a general equilibrium is not a figment of the imagination but a necessary feature of capitalism vindicates the working of the law of value.

But the state of general equilibrium, towards which the capitalist economy really tends, can be understood at two different levels, *formally at the level of prices and substantively at that of values.* There is nothing wrong in distinguishing them. It is not only legitimate but essential to distinguish between these two dialectical levels of abstraction, which must not be confused. One level has to do with the *price system,* which is specific to capitalism, and the other level with the *value system,* which retains something in common with all other societies. Nor is it disturbing to have to choose, on practical grounds, one suitable "invariance postulate"[15] among many to relate the two parallel systems, so as to make values and prices directly comparable in quantitative terms. One should, however, not expect to have a privileged postulate of invariance, a special pathway that connects the two systems operating at distinct dialectical levels, which is deemed better than any other. For the direct comparison of values and prices in quantitative terms can be achieved equivalently with any postulate of invariance.

It may well be true that one of Marx's two so-called aggregate equalities should be interpreted as the equality of the value and the price of the net (as opposed to the gross) product.[16] But that fact hardly justifies a rejection of the so-called "dualistic" approach in favour of a "single" system approach to value-and-price theory. For we gain nothing in conceptual terms by putting prices and values in one system by merely stipulating a "value of money", a "monetary expression of labour" or a "conversion rate of labour into money", these being all synonyms with a particular postulate of invariance. It may, on the other hand, lead to an untenable confusion of that which is confined to the capitalist market with that which leaves open an avenue to human societies in general. Yet such a single-system approach which allegedly abolishes the transformation problem, has been vigorously promoted with the vague hope of bringing the labour theory of value to bear upon (ideologically more acceptable) interpretations of the existing price data of contemporary economies. However, the labour theory of value, as I have repeatedly emphasized, is *a conceptual theory indispensable for the definition of capitalism by capital itself, and certainly not an instrument of empirical studies in Marxian econometrics.*

I will, however, not pursue this issue any further.[17] For, my purpose here is not to criticize other interpretations of the labour theory of value, but to state as clearly as possible the Unoist position on that theory. At this point, however, it becomes necessary to highlight certain basic characteristics of the Unoist doctrine, or the approach of the dialectic of capital, for the benefit of those to whom it is new.

The method of the dialectic of capital

Marxism always involves a critique of capitalism, but, in this, there are in fact two distinct types. One denounces capitalism as an *unjust* society, in which exploitation, class struggles and repression repeat themselves. Since such a society can be terminated only by means of a revolutionary action, Marxists are primarily called upon to rally for such an action, according to this type of critique. The second type criticizes capitalism as an *inverted* market economy, in which human priorities are subordinated to the market priority of capital. This school, therefore, calls for the suspension of the primacy of capital and the liberation of humankind from its tyranny, but that presupposes a full comprehension of what capital is all about. Marx's writings contain elements of both these arguments. Yet most Marxists seem to have followed the first, easier path with religious fervour and conviction, if they have also at times paid lip service to the second type of critique. I would say that the first type stands in the political and ideological tradition of Marx, while the second remains in the intellectual and conceptual tradition of Marx. The adherents of the first type are very attached to Marx's materialistic conception of history, while those of the latter lean more heavily on the reading and comprehension of Marx's *Capital*. Uno's approach clearly belongs to the second type.[18]

Kôzô Uno (1897-1977) was one of the first Japanese economists who studied *Capital* seriously, but, unlike others, he was determined to extract from it only that which really made sense to him, impervious to the ideological and political aura that surrounded the book. After years of concentration, he concluded that the essence of *Capital* resided in the dialectic of capital (or in his words, *genriron*), even though it might also contain other useful information. In other words, he was convinced that the content of the three volumes of *Capital* constituted a self-contained logical system, just like Hegel's *Science of Logic*. Uno decisively rejected the popular idea that *Capital* had remained incomplete, in the sense of constituting only a small part of Marx's larger theoretical project, which he outlined in his various Plans. From that point of view, Uno reorganized the contents of *Capital*, rearranging to some extent the order of exposition of the materials.

Uno's rearrangement of materials is reproduced in my *Outline of the Dialectic of Capital* (1997) to which I beg to refer the interested reader for details. There he/she will find that the first two parts of volume I, which treat the three simple circulation-forms of the commodity, money and capital, are put together into the *Doctrine of Circulation*, a structure which closely corresponds with Hegel's Doctrine of Being. Then the rest of volume I (apart from its last chapter on primitive accumulation) and the whole of volume II are integrated into the *Doctrine of Production*, which corresponds with Hegel's Doctrine of Essence. Here, the production-process of capital, the circulation-process of capital and the reproduction-process of capital are investigated. Essentially, this doctrine treats the production of commodities *as value* first inside the factory, then outside it, and thirdly altogether in the macro-interaction of the process of accumulation of the aggregate-social capital. Finally, all of volume III belongs to the *Doctrine of Distribution*, which corresponds again with the tripartite structure of Hegel's Doctrine of the Concept, with its parallel division into the chapters on Profit, Rent and Interest. Yet, the order in which these three revenue-forms appear differs from Marx's arrangement in *Capital*. Details apart, the fact that Uno's reformulated dialectic of capital (rather inadvertently) reproduced the structure of the Hegelian logic is quite significant. This would mean that, just as Hegel's logic, "which coincided with metaphysics",[19] was "the exposition of God in his eternal essence before the creation of nature and a finite spirit"[20], Marx's dialectic of capital, which coincides with economic theory, is the exposition of capital's own definition or specification of capitalism before this latter actualized itself in the history of humankind. In other words, *economic theory is essentially the inner logic, programme or software which capital uses to manage and reproduce capitalism (as opposed to being something we humans have devised for the organization of our minds)*.

Understood in this way, Uno's approach offers a radically new methodology for Marxian economics.[21] It is significant, in particular, in that it unambiguously departs from the natural scientific method, which Marxists have borrowed unwarrantably and inappropriately as a matter of expediency. *Nature and society are two altogether different things and cannot be studied in the same way*. In the study of nature, all we can do is to observe it from the outside in its various specific contexts, and find some regularities of its motion. So the knowledge of nature is necessarily "partial" and tentative. Even then, our knowledge of nature is often good enough to enable us to make a reasonably accurate "prediction" of what it might do next in the same or a similar situation. Natural science seeks this kind of limited knowledge the application of which, though rich in technical applications, does not enable us to radically alter or suspend the laws of nature. It is, therefore, a matter of practical wisdom for us to conform to the given order of nature and piggyback on its blind forces if that seems feasible. If, however, we exceed our own limits in our undue eagerness to "master" and "conquer" natural forces, we are bound to be punished by environmental disasters of one sort or another. This much is clear and is today more and more widely understood. For, after all, it only means the obvious fact that we are not ourselves the creator of nature.

However, when we study "society" as distinct from nature, we clearly do not seek the same sort of knowledge. Society is that which we ourselves make; we are its creator whether we are conscious of it or not. Thus, we are, and should be, perfectly capable of divulging (or "laying bare") its inner structure (its operating mechanism, its software, etc.). It would be hypocritical for us to pretend that, since the latter involves an unknowable thing-in-itself, we must observe it from the outside, in the style of the natural scientist, and aim only at gaining some "predictable" but partially limited knowledge thereof. All we could do then would be to derive some useful "policy recommendations", making sure that we do not offend the existing social order. Only those who have stakes in the existing social order would seriously claim that we must never seek to abolish capitalism, since it is ordained by Providence. No Marxian thinker can concede to this kind of bourgeois charade. Yet few realize that the adoption of a natural scientific method in the study of capitalism amounts precisely to making an irrevocable concession to just that, because *it is equivalent to accepting that the inner programme of capitalism, that which makes capitalism what it is, cannot be divulged in its totality.*

Perhaps Marx was quite aware of all this, but he did not expressly warn against dependence on the natural-scientific method in the study of capitalism. Moreover, commonsense and bourgeois economics have always promoted the idea that being scientific meant "acting like a natural scientist", giving the false impression that economics too should be a positive-empirical science. Consequently, many simple-minded Marxists have been misled into believing that a happy union of the natural-scientific method and Marx's enigmatic "materialist dialectic", yet to be fully understood will one day accord them superhuman insight, which would put all the vulgar bourgeois ideologues to shame. In the meantime, however, unable to formulate a new and credible scientific method appropriate to the acquisition of total knowledge of society, they have remained hesitant to openly abandon the positivist-empiricist method designed for the study of natural phenomena. But total knowledge of capitalism does not require knowing it in all its empirical detail. It only requires the exposition of the dialectic of capital as the definition of capitalism by capital itself or what we might call today the "software" of capitalism which capital may be deemed to have conceived before putting it into practice in the world of humans. That is precisely what Uno has accomplished. He appropriated the dialectic of capital in this sense through his idiosyncratic reading of Marx's *Capital.*

The dialectic of capital thus constitutes the core of the Unoist approach to Marxian economics. For real capitalism which operates in human history must always embody this definition of capitalism by capital itself. If I use the term "use-value space" to mean the concrete-specific context within which the real economic life of society evolves, an enormous variety of use-value spaces must have existed throughout our history, not all of which can be organized or integrated by the logic of capital. Only those spaces in which many key use-values are capitalistically producible as commodities can be subsumed under the logic of capital and are, hence, amenable to its control.[22] Of these use-value spaces, three conspicuous types are identified as the mercantilist, liberal and imperialist. With each of these are associated a specific level of technology which is consistent with the type of use-value production dominant in that era and, therefore, also with a peculiar style of capital accumulation. These three types, moreover, mark the specific *stages of the world-historic development of capitalism.* Uno's doctrine makes use of these three typical stages to mediate between the dialectic of capital and real capitalism in history. For in the absence of such mid-range stages-theory, we run the risk of unduly historicizing theory and of unduly theorizing history, of which the worst example is the now discredited "logical-historical method". The three stages also characterize the typical economic policies enforced by the bourgeois state in each era.

What makes the study of capitalism difficult is that the dialectic of capital can be formulated only when the use-value space is rarefied and made abstract (unreal), whereas real capitalism presupposes a very concrete-specific use-value space, which, as a matter of fact, is never completely subsumable under the logic of capital. This implies that in real capitalism there are bound to be "externalities" i.e., factors that exceed the operating mode of the capitalist market. That is the reason why the bourgeois state had to devise a suitable economic policy, even at the very height of the liberal era, with a view to internalizing the prevailing "externalities". What this implies is simply that human society is never completely reducible to the capitalist market, contrary to the facile presumption of bourgeois economics. At the same time, we cannot overlook the fact that *the scope of economic policy under capitalism is limited to the internalization of externalities.* For under capitalism the principal actor remains the capitalist market, to which the economic policy of the state plays only a subsidiary role. Thus, we may say that real capitalism exists only when the existing externalities are "internalizable" by the policies of the bourgeois state.

Now it is this condition that became increasingly untenable after the First World War. Elsewhere, I have explained the circumstances under which the bourgeois state gave way to the welfare state in the depth of the Great Depression putting an end to the classical form of capitalism and introducing a new regime which I call the *process of ex-capitalist transition*. Under this regime, the government interferes with the national economy much more vigorously than under capitalism. It routinely takes on the management of the currency and of aggregate demand, and also resorts to supply-side policies that involve the regulation of technology and labour-power. The economic policy of the welfare state is thus much more extensive and far-reaching than that of the bourgeois state, precisely because the capitalist market has been radically adulterated, and can no longer function without being assisted by the economic intervention of the state, both in quantitative and qualitative terms. Under the circumstances, what is the relevance of the labour theory of value to the contemporary economy?

The labour theory of value and the contemporary economy

Before facing this issue, however, I wish to remind the reader that, unlike natural-scientific knowledge, social-scientific knowledge distinguishes itself by virtue of the fact that it is not "predictive", and, hence, it does not lend itself to any technical application. The social scientific knowledge which we seek is, if anything, "post-dictive" in the sense that it explains the reason why reality has evolved as it has *ex post facto*. (Hegel would describe this kind of knowledge as "grey".[23]) The knowledge of the dialectic of capital, for instance, tells us merely how capitalism was, in fact, programmed to operate the way it did. It reveals, as I said earlier, the inner logic (or the software) of capitalism, which has already evolved historically in human history. It, therefore, provides us with *a conceptual (or dialectical) theory*, and not an instrumental theory. A conceptual theory does not predict, nor does it offer any tool of analysis. It only provides us with a suitable *referent point* relative to which we may judge or evaluate the economic life of the present or of the past. This may sound rather disappointing, but it cannot be otherwise. For history moves one way inasmuch as time is non-empty and irreversible. We step backward into the future (*"Nous entrons dans l'avenir à reculons"*), as Paul Valéry aptly said. It is for this reason that I already dismissed as futile any attempt at interpreting the labour theory of value as an operational tool of economic analysis. It is not made for that purpose. As a conceptual theory, the labour theory of value forms an essential ingredient of the dialectic of capital, which provides us with a referent point. From this point of view, what devolves on me is not to demonstrate how that law of value actually enforces itself in the present-day capitalist economy, but the exact opposite. I should, on the contrary, demonstrate *how that law has become inopera-*

tive today since we now find ourselves in the process of ex-capitalist transition, i.e., in a process of disintegration of capitalism, and that is what I intend to do in what follows.

There are presumably different ways to argue that the typical use-value space today, be it in Japan or in the United States; is no longer organized or integrated by the dialectic of capital, which is merely assisted by the "internalizing" policy of the bourgeois state. Whatever approach one uses, it must be recognized that the welfare state must intervene much more actively and vigorously in the overall management of the national economy. Externalities are far too unwieldy in the contemporary period to be internalized by means of a series of regulatory legislations and tax-subsidy combinations that fall within the purview of the bourgeois state. But, in the light of our previous arguments pertaining to the law of value and to the law of population I would place the focus on the following two points: (1) The state deeply intervenes in the process of the adoption of society's industrial technology and also in ensuring the supply of labour-power, so that the wage-rate has in effect become an administered or controlled price; and (2) the prices of commodities are determined arbitrarily, that is to say, strategically on the supply side with little consideration of the demand side, so that there can be no general equilibrium prices in the Walrasian sense, and, if, at any moment, a Nash equilibrium chances to be achieved, that can imply the least (and not the most) desirable allocation of society's resources.

During the interwar era of "the great transformation"[24], the bourgeois state, caught in the cross-fire between the collectivisms of the right and of the left, had to embrace social-democracy so as to mitigate the bitterness of class struggles and ensure at least its partial survival. This entailed the introduction of a welfare state which established itself firmly only after the Employment Act of 1946, and served well through the period of Fordism and consumerism. The state committed itself to macro policies for full employment and nearly achieved that goal, but it also rendered the national economy inflation-prone.[25] Industry accepted the system of collective bargaining with trade unions, which also worked towards wage inflation. Under the circumstances, a tendency towards a *de-commodification of labour-power* could not be avoided. It was under this regime that the "affluent" mass-consumption society was realized for the first time in history, while significant social progress was made as well. Yet the system in time became dysfunctional for two reasons. First, as the consumer, increasingly satiated with standardized commodities, looked for more diversified and sophisticated goods, the American-style Fordist factories were not up to the task. Secondly, the inflationary chemistry of liberal-democratic America went increasingly out of control. These two problems plunged the United States into the stagflation of the 1970s, the solution to which required a radical reorientation.

Throughout the 1980s and 90s, the supply-side remoulding of the U.S. economy proceeded, guided by the anti-Keynesian neo-conservative ideology, which rehabilitated the once discredited financial interests and depriving in the process industrial interests of their erstwhile protection. Extensive deregulation took place as re-activation of the private sector was called for. The whole project gave the impression of a return to the capitalism of old, and this impression was reinforced by the sudden, unexpected collapse of the Soviet Union, (which perversely led to the jubilant celebration of the victory of capitalism). Yet, in reality, no bourgeois state returned to supplant the welfare state, when economic policy shifted its emphasis from the demand side to the supply side.[26] The Trade Act of 1988 marked a new trend in which the U.S. government took upon itself the promotion of new technologies in industry under the guise of "competitive-power promotion policy". Manifestly, the government today intends to guide and assist the R&D operation of firms, rather than leaving it simply to their capitalist instincts.[27] And that is as it should be. The reason is that technological progress today has become "qualitative" rather than remaining "quantitative".

As I explained above, the law of relative surplus population entails the adoption by the aggregate-social capital of new technological advances in clusters in the depth of depression, so as to ensure the needed supply of labour-power for its continued accumulation. However, what is involved in this case is a "quantitative" innovation such as, for instance, replacing an old spinning machine with 8,000 spindles with a new one with 10,000 spindles, and not a "qualitative" innovation such as a shift from light technology (as in textiles) to heavy technology (as in iron-and-steel). In the halcyon days of classical capitalism, capitalists rarely faced the need for a qualitative innovation and, if they did, they surely needed greater-than-usual assistance from the state.[28]

At present, we live in an age of accelerated technical progress. The winning technique today is something one never even dreamed of scarce months ago. Precisely for that reason, a huge amount of capital must be invested in R&D to explore possible breakthroughs, and that is not only a costly but also a highly risky operation.[29] Under the circumstances, similar innovations do not occur in clusters in a predictable fashion, but unexpected ones appear sporadically at any moment. That is reason enough to put an end to Juglar type rycles.

The shape of business cycles had already changed under the regime of Fordism, but during the 1990s it changed again with the advent of the much touted "new economy" and that was only to be expected. If qualitative innovation tends to occur at random, the alternating pattern of "widening" and "deepening" in the accumulation process of capital will not be reproduced. Business cycles then become irregular and fail to reproduce a clearly identifiable period of "average activity".[30] That, in turn, will mean that an automatic, self-regulating mechanism which would bring the demand for and the supply of labour-power closer together, operates no longer. The state then has to see to it, willy-nilly, that the existing supply of labour-power is adequate to permit an accumulation of capital that is consistent with the existing state of technology. The value of labour-power thus becomes arbitrary. Under the circumstances, the capitalist market can in no way tend to move autonomously towards a state of Walrasian general equilibrium, which would imply an optimal allocation of resources. Thus, neither the law of population nor the law of value can be said to enforce themselves automatically. But that is equivalent to saying that the present-day economy is no longer "capitalist", in any meaningful sense of the term. It is thus futile to try to discover an operation of the law of value in it. It is, on the contrary, the absence of capitalism that should tell us something about the nature of the contemporary economy.

The reason why the dominant technical progress has become qualitative rather than quantitative is that it originally arose in a military, rather than an industrial, context. For a long time, the United States denounced the Japanese government's industrial policies as smacking of a developmental dictatorship, but all along they themselves kept pouring public funds liberally into explorations in military technology. During the cold war, the industrial application of military technological achievements was, of course, severely constrained. It was only in the late 1980s, when the threat of the Soviet Union receded, that the U.S. military-industrial complex began to release some of their newly acquired high-technologies for wider industrial use. The result was remarkable. By that time, the United States had lagged behind Europe and Japan in quantitative progress in older-generation conventional technologies, be it in steel, automobile, home electronics, engineering robots and what not. But they clearly had an edge in the ICT (information and communication technology). It was only natural then that, from around the end of the 1980s, the supply-side economic policy of the state was geared to capitalize on this advantage, and the direction of America's re-industrialization on a high-tech basis was set. The trend was reinforced under the Clinton administration until the "new economy" boom in the late 1990 was realized.

When new products embodying qualitative innovations appear in the market and set the tone of international mega-competition, consumers, whose "sovereignty" the market is supposed to uphold, become increasingly irrelevant in the pricing of commodities. For, the consumers cannot, without often prohibitive costs, obtain enough information regarding the true quality of the product, which the producers automatically possess. The consumers must struggle with complicated "manuals" to learn how best to use the item they purchased, while customer services in trouble-shooting that the supplier offers are bound to be limited. In order to be a winning purchaser, one must today bear substantial transactions costs, by either hiring an expert consultant or training oneself to become one. To ignore expert opinion in shopping has become a risky affair even with regard to products which *prima facie* do not look particularly knowledge-intensive. For example, consuming food whose nutritional value or traceability is suspect can cause a serious health hazard. Yet experts themselves can work more lucratively for the powerful producers than by doling out small favours to dispersed individual consumers. It is only natural then to expect that the pricing of commodities in the producer-dominated market becomes strategic or game-theoretic, since oligopolistic suppliers worry more about their rivals than their customers.

Concluding remarks

By now I have said quite enough to be able to conclude that we cannot observe the slightest sign of the working of the law of value in the contemporary economy. I have also shown why, given the well known features of the contemporary economy, that indeed must be the case. On the other hand, this fact in no way diminishes the validity and importance of the labour theory of value as an integral part of the dialectic of capital, the only definition of capitalism by capital itself. If the theory says that the labour theory of value should enforce itself in capitalism, and yet, at the same time, the contemporary economy shows no sign of it, the only reasonable and possible conclusion that we can draw under the circumstances is that, vulgar opinions notwithstanding, capitalism no longer really survives, and that what we see in front of us is no more than a pale shadow of what capitalism once was.

Once again, I wish to remind the reader that the dialectic of capital is a conceptual theory and not an instrumental theory. Therefore, the labour theory of value, as an integral part of it, does not and need not provide us with "tools of analysis" whereby to derive convenient policy recommendations or self-serving revolutionary practices. Beware of the loud street hawkers flaunting the Marxian theory of value as a crystal-ball in which to see the world as they want you to see it.[31]

Notes and References

[1] For further exposition of this subject, see Sekine, *An Outline of the Dialectic of Capital* (London: Palgrave, 1997), vol. I, especially pp. 129 ff.

[2] Perhaps Marx himself used the term "value" less stringently. But that was understandable given the fact that the concept of general equilibrium was not yet as well known then as it is today.

[3] On the relationship between the Hegelian dialectic and economic theory, see Sekine, „The Dialectic of Capital: An Unoist Interpretation", in this volume, and Sekine, The Dialectic, or Logic that Coincides with Economics", in this volume.

[4] Sekine "Uno School Seminar on the Theory of Value", in this volume. See especially pp. 80-81.

[5] Steedman, Ian, *Marx after Sraffa* (London: New Left Books, 1977).

[6] Sekine, *An Outline of the Dialectic of Capital*, vol. II. See especially pp. 12 ff.

[7] Freeman, Alan and Carchedi, Guglielmo, *Marx and Non-Equilibrium Economics* (Edward Elgar, 1996).

[8] There is a widespread misconception that value is first produced and then realized, with a suggestion that "realized value" may be less than "produced value". The dialectic of capital considers that to be impossible. For no unrealized value can be deemed produced. This error may originate in Marx's imperfect usage of the term. See above footnote 2.

[9] The phase of prosperity in business cycles can be divided into the three subphases of "recovery", "average activity" and "precipitancy (or overheating)". See Sekine, *An Outline of the Dialectic of Capital*, II, pp. 156 ff.

[10] Freeman, Alan, "The Psychopathology of Walrasian Marxism", in: Freeman and Carchedi (*Marx and Non-Equilibrium Economics*).

[11] For a theory not to be a mere figment of the imagination it must be able to defend itself by demonstrating that it treats something that really occurs. Bourgeois economics justifies the approach of the capitalist market to general equilibrium on the grounds of religious faith in the Invisible Hand of Providence or equivalently of the ideological credo of liberalism. In contrast, Marxian economics does so by showing the fact that the actual process of capital accumulation never fails to pass through the phase of average activity.

[12] The term "capitalism" is used quite loosely in day-to-day language without rigorous definition. There is no problem about that. But for economic theory to be more than a joke, we must have an adequate definition of capitalism. The dialectic of capital provides us with such a definition, which moreover is not a subjective definition by us but an objective one by capital itself.

[13] In Marxian economic theory, the micro value theory (the law of value) takes the value of labour-power as given. The value of labour-power consistent with the prevailing state of technology can be determined only in macro accumulation theory, as the actual process of capital accumulation passes through the phase of average activity, in which the demand for labour-power tends to be equal to the supply of it. It is not sufficient simply to say that the value of labour-power is equal to the value of a basket of wage-goods, the assortment of which is physiologically or socio-culturally given and is "practically known as a datum". Sekine, *An Outline of the Dialectic of Capital*, vol. I, p. 111. Nor is it justified to "prescribe" it in terms of a "labour-feeding technology approach". Sekine, *An Outline of the Dialectic of Capital*, vol. II, pp. 23-25; Duménil, Gérard, *De la valeur aux prix de Production* (Paris: Economica, 1980), pp. 123-25. The right assortment of wage-goods which just reproduces labour-power tends to be determined macro-economically, i.e., relative to the prevailing state of technology, in the course of business cycles as the economy undergoes the period of average activity. Sekine, *An Outline of the Dialectic of Capital*, Vol. I, p. 224 ff.

[14] See Sekine, *An Outline of the Dialectic of Capital*, vol. I, pp. 215 ff., vol. II, pp. 61 ff., pp. 156 ff.

[15] The separation of the value system and the price system dates from von Bortkiewicz. Morishima (*Marx Economic's,* Cambridge: Cambridge UP, 1973) most clearly reproduces this approach. The concept of the "invariance postulate" is due to Seton, Francis "The Transformation Problem", in *Review of Economic Studies*, 20 (1957), pp. 149-60. None of these authors were conscious of the distinction between the two dialectical levels. Yet, they were intuitively right in accepting the logical indeterminacy of the postulate of invariance as a matter of course. The more recent critics of this postulate merely reveal their blind adherence (and adoration) of formal logic, which alone will not be sufficient for an adequate understanding of the dialectic of capital.

[16] Duménil, *De la valeur aux prix de Production* and Duménil, "Beyond the Transformation Riddle, a Labour Theory of Value", in *Science & Society*, 47/4 (1983), pp. 427-50; Foley, Duncan, "The Value of Money, the Value of Labour Power and the Marxian Transformation Problem", in *Review of Radical Political Economics*, 14/2 (1982), pp. 37-47. There is much to learn from these works, since the technical competence of these authors is undoubted. But they both adopt an "instrumental" approach to Marxian value theory, which conflicts with my "conceptual" approach to the same.

[17] It may, however be useful to simply list here the three main points of objection to that approach from our point of view, two of which have already been mentioned. *First,* this approach, as many others, uncritically applies the method of linear production models in determining meaningless values and production-prices which are invariant to activity levels, i.e., regardless of the demand conditions. In linear production models, values and prices are determined only in the

light of technical coefficients (and even the general rate of profit from the Frobenius root of their matrix). This method, which surely has many advantages, if carefully used, has had pernicious effects on the interpretation of Marxian value theory, as it gives the facile and false impression that a state of general equilibrium could be identified without regard to the demand-side conditions. If an economy were in the same equilibrium, whether it produces steel and corn in the ratio of 1:2 or in that of 2:1, it would certainly be meaningless to talk about values and equilibrium prices in it. *Secondly*, as mentioned in footnote 15, the single-system approach ignores the dialectical significance of the indeterminacy of the "invariance postulate". *Thirdly*, as just mentioned in the text and in the previous footnote, this approach implies an interpretation of Marxian economic theory as a natural-scientific (instrumental) theory, and not as a social-scientific (conceptual) theory. I have more to say on this issue in the next section.

[18] About two Marxisms, see Sekine, *An Outline of the Dialectic of Capital*, vol. I, pp. 1-2, and Sekine "Polanyi, Marx, et Uno", in *Shôgakukenkyû* (Aichi Gakuin University), 42/1-2, pp. 53-78.

[19] Quoted from Wallace, William, *Hegel's Logic* (Oxford: The Clarendon Press, 1975), p. 36.

[20] Quoted from Miller, V., *Hegel's Science of Logic* (New Jersey: Humanities Press, 1969), p. 50.

[21] For more discussion on the theme of this and the next paragraphs, see Sekine, "The Dialectic, or Logic that Coincides with Economics", in this volume.

[22] For more discussion on the theme of this and next two paragraphs, see Bell, John and Sekine, Thomas T., "The Disintegration of Capitalism: A Phase of Ex-Capitalist Transition" in R. Albritton et al. (ed), *Phases of Capitalist Development, Booms, Crises and Globalizations* (Basingstoke: Palgrave, 2001, pp. 37-55); Sekine "Une réflexion sur les tendances actuelles de l'économie mondiale", *Chiiki-Kenkyû* (Aichi Gakuin University), 37/1 (1999a), pp. 17-25.

[23] For more on this theme, see Sekine, *An Outline of the Dialectic of Capital*, vol. I, pp. 10-13.

[24] This expression is inspired by the title of Polanyi, Karl, *The Great Transformation, The Political and Economic Origins of Our Time* (Boston: Beacon Press, 2001).

[25] This fact has been cogently pointed out, and early, by James Buchanan. See, for example, Buchanan, J. M. and Wagner, R. E., *Democracy in Deficit, the Political Legacy of Lord Keynes* (New York: Academic Press, 1977).

[26] Although the welfare state has since become distinctly less labour-friendly and less business-regulatory and repudiates the idea of "big government", it is difficult to say that it has been supplanted once again by the bourgeois state. The most that can be said is that the welfare state has been modified and has become less "liberal" (munificent) in the sense of social-democratic.

[27] I owe this and other information to three recent Japanese studies on the American economy: Tate-ishi, Takeshi (2000), *Beikoku Keizai Saisei to Tsûshô-seisaku* (The Re-Birth of the U.S. Economy and its Trade Policy), (Tokyo: Dôbunkan, 2000), Miyata, Yukio, *Amerika-no Sangyô-seisaku* (American Industrial Policy), (Tokyo: Yachiyo Shuppan, 2001) and Kawamura, Tetsuji, *Gendai Amerika Keizai* (The Contemporary American Economy), (Tokyo: Yûhikaku, 2003).

[28] The development of capitalism from its liberal stage (based on light industries such as textiles) to its imperialist stage (based on heavy industries such as iron and steel) involved far more than mere quantitative innovations. The British steel industry which had invested too heavily in the Bessemer technique found itself unable to compete with its Continental European counterpart, which shortly afterwards, introduced the more advanced Siemens-Martin method. This, among other things, led to the demise of British hegemony in manufacturing and the shift of the industrial centre from Britain to Germany in subsequent years. When such a technical progress of the qualitative type occurs, it can change the nature of the use-value space and the life-style of society as well, with the result that capitalism may or may not subsequently survive. It is not capital but the state that must brave such a challenge.

[29] This is well documented in studies included in Krugman P. R (ed), *Strategic Trade Policy and New International Economics* (Cambridge, Mass.: MIT Press, 1986).

[30] If an "average activity" situation did occur, we would have observed a tendency for profit-rate equalization at the margin of all industries. Nothing of that sort has been seen for a long time in the present age of rent-seeking.

[31] This article was written for presentation at the International Roundtable of the Korea Social-and-Economic Studies Association, held on July 4, 2003. It parallels in content with my similarly entitled work "What We May learn from Value theory?" which has just appeared in Richard Westra and Alan Zuege ed., *Value and the world Economy Today, Production, Finance and Globalization*, Palgrave, 2003, pp. 188-204. Here the same theme is treated afresh with further thoughts of the author.

III. A New Essay

Towards a Critique of Bourgeois Economics

I

Economics is a product *par excellence* of the modern age. Modern societies evolved world-historically, as the mediaeval, feudal societies in the West gradually disintegrated over a lengthy period of time. The word "capitalism" will be used, in this essay, in the sense of the economic base (or substructure) of modern society. In other words, the latter's economic life is, in principle, believed to be supported by the capitalist commodity-economy, or more simply "capitalism", in which the commodity-economic logic of capital holds sway.[1]

Towards the end of the mediaeval age, in the West, the increasingly frequent movement of people and goods stimulated commerce, while the level of productive powers in traditional societies generally rose. At the same time, the hierarchical order, both political and religious, that had united local feudal units, dispersed over an extensive territory, could no longer be easily maintained. There arose battles amongst warlords, with the stronger ones subjugating the weaker, until the most powerful, allied with the rising class of the bourgeoisie, succeeded in unifying particular nation-states, thus becoming absolute monarchs over their territories. Subsequently, in what is typically referred to as the *early-modern* period, the absolute monarchs energetically pursued mercantilist policies so as to promote the national (or home) market, while building strong armed forces as well as industry within their respective jurisdictions. Such efforts eventually paved the way for the Industrial Revolution and the evolution of the labour market, while shifting the locus of commodity production from farm cottages to town factories, which led to a tremendous elevation of the productive powers. By the time the capitalist commodity-economy had begun its autonomous operation, however, the bourgeoisie no longer needed the absolute monarchy for its protection; thus, it eventually brought down the so-called *ancien régime* by a series of bourgeois revolutions and established truly "modern" society, with a self-regulating capitalist mode of production at its base. It was against this background that economics emerged as science or a systematic body of objective knowledge.

Up to that time, economics had remained partial and fragmentary (i.e., unsystematic) knowledge. This reflected the fact that the commodity-economy itself had never involved the whole, or an integral part, of society's economic life, but operated only partially or peripherally, i.e., interfering with it, if at all, in non essential ways. When, after the Industrial Revolution, modern society established itself fully, however, its substructure, i.e., capitalism, engulfed society's economic life integrally, so that, without comprehending the "inner logic" (or "laws of motion") of capitalism, the modern person would remain unaware of the world in which he/she lived. It was for that reason that economics and the other modern social sciences were called upon to explain how capitalism, or the material base of modern society, actually operated. Indeed, in pre-modern societies, such essential concepts (or even words), employed by modern social scientists as "society", "economy" and "the nation-state" did not even exist, because religious cosmology prevailed there, and taught that inter-human relationships must reproduce, or at least remain consistent with, the more fundamental hierarchical order that existed between God and humans, or between heaven and earth. In this way, the master-servant relation based on one's status in society (rather than contracts between individuals) was naturally accepted, and the authority of the supreme ruler, be it king or emperor, was to be regarded as, in some ways, ordained by the Almighty. The modern outlook on the world was, however, to be radically different; it was to be secular (this-worldly) and more anthropocentric. It sought a scientific, rather than a metaphysical, explanation of the world. It was for that reason that not only mechanics and the other natural sciences, but also economics and the other social sciences were increasingly in demand.

Economics began with polemical pamphlets justifying the mercantilist policies of one sort or another but, by the time of the French Physiocrats (represented by François Quesnay), and of the Scottish Moral Philosophers (such as David Hume and Adam Smith), it began to be expounded in more systematic manner in lengthy treatises. That was during the late 18th century, when a series of bourgeois revolutions were heralding the end of the absolute monarchy. Then, shortly after the Napoleonic wars, in the early 19th century, the Free Trade Movement arose in England under the direct influence of the classical school of economics, and began dismantling the mercantilist restrictions on trade, domestic and international.

The story thus far recounted might give the false impression that prosperity in commerce automatically leads to the modernization of society; but such a thing did not occur in ancient times, even though many independent (near autarkic) communities were then also exposed to active merchant trade. A barely self-sufficient economy with little surplus,

and thus not yet attuned to commodity production, can easily be devas-
tated or destroyed, by being exposed to external trade. Its productivity is
still too low to benefit from contact with other economies. Perhaps the
case of "silent trade" most graphically illustrates the wariness of isolated
natives faced with foreign traders.[2] As Marx points out, the exchange of
commodities originates in the interstices of independent economic communities;[3] that is to say, trade arises originally as external relations to the
community. Only when the latter, can, to some extent, "internalize" these
external relations, does trade become regular; and that would occur only
when external trade stimulates the internal economy to produce more
commodities. In other words, there must be some internal production of
commodities already, before the community can profit from external
trade. This was the case, both in the West and in Japan, when the so-far
predominantly agricultural, mediaeval societies turned to a more vigorous production of commodities, when exposed to external trade. That
also explains the collusion of the bourgeoisie and the absolute monarchy
in the early modern period in Europe (and in the longer Tokugawa era in
Japan), which prepared the ground for more radical modernization and
industrialization, subsequently. If one looks at the same process from
another angle, that which made "modernization" possible, in both cases,
was the fact that the use-values, which constituted an important part of
the real economic life of society, were then relatively easily producible as
commodities. In other words, the so-called "contradiction between value
and use-values" (inherent in the commodity)[4] could then be relatively
more easily surmounted. For, only in that case, could the commodification of the national economy be accelerated under the mercantilist policies of the absolute monarchy, preparing the ground for the Industrial
Revolution and the concomitant evolution of the labour market.

II

Having satisfied this crucial condition, genuine modern-bourgeois society
emerged in the early decades of the 19th century in England, and
reached its acme in the middle of the 1860s. The Free Trade Movement
arose in that country, as already mentioned, under the direct influence of
the classical economic doctrine, quickly dismantling mercantilist restrictions on trade, both internal and external. The British could also "interna-
tionalize" this movement by concluding treaties, containing the so-called
"most-favoured nation clause", with their trading partners. The Anglo-
French Commercial Treaty of 1860 (otherwise known as the "Cobden-
Chevalier Treaty") was perhaps the capstone of their achievement, in-

asmuch as 19th century international trade was never freer from impediments than under that treaty. The reason for such a resplendent success in free trade then was due to the fact that the British cotton industry was by far the most advanced producer of commodities, for both internal and external markets, which enabled Britain to retain the so-called "monopoly of industry".[5] With this privileged position, Britain occupied the central place in the then international division of labour, in which other nations remained essentially agricultural suppliers of food and raw materials to Britain. This was also the time when the world-historic development of capitalism achieved the highest degree of self-regulation, as the commodity-economic logic of capital held increasing sway. If the world-historic development of capitalism could be represented by the cubic growth curve, this must have been the time at which it was passing near its saddle-point, at which its increasing rate of growth up to then, having reached its maximum, turned to a decreasing rate of growth.

The significance of this fact cannot be overrated. For capitalism, as the object of study of economics, was then manifesting a tendency to "purify itself". It does not mean that it ever became pure in fact; it would have, however, had the growth rate of capitalism maintained its maximum speed experienced at the saddle point of its growth curve (that is to say, had its growth curve turned into a straight line after reaching its saddle point!). Economic theory became a systematic knowledge because the perfectibility of capitalism could then be glimpsed (perceived) as the end point of its own development. The ideal image of pure capitalism is, therefore, not a mere fantasy; it is a "copy" of the real movement that capitalism itself manifested in its world-historic development, at the time when the British cotton industry dominated the world's commodity-production. Economists could thus learn, more or less adequately, the "definition of capitalism by capital itself". The dialectic of capital, or Uno's *genriron*, reproduces it, however, more consciously and thoroughly, by pre-supposing, in effect, that use-values would become more easily commodifiable than they actually were in the mid-19th century Britain. At that point in time and place, the "definition of capitalism by capital itself" loomed more or less clearly, thus appealing to the mind of the theorizing economist. It was surely not a mere ideal-type that economists arbitrarily concocted as a "model" because, in this case, real abstraction lay behind mental abstraction. Not only does this remind us of Hegel's object-subject identity, but it also constitutes the confluence of the real movement and its mental reflection, or of the ontology and epistemology of capitalism. In fact, the so-called "materialist copy-theory" has never been more strikingly illustrated than by this fact, on which Uno definitively laid his finger, while Engels and Lenin who had meant to expound the same theory never achieved as convincing a defence of it.[6] A matter of this importance, however, seems to have wholly eluded economists (both bourgeois and Marxist), which fact spells the doom of their ideologically-motivated, haphazard knowledge that lacks any satisfactory scientific foundation with regard to method.

Nevertheless, one must not overlook the fact that capitalism, being a once-for-all historical occurrence, cannot consummate its self-purifying tendency. For, that would mean the complete emasculation of use-values, which represent the concrete-real substance of wealth. Use-values in history do continue to resist value categories, or the abstract-general (mercantile) forms of the commodity-economy. Indeed, in the 1870s, new industrial nation-states, such as Germany and the United States emerged, challenging, and terminating, the "monopoly of industry" by Great Britain and the international division of labour between that country and the agricultural ones which surrounded it. At the same time, the development of the railroad system and the frequent use of steam-ships stimulated heavy industries notably iron and steel, which replaced light industries such as cotton and other textiles at the core of commodity-production. Improvements in long-distance transportation were also accompanied by massive international flows of agricultural as well as heavy and light industrial products in the world market. This meant that the age of free competition among atomistic small firms had to give way to the age of a small number of monopolies and strong customs protection to suit them. It was from this perspective that Britain lost its industrial hegemony to the newly emerging Germany and United States, lapsing gradually to a rentier state. As the liberal age was thus supplanted by the age of imperialism, the self-purifying tendency of capitalism, too, lost steam, and was eventually reversed. In the emerging new industrial states, the "impurities" (i.e., pre-modern residues), especially in the agricultural sector, tended to be tolerated and retained, because the "mechanized industry" that these countries could import ready-made from Britain was already productive enough not to require a radical dissolution of the old customs and practices to be competitive. Thus, "uneven" economic development became the rule and was accelerated in these countries.

This new trend was already making itself felt in Marx's lifetime, yet its eventual course was not yet sufficiently evident to let him realize the advent of "imperialism" as the new (and highest) stage of development of capitalism. WWI which was its necessary consequence could hardly be foreseen yet by anyone. As the trend proceeded subsequently, however, the gap opened wide between what Marx taught in *Capital* and the evolution of real capitalism, which deeply confused and tormented Marxists.

They were divided between the Orthodox and the Revisionist Marxists, unable to settle the basic conundrum that confronted economics. Even Lenin's widely read pamphlet, *Imperialism, the Highest Stage of Capitalism (A Popular Outline)*, published in 1917, could not in the end settle their dispute. As the acute political urgencies of various class struggles increasingly overwhelmed them, they had little time or energy left to spare for the resolution of the fundamental difficulty facing economics, namely, how to bridge the gap between the theory (logic) and history (reality) of capitalism. (As I will show presently, the problem of the gap between "theory" and the "real world" plagued bourgeois economics as well, and perhaps even more so). With the birth of the Soviet state in Russia, those who became purveyors of official doctrines contributed towards the vulgarization of Marxist economics, being oblivious of the need to critique bourgeois economics at its root, despite the object lesson Marx himself had left behind decades ago. This ideologically active Marxism thus sank deep into the "poverty of economics", until Kôzô Uno finally blazed the correct trail out of this quagmire in the interwar period. Before discussing the nature of his seminal contributions, however, I wish to reiterate that Marxists were not alone in being stalemated by the "poverty of economics". Almost as soon as capitalism entered its liberal stage, bourgeois economics too began to suffer from the same traumatic state, unable to decide what to make of capitalism.

III

Marx was widely credited with being the first to talk of "classical" political economy. However, under this rubric, he included only a select group of economists "beginning with William Petty in Britain and Boisguillebert in France, and ending with Ricardo in Britain and Sismondi in France",[7] without mentioning such illustrious names as Jean-Baptiste Say, Robert Malthus and John Stuart Mill, whom he rather considered to belong to the class of "vulgar" economists. The present day usage, in contrast, is far more inclusive. Not only does it contain the three names mentioned, but practically all notable economists prior to the so-called the Marginal Revolution[8] which occurred in the early 1870s. Even in the latter case, what remained central to the classical school of economics was the doctrine that Ricardo inherited from Adam Smith, others being regarded somewhat peripheral to this mainstream. Yet, as soon as Ricardo enunciated his own doctrine in the early decades of the 19th century, it was exposed to persistent criticisms by Samuel Bailey and Robert Malthus among many others,[9] largely because his "embodied" labour theory of value did not appear to sit well with the equalization of profit-rates in different industries. Marx commented at length over the "disintegration of the Ricardian school" in chapter 20 of his *Theories of Surplus Value*.[10] This suggests that, in the golden age of liberal capitalism in Britain, from the early 1820s to the late 1860s, classical economics was already in disarray, so that the only major economist who built on the quintessence of Ricardo's doctrine (i.e., that which bears on the "definition of capitalism by capital itself") was Karl Marx, who was engaged in economic studies from the second half of the 1850s to the first half of the 1860s. In other words, Marx's *Capital* is the work that links Ricardo's *Principles* with what is known today as the dialectic of capital. The revolutionary significance of Marx in the history of economics is rarely noticed. Yet, he, nevertheless, made one decisive step towards genuine economic theory (in the sense of capital's own definition of capitalism) for two reasons. First, he himself lived through (and so experienced in his personal life) the process of capitalism's increasing self-purification, which occurred near the saddle-point of its growth curve. Secondly, he was acutely aware of the fact that capitalism was a once-for-all, transient economic order, not a permanent and eternal one, as the classical economists wanted to believe.

Prior to undertaking his economic studies, Marx formulated the so-called "materialist conception of history" (otherwise known as "historical materialism") on the basis of his earlier affinity with the German philosophical tradition.[11] Many Marxists believe, quite unwarrantably, that historical materialism by itself constitutes a "social theory" or scientific knowledge of some kind. In fact, it has no scientific content at all; it is merely an ideological hypothesis that served him as a "guiding thread" to the study of economics. As I explained elsewhere,[12] it is based on the following three hypothetical principles: (a) In any society, the ideological superstructure stands on a material base (or economic substructure); (b) In any society, the prevailing production-relations correspond with the existing level of productive powers; (c) Capitalism is the last class-antagonistic society. None of these three general principles has been scientifically established to be true (nor are they so formulated as to be susceptible of "demonstration" in any conventional sense of the term), even though, according to Uno, Marx's economic work implicitly corroborates that all these principles do apply insofar as "capitalism as a historical society" is concerned. (Uno calls this special application of the three principles to capitalism the "epitome" of historical materialism). What is more important here, however, is to understand the way in which the materialist conception of history served as the "guiding thread" to Marx's study of economics. In a nutshell, it protected Marx as an antidote against infection by the "modernistic, bourgeois-liberal and capitalist" ideology that is so deeply ingrained in economics, so much so that anyone who studies economics, unprotected by this sort of antidote, is bound to be irrevocably contaminated by a rabid bourgeois bias, to the extent of forgetting that capitalism is a historically transient and once-for-all economic order.

Economics was, in the first instance, discovered and constructed as the knowledge that powerfully supports the superiority of modern society over all preceding societies. Indeed, the role assigned to the classical political economists was to uphold the idea that capitalism constituted an ideal form of human society. Adam Smith already had talked of the *Invisible Hand of Providence*, which coordinated and reconciled all disparate and conflicting interests of blind human beings (like "monads") into a world of the (Leibnizian) Pre-established Harmony.[13] Perhaps the idea that the free and unobstructed working of the capitalist market led eventually to a Pareto-optimal[14] general equilibrium was not as clearly grasped by the early Whigs, as it was later by the Harmonists and neoclassical economists. Yet, it is noteworthy that the bourgeois-liberal belief in the perfectibility of the capitalist market became prevalent, thanks to classical political economy, quite early in the formation of modern society. This undoubtedly reflected the emergence of the bourgeoisie as the unchallenged master (or caller of the tune) of that society.

Interestingly, however, by the time Ricardo completed classical political economy, modern society, which stood on the material foundation (or base) of the capitalist mode of production, was already beginning to show its true face. It was composed of the three major classes of the capitalists, the workers and the landlords, and was plagued with periodic industrial crises. Far from being a happy world of pre-established harmony, real capitalist society involved disagreements and conflicts among the three classes. The increasing gap between the rich and the poor meant that class struggles between the capitalists and the wage-earning workers kept intensifying, so that a faction of the Ricardian school eventually shifted towards socialism.[15] Even the landlords, who established a "teleological coexistence" with the capitalists, could not necessarily buy into the bourgeois view of the world.[16] For, even though they grew richer with the growth of capitalism, they could not spend all of their incomes for consumption. Had they invested the remainder, they would have become half-capitalists themselves, while, if they had consumed less than their incomes, they would have been stuck with idle monetary savings inconvertible into capital, which would have led society to deflationary under-consumption. Malthus may have been obsessed with such an image, when he defied the classical Say's law. In any case, it was obvious that economic theory had to surmount the bourgeois bias in order to be objective. Yet, the Ricardians, stuck with the bourgeois illusion that capitalism was a permanent and eternal economic order, instead of a once-for-all and transient one, could not. Those who shunned socialism then had to become rabid believers in the pre-established harmony. Thus, the Ricardians were split into the two camps of the Socialists and the Harmonists, and became, in both cases, more "ideologues" than economists.[17] Herein lay the seed of the aforementioned "poverty of economics".

Only Marx was spared from that degradation, the reason being that, contrary to the popular opinion, he had the wisdom of controlling his own ideology. No one denies the fact that he was the foremost socialist revolutionary and ideologue. Yet, he did not allow himself to be blinded thereby and thus be deterred from penetrating to "capital's own definition of capitalism", which constitutes the kernel of economic theory. Armed with historical materialism, the antidote against bourgeois-liberal biases, he could study far more thoroughly than any of his contemporaries economics as it then existed, and, thus, was able to distinguish "classical" from "vulgar" economics, where the former touched on the kernel of economic theory, while the latter merely recited a litany of the semi-religious Harmonist faith. With all these accomplishments, however, Marx did not quite complete his "critique of political economy", his life-long project, and could not, therefore, clearly show the decisive recipe whereby to break away from the stalemate of post-Ricardian economics. In the following section, that problem will be faced.

IV

Marx did not wish to remain at the level of the utopian socialists. He felt that, in order to critique the capitalist mode of production (which we call "capitalism" here for short), he needed to fully comprehend its law of motion (internal logic), and that, to that end, he needed to study economics thoroughly, i.e., to come to grips with that which makes capitalism what it is. The latter is equivalent to the "definition of capitalism by capital itself" or a systematic exposition of capitalism in its "pure" form. Capitalism is said to be "pure", when "the use-values in it are thought to be much more easily commodifiable than they actually are". The commodity, it will be recalled, consists of value, which represents it as abstract-general (mercantile) wealth, and of use-value, which represents it as concrete-specific (material) wealth. Capitalism is synthesized in terms of value by capital's commodity-economic logic, but it must also remain a "use-value space", i.e., real economic life of a human society. Use-values are each a concrete-specific object, which, in one way or another, resists (i.e., does not automatically accept) the generalizing and unifying principle of value. It is this fact that is referred to as the "contradiction between value and use-values". The word "contradiction" is here used in the dialectical, and not in the formal-logical, sense. It simply refers to a gap (cleavage, tension, discrepancy, conflict, stress and the like) between the two aspects of one and the same thing. (Certainly, that does not in any way offend the law of contradiction in the formal logic.) Indeed, some use-values that we produce and consume in our own daily lives are more easily handled as commodities than others. By the same token, some "use-value spaces" can be more readily operable than others by means of the capitalist commodity-economy.

Of course, Adam Smith taught long ago that the word "value" meant sometimes "value in use" and sometimes "value in exchange"; and the same idea was faithfully reproduced by Ricardo.[18] But, in striking contrast to Marx, the classical economists never recognized a dialectical "contradiction" to be surmounted between them. It is for that reason that they always remained impervious to the dialectic in the style of Hegel, even though, as it turns out, (scientific) economic theory can never be brought to completion without it (i.e., without being synthesized, step by step, by overcoming "dialectical contradictions" which reappear at each step except the last). In fact, the classical economists implicitly postulated that there was no contradiction (or tension) at all between use-values and value, between the real-economic and the commodity-economic, which was, in effect, equivalent to asserting that capitalism had always existed and would last forever, since all use-value spaces would then be, by definition, equally "subsumable" under the commodity-economic principle of capital. Marx adopted the diametrically opposite position with regard to capitalism, which, to him, was a historically unique, once-for-all and transient economic order. It was, therefore, entirely consistent for him to begin his economic theory with the "dialectical" contradiction between value and use-values. For, only when, and to the extent that, capital succeeds in "sublating" (resolving) that contradiction, can capitalism exist at all. Thus, his "critique of political economy" amounted, in effect, to exposing the unreasonable classical dogma that capitalism was part of the natural order.

Yet, economic theory, classical or Marxian, cannot even begin without admitting the possibility of a perfectly competitive commodity market, which automatically tends towards a general equilibrium. In other words, economic theory must always presuppose an "ideal" working of the capitalist market, which means that use-values must be neutralized, or "nominalized", therein. In theory, in other words, they are viewed only as names of different objects for use or consumption (direct and productive), and conform always to capital's wish to treat them as value (i.e., as abstract-general, mercantile wealth). The difference between Marxian and classical approach lies in how such an image is obtained. In the Marxian case, as already explained, it is obtained by copying the real movement towards pure capitalism, which could be observed in the development of capitalism in history. When capitalism passes near the saddle-point of its growth curve, an ideal working of the capitalist market can be perceived (foreseen), as a state in which the use-value resistance against the dictates of the value principle "asymptotically approaches zero" (i.e., almost evaporates). There is, in this case, nothing normative about letting capital pose its own ideal state. In the classical case, in contrast, the ideal state of the capitalist market (the pre-established harmony) is a norm or "ought" (perhaps ordained by Providence or the Infinite), which can be disturbed only by the aberrant behaviour of finite human beings. The methodological difference thus explained between the two approaches may appear rather academic at this point; however, when the real and the ideal of capitalism diverge from each other, the two approaches manifest completely distinct responses. If the real diverges from the ideal, the Marxian response will be that use-values turn out, in reality, to be more recalcitrant (less amenable) to the aim of capital than is supposed in theory, while the classical response will be that there are aberrant interferences with God's plan, where the latter must be obeyed by removing the former.

In the first case, one has to investigate the relationship between the actual "use-value space" and the capitalist form that subsumes it. The pure form of capitalism, however, exists only in theory and not in reality, so that real capitalism is always an imperfect embodiment of the commodity-economic logic of capital. That is why the real and the ideal must be mediated by the world-historic developmental stages of capitalism.[19] Specifically, in the nascent (mercantilist) stage, use-values were predominantly of a type reminiscent of the woollen and worsted goods produced "domestically" in British farm cottages in the 17th and 18th century. In the more vigorous (liberal) stage of capitalism, typical use-values were more reminiscent of the cotton goods, produced by many small, competitive British factories in the middle of the 19th century. In the declining (imperialist) stage, leading use-values were of the type represented by iron-and-steel goods produced and marketed by large monopoly organizations in Germany or the United States, between the late 19th century and the war of 1914. For all these cases, the typical "use-value space" was quite distinct, depending on the leading industry's level of technological development and the corresponding life-style of the consumers. Thus, the actual capitalist economy in empirical history cannot be related to the purely theoretical definition of capitalism by capital, unless mediated by these stages. There is also bound to be the possibility that none of these stage-theoretic types can mediate between the actual "use-value space" and the pure form of capitalism that economic theory exposes, suggesting that the economy in question is no longer (or not yet) a "capitalist one".

Unlike the first (Marxian) case which thus opens the door to so many different new paths of further exploration, the second (bourgeois) case puts the whole onus on the real, and none of it on the ideal. For, the latter is deemed divine, whereas the former is only human. In other words, reality must be either chopped or stretched to fit the Procrustean bed of pre-established harmony.[20] The poverty of economics in the classical approach (especially in its vitiated, bourgeois "Harmonist" form) is, thus, made obvious. Only the Marxian approach enables us to liberate ourselves from the quagmire, into which the disintegration of the Ricardian school has led us. Yet, Marx himself, whose "critique of political economy" was only half finished, did not quite see the full import of his own approach. The reason is that he came to this world too early to see the end of capitalism, so that the owl of Minerva had not yet quite spread its wings by the time he died in 1883 (though it was about to). In short, he could not fully evaluate "imperialism, as the highest (last) stage of development of capitalism". Had he done so, he would have realized that the study of economics must be undertaken at three distinct levels of abstraction (the purely dialectical theory, the stages-theory of development and the empirical history of capitalism). For that insight, however, one had to wait for the arrival of Uno, upon whom that idea dawned in the interwar period.

V

The fact that Marx himself did not realize the full implication of his own (dialectical) method was unfortunate, but unavoidable given the fact that he died in 1883, which was only a little over a decade after capitalism had entered the last stage of its development, known as imperialism. He, in effect, knew only the first two stages of capitalist development, mercantilist and liberal, which he simply distinguished as the old and the modern. Therefore, when the last volume of *Capital* was published by Engels in 1894, this magnum opus contained in it elements of the purely logical theory of capitalism, their illustrations drawn from the empirical history of its first two stages of development, together (perhaps occasionally) with some stage-theoretic determinations pertaining to these two stages, but without maintaining a clear and consistent distinction of the three levels of abstraction (purely logical, stage-typological and empirico-historical). By the end of the 19th century, however, the imperialist stage of capitalism's world-historic development had proceeded far enough to have manifested many novel characteristics, so that a quite considerable gap opened up between Marx's economic teachings in *Capital* and the evolutions of actual economic life in the age of imperialism. It was this fact that confused and tormented Marxists of the Second International, as I remarked earlier. In the meantime, however, there had occurred an important change on the side of bourgeois economics, known as the Marginal Revolution, which gave birth to the presently dominant neoclassical school.

After the disintegration of the Ricardian school, the Harmonists wished to abandon the (objective) labour theory of value in favour of the (subjective) utility theory under the influence of Condillac and Say, but they remained indecisive until the so-called Marginal Revolution occurred in the early 1870s, when the concept of "marginal utility" was adopted independently and simultaneously by Carl Menger, Stanley Jevons and Léon Walras.[21] By replacing "labour" with "utility" in the theory of value, these three authors could re-establish consistency between that theory and the equalization of profit-rates in all industries, and thus launch the new school with (what they thought to be) a logically defensible system. Their major innovation consisted of the application of mathematical analysis to economic theory, which replaced the traditional method of numerical illustrations. In this way, economists learned to speak the same language as physicists, and thus could formulate their theory in much more general and precise terms than formerly. For example, Walras' formulation of general economic equilibrium in terms of simultaneous equations is believed to have been inspired by Laplace's similar treatment of celestial mechanics.

For about forty years or so prior to the First World War, the leading economists of this school, in two generations, made outstanding contributions towards reformulating how the operation of the perfectly competitive market would lead the whole economy to a state of Pareto-optimal general equilibrium. Even though their economics did not depart from the narrowly one-sided Harmonist view, the technical innovation and refinements that they brought to bear on rigorous economic analysis were quite remarkable. Some, including Walras, were apparently socialists, but they preferred to stick to their ivory-tower, Parnassian approach, insofar as pure economic analysis was concerned. Interestingly, and ironically, it was at the time when real capitalism, in its imperialist stage of development, reversed its former trend to approach an ideal state of competitive general equilibrium, but rather tended to increasingly diverge from it. Newly emerging industrial nations, such as Germany and the United States, challenged the "monopoly of industry" that Britain had enjoyed, together with the international division of labour surrounding it. The liberalization of international trade then gave way to tariff wars and dumping. For, with the advent of heavy industries, centering round coal, iron and steel, the "bulking large of fixed capital" promoted a small number of dominant monopoly organizations, which tended to displace free competition among many small capitalist firms in those industries. The mode of accumulation of finance-capital overwhelmed that of industrial capital, which fostered uneven capitalist development between sectors rather than balanced growth, especially in newly industrialized nations where the economy remained "dual", in the sense that a highly productive heavy-industry sector operated side by side with traditional agriculture and light industry. In short, the operation of real capitalism increasingly deviated from the norm of Pareto-optimal, competitive general equilibrium. All that, however, hardly disturbed neoclassical economists. They were absorbed in polishing the heavenly norm of pre-established harmony, aloof from the more burning policy issues of the real economy. Only the German *sozialpolitiker* of the Schmoller school addressed such issues, until their influence quickly waned after the First World War.[22]

Looking at the "moral fortitude" with which the mathematically oriented, neoclassical economists concentrated on the intellectual refinement of the heavenly "harmony" of interests, untroubled by the vicissitudes and travails of this world in the imperialist age, one cannot help being reminded of the Benedictine and Cistercian monks in the mediaeval age, who withdrew to the interior of their monastery walls to quietly reflect upon the religious cosmology, which was then believed to dictate the ultimate fate of this world. In both cases, they were the intellectual elite of the age, whose assigned role was to uphold and reproduce the dominant ideology of the existing society. It is important to recognize the meaning of neoclassical economics in that light. The esoteric stance, accentuated by its mathematical elegance and disengagement from this fleeting, fallen world, was perhaps deliberately adopted, since, in that way, it became all the more powerful as the weapon to defend the declining (i.e., increasingly eviscerated) bourgeois society. Surely, it was more than merely the "economics of the leisure class" to be lightly dismissed and forgotten.

All societies combine an ideological (political, juridical, ethical, cultural, informational, educational, recreational, etc.) superstructure and a material (economic) substructure. In general, if the substructure is stable, so is the superstructure. This however, does not mean that the super-structure has no active role of its own to play, and need only remain passive. The stability of the economic base, of course, reflects the state in which society's existing production-relations remain compatible with the available level of productive powers, but the latter do not remain stationary. Under capitalism, especially, innovations in the method of production occur frequently, which builds stress in the prevailing production-relations and calls for suitable adaptations in super-structural institutions. The latter, however, have been carefully fashioned to suit the dominant ideology, which defines the conventional world-view that holds sway in society. In order for society to remain cohesive, the leading or dominant ideology, i.e., the one held by the more powerful and privileged classes, and which legitimizes the existing hierarchy, must be constantly reproduced and reinforced, until it becomes axiomatic, that is to say, part of the commonsense or conventional wisdom in society, and permeates through the whole of its super-structural institutions. To that end the intellectual elite of society must be mobilized. The role of the educational system and cultural/informational networks (depending today especially on mass communications channels) is paramount. Those who contribute, in one way or another, to the apologetic of the existing order are generously rewarded with comfort, status and honour. In contrast, a critical ideology that challenges the status quo, will be suppressed ruthlessly in a dictatorial régime, though tolerated as a "minority opinion" in modern democracies within limits, that is to say, to the extent that it does not become destructive of, or dangerous to, the existing social order. Clearly, the dominant and the critical ideologies are not equally matched. It is for this reason that ideological battles are often fruitless, unless a newly arriving society is already at the door and its image is clearly grasped by the majority.[23] Prior to that stage, one could do no better than to follow Marx, and show that the dominant ideology, too, is a mere ideology, and that its pretension to objective (or universally accepted) truth is completely ungrounded.[24]

VI

The world economy after the Great War (1914-1917) does not, according to Uno, mark any new "stage of development" of capitalism, and so must be studied directly as economic history.[25] This presumably means that the world economy today no longer reflects the working of the laws of capitalism in any consistent and conclusive manner, but that, instead, their non-working, or working in deviant or adulterated ways, fails, in the end, to bring together a proper operation of capitalism. Of course, I here continue to use the term "capitalism", as defined above, in the strict sense of the self-operating capitalist commodity-economy, and not in the broad and more colloquial sense of just "being, or acting, capitalist-like". Thus, from the Unoist point of view, it is best to describe the world economy today as being in the process of the "disintegration of capitalism", or in that of "ex-capitalist transition". This judgment might strike many as strange, because after WWI (and after WWII even more), the scope of the commodity-economy seems, at first sight, to have expanded rather than contracted. Yet, I wish to show below that the two essential laws of capitalism, viz., the laws of value and of (relative surplus) population, are no longer effective or in force. In the light of that fact, I wish to assert that we are today in the process of transition away from capitalism to another historical society.

The First World War was a "total war", which involved not only the military but the civilian population as well, and massively; it had, therefore, devastating effects, which completely transformed the nature and structure of the world economy. Yet, how deeply and in what specific ways were not immediately apparent to those who were in charge of the world's economic and political management after the peace of Versailles. Most of them stuck to the old-fashioned idea that the postwar reconstruction of the world economy could not (and indeed must not) be expected, without the prewar gold-standard system being first restored, the system which had "symmetrically" mediated international trade and investment.[26] As it turned out, the United States was the only country which could restore the prewar gold standard immediately after the war, while the other major powers had to wait until the return of so-called "relative stability" in the middle of the 1920s to do so, and, in most cases, at the cost of exacerbating already severe deflation. After the crisis of 1929, which introduced the Great Depression, they all had to abandon gold as the standard money, Britain and Japan in 1931, the United States in 1933, France in 1937, and so forth. It is thus clear that, after the war of 1914-17, some key condition was lost that would have enabled the world economy to revive a commodity-money such as gold. As the dialectic of capital shows, a commodity money, unlike fiat money, is that which the logic of commodity exchanges automatically entails. If that logic does not work, one has reason to suspect that something is amiss with capitalism.

After WWI, as the centre of commodity-production shifted from Europe to the United States, a new mode of operation sometimes referred to as "Fordism", which consisted essentially of the "production of durable commodities by means of durable commodities"[27] in the hands of oligopolistic large firms, established itself in the world economy. This point has already been made, especially by Hyman P. Minsky. But anyone familiar with the dialectic of capital should immediately realize that the introduction of "durable goods" into the capitalist reproduction system would cause many awkward problems, because there is no capitalistically rational method of depreciation. It is due to the fact that the use-value of a durable commodity does not diminish over time pari passu with its value. In other words, durable use-values resist the mercantile principle of value more than non-durable use-values. The "production of durable commodities by means of durable commodities" is, therefore, bound to sabotage the working of the law of value.[28] Yet, even before one gets involved with that problem, Fordism already differs from capitalism proper in this, that oligopolistic firms faced with reduced demand for their product do not bring down its price, but instead directly cut back production, and employment along with it, thereby destroying incomes.[29]

It will be recalled that the actual process of capitalist accumulation alternates between the "widening" phase, where the organic composition of capital is held constant, and the "deepening" phase, where it is elevated. If accumulation continues "extensively" with a given state of techniques (i.e., undergoing the "widening" phase), real wages will rise gradually and will eventually cause a "profit squeeze", which will end in a crisis. However, in the ensuing phase of depression, characterized by a general fall of commodity prices, competition among capitalist firms intensifies, and forces them to adopt new techniques , which permit them to earn adequate profit, even at prices lower than before. This deepening, or "intensive" capital accumulation, which involves technical progress that enables capitalist firms to produce their products at reduced prices, raises the organic composition of capital, and will lead to business recovery, launching another round of extensive accumulation at a higher organic composition of capital than before.[30] Marx recognized the salutary effect of these periodic crises which ensured the survival of the "fittest" capitalists, and Schumpeter eulogized capitalism's "creative destruction". Key to this mechanism of "automatic recovery" from the devastation of an industrial crisis is the general fall of prices. This desirable feature which ensures the resilience and staying power of capitalism can be preserved, so long as prices fall when the demand for commodities contracts. This signifies that the law of relative surplus population peculiar to capitalism is at work. For, when extensive accumulation brings about a severe shortage of labour, intensive accumulation, which raises the organic composition of capital, in effect, eases the demand for labour per unit of capital.

Even though, in the stage of imperialism, the decennial periodicity of the capitalist crises had to be somewhat warped, due to the advent of heavy industries (such as coal, iron and steel) and to the consequent decline of free competition among small firms in the face of powerful monopolies, the prices of their products (such as coal, iron and steel) fluctuated sharply in the course of business cycles. Thus, the pure theory of crises and actual crises in the empirical-historical space could still be mediated through the stage-theoretic determinations of imperialism, so that the operation of capitalism could be preserved. Under Fordism, however, this connection was broken, as oligopolistic firms no longer allowed the price of their product to fall, but, instead, directly reduced the quantitative scale of their production together with employment. The consequence of this behaviour was graphically illustrated by the Great Depression of the 1930s, from which an automatic recovery of capitalism could, in no way, be expected. With the dysfunction of the law of population, capitalism proper was by then dead.

Indeed, if the law of population fails, it means that the value of labour-power cannot be determined; for, its determination must be grounded on the real tendency that the demand for, and the supply of, labour-power tend to be equalized in the sub-phase of "average activity" (which follows the sub-phase of "recovery", and precedes that of "over-heating or precipitancy"), during the prosperity phase of business cycles, which is just another name for the phase of extensive (or widening) accumulation. Only during the sub-phase of "average activity" does the law of average profit (i.e., the law of value as it appears in the capitalist commodity market) tend to hold, as wages tend to converge to the value of labour-power. In other words, the micro law of value (or of average profit) would be meaningless, unless the macro law of population (or of the falling rate of profit) determines the value of labour-power at the same time.[31] The dialectic of capital regards "capitalism" to be in operation if, and only if, the course of extensive capital accumulation (or of prosperity in business cycles) undergoes the sub-phase of "average activity", in which the micro law of value meets the macro law of population. Since Fordism as defined above contravenes this condition, it cannot be recognized as constituting "capitalism", properly speaking.

My purpose in what follows is not to discuss in detail the evolution, after WWI, of the process of transition away from capitalism to another historical society, but rather to relate some salient features of this process to new developments in bourgeois economics, notably in the United States. It is, indeed, in that country that bourgeois economics has witnessed the most vigorous development, as it served as the ideological background of the U.S. international strategy, viz., that of the globalization of the world economy under American hegemony. It is necessary, however, to first review the process of the "disintegration of capitalism", which, as is well known, has gone through the following three periods: (1) The Interwar Period of Great Transformation;[32] (2) The Golden Age of Keynesian Social Democracy and its Lapse into Stagflation; (3) The Age of Neo-Liberal Counter Revolution, leading to the Financial Domination of the World by the United States. Each of these three periods has manifested some distinct features. I will summarize these periods as briefly as possible, in the following section.

VII

In the first period of the "Great Transformation", which roughly covers the 1920s and 1930s, the centre of the world's commodity-production shifted definitively from Europe to the United States. For, by the end of WWI, Europe had contracted an enormous amount of debt to the United States. The Americans had never wanted to take part in that war, which they considered to be strictly a European affair. All they intended was to be paid interest on the loans they granted, on a strictly business-like basis; and, this position did not change even after they finally sent troops to Europe, galled by the German submarine attacks on their commercial vessels. However, the Europeans had borrowed so much from the United States that, after the war, their gold steadily flowed away in the latter's direction. Thus, unless the Americans invested their money first in Germany, so that the latter could pay part of it as reparations to its former enemies, Europe had little cash to finance its reconstruction. Only in the mid-1920s did this happy circuit appear to have been realized, materializing the so-called "relative stability" of the world economy. By the end of the decade, however, the unprecedented American boom, turning into a bubble, called back all the money previously lent to Europe, which, of course, bled the latter white. Then, in no time, with the bursting of the bubble in 1929, the U.S.A. itself was caught by the Great Depression, not because of any policy mistake, but because, given that key prices had not fallen, production and employment had to be cut back. This income destruction naturally led to another fall of aggregate demand, which, in turn invited more contraction of production and employment, and hence of incomes, that then started a fatal spiral of deflation in the private sector of the economy. With the collapse of the American economy, the whole world was prostrate; the bourgeois democracy was understandably challenged, and then besieged, by the collectivisms of the right (fascism) and of the left (bolshevism). The Second World War

(1939-1945) thus became inevitable. The only way to escape the horror of a deflationary spiral would have been for the public (non-private) sector to spend more than it received. Pre-Keynesian economics, however, had no inkling of that lesson. True, the New Dealers did experiment with this policy rather hesitantly with a limited success; but, it was the war in Europe that compelled all powers to suddenly resort to "deficit (public) finance" under duress, Keynes or not, which immediately led them out of the depression.

The second period covers the 20 halcyon years (1945-65) of strong American leadership after WWII, and the messy 15 years (1965—1979) of instability and stagflation which followed. At the beginning, the supremacy of the United States in economic and political power among the victorious Allies was uncontested. It was only natural that the postwar world order had to be built under the aegis of Washington, which assumed leadership in designing and enforcing the postwar IMF-GATT system. This system established a gold-exchange standard based on the U.S. dollar, on one hand, and the rules whereby to reciprocally liberalize international trade among the contractual parties, on the other. In order to make it easier for as many countries as possible to join that system, in the early postwar world that was plagued by the "dollar shortage", the U.S.A. offered the Marshall Plan in order to supply $12 billion aid for European reconstruction over 1948-51. Yet, this had the side-effect of heating up the Cold War that was already brewing, as it divided the world into the Western camp, which accepted the American offer, and the Eastern camp, which fell under Soviet rule. Domestically, the United States instituted the Employment Act in 1946 with a view to officially aiming at both "full employment and price stability". Under the Cold War, the Americans were forced to favour "industrial peace" over "class struggles", and, thus, to concede to "social democracy" despite their natural aversion to socialism. To that end, they made use of Keynes, who at least passed outwardly for a liberal. He favoured working entrepreneurs and labour, but harboured antipathy towards rentiers, whose "euthanasia" he openly professed. In this way, he could be accepted by the New Dealers, if not by American conservatives. Yet, the reluctant adoption of Keynesian fiscal policies worked wonders, and soon produced the golden age of Keynesianism, together with Affluent Society, which tolerated mild inflation and favoured borrowers over lenders, in addition to an increasing class reconciliation between employers and the employed. In the meantime, the financial interest, which was severely regulated, nursed grudge against this social-democratic trend. However, the main reason why fiscal Keynesianism worked well, especially in the first half of the 1960s, was that the "unit labour cost" tended to fall, as the productivity of labour increased faster than money wages. Presumably, the rise of productivity in industry was mainly due to the advances in petro-technology.

Though itself a fossil-fuel like coal, oil can do a lot more than coal, not only because it can power the internal combustion engine, but also because, through innovations in petro-chemistry, it can substitute plastics, detergents and chemical fibres for primary natural materials. No wonder the age of affluence and high consumption could be achieved by the easy availability of oil (if at the hidden cost of environmental devastations). Yet, the United States and other advanced economies could not forever benefit from the import of cheap oil. When OPEC formed a cartel (in bitter reaction to the aborted dream of NIEO) to elevate the price of oil, petro-technology could no longer be counted upon to raise productivity of labour any faster than money wages; thus, the falling trend of unit labour cost ceased and was reversed. With that, the golden age of fiscal Keynesianism was over, and gave way to the age of instability and stagflation. Even prior to that conjuncture, the gold exchange standard, anchored on the U.S. dollar, had to be abandoned, as the United States built a considerable current account deficit vis-à-vis the rest of the world; by the end of the 1960s, it had lost practically all the gold that it had gained during the 1930s, having clung for too long to the external convertibility of the U.S. dollar into gold, which President Nixon finally revoked in 1971. The difficulty of controlling inflation by means of Keynesian fiscal measures then ended by giving undue credence to monetarism, while the recycling of petro-dollars which gave a lucrative opportunity to unregulated offshore banking revived Wall Street (the financial interest) from an extended period of inertia, within the national boundaries, under the strict New Deal regulations. The conditions were ripe for a neo-liberal counter-revolution.

The third period covers the neo-liberal era (1980-2010), which stretches over three decades since the beginning of the 1980s, and still continues unabated to this day. It began with monetarism and Reaganomics. Milton Friedman had long fought against the idea that the Keynesians had a monopoly over macroeconomics, and had aimed at building a "neoclassical macroeconomics", based on the quantity theory of money. Monetarism is an extension of that theory which claims that the money supply (M) is a policy variable, to which the nominal value of national product (PQ) will respond, given the velocity of monetary circulation (V). Thus, under full employment, an increase in the money supply will lead to a rise in the price level, but, under less than full employment, to a quantitative growth of national product at a near constant price level. Although this theory does not always work, since no monetary authority can unilaterally dictate an increase in the money supply, in the absence of a strong enough demand for bank-loans, it may work in the other direction, inasmuch as the money supply can always be held constant (or even contracted) by policy, when there is too vigorous a demand for loans. Indeed, the central bank can hold back the money supply, by restricting the base-money in the banking system, and, if the quantity of national product stays as it is, so must the price level.[33] Paul Volcker's anti-inflationary FED policy was essentially of that type. As the money supply was held constant, though the demand for bank-credit remained quite strong, rates of interest skyrocketed; but that eliminated inflation. While such a truculent policy was being enforced, newly elected President Reagan introduced a policy aimed at "small government", meaning deregulation and tax reduction, in the hope of re-activating the private economy. What he did in fact was to forcibly arrest the further increase in money wages, which stopped and reversed the upward trend of unit labour costs. He also spent more on the military budget. The private sector was stimulated by these measures, if not by deregulation and tax reduction.

Simultaneously, the exceptionally high rates of interest led to serious "debt problems" at the expense of the developing countries, which had borrowed so many petro-dollars at low debt-servicing costs. The high interest rates also encouraged the inflow of foreign savings into the United States, and strengthened the value of the U.S. dollar, to a greater extent than was desirable with respect to the American balance of trade. Thus, in his second term, President Reagan sought a "realignment" of the U.S. dollar with foreign currencies, and, in effect, obtained its considerable depreciation via the Plaza Accord (1985). Whereas this move had doubtful effects on the promotion of American trade with the rest of the world, the high rates of interest created a far more serious bind for U.S. commercial banks, which, because of the so-called regulation-Q (of the Glass-Steagall Act), could not pay adequate interest on their time-deposits. They naturally saw these deposits quickly withdrawn for more lucrative investments elsewhere. By that time, the gap between the strict regulations on banks inside US borders, in contrast to no regulation outside them, was becoming untenable, so that the rates of interest on bank deposits were liberalized in 1983, which lent an impetus to a more general deregulation of banking and finance. Thus, in the second half of the 1980s, an A&M boom occurred, restructuring American industry. Behind this lay two important facts. First, the nature of finance in the system that "produces durable commodities by means of durable commodities" lacks the commodity-economic rationality of capital. Secondly, in the present world economy, idle money that is extensively saved and remains convertible into real capital is no longer scarce, so that it can be used directly (and probably even more lucratively) as the instrument of money games. Wicksell has already warned against a "cumulative process" that may damage industrial activity, when the money rate of interest (return on money games) is held at a higher level than the real rate of interest (return on real investment).[34]

VIII

Now, returning to the end of the First World War, let us recall that, as the German influence in economics (among other fields) waned rather quickly, the relative importance of the Anglo-American neoclassical school increased, in which more American names stood out than before. In Harvard and the University of Chicago, some great teachers were training the following generation of world-famous economists, even though their teaching rarely clarified the nature and the causes of the Great Depression, except to say that wages were much too high. In the meantime, in England, Keynes was writing energetically on economic affairs of the day, but without much impressing the established economists in the Marshallian tradition. In the early 1930s, however, a large number of Harvard economists went to Washington to assist and advise the New Dealers, though they were themselves not yet Keynesians. At Harvard, in the meantime, economists of the younger generation, junior instructors and graduate students, were beginning to be informed of Keynes' new ideas by his former students at Cambridge, England. Thus, by the time the *General Theory* was published in 1936, Keynes' fame was already well established, though it is doubtful that its revolutionary message was correctly understood or appreciated at that point.[35] Some American Conservatives naïvely denounced Keynes as a covert communist, while many professional economists made painstaking efforts to integrate Keynes' new ideas into their more traditional neo-classical framework. The so-called "neo-classical synthesis", promoted especially by Paul Samuelson and his students, which amounted to an eclectic parallelism of the classical "micro" price theory and the Keynesian "macro" income theory, was one of such schemes. But, in this manner, only a part of Keynesian theory, specifically the multiplier theory of consumption, was accepted in undergraduate textbooks on economics, its more significant "uncertainty theory of investment" being largely ignored. Even then, the coming of Keynes to America and its partial acceptance had a far-reaching effect on the subsequent development of bourgeois economics, especially in the first twenty years after the end of WWII.

As recounted above, Keynes and petroleum were the two principal players in the second period of transition away from capitalism. In its first twenty years, fiscal Keynesianism seemed to work quite well to promote a sort of social democracy within the framework of affluent, mass-consumption society, by being able to benefit from the development of petro-technology, which steadily raised the average productivity of labour more quickly than money wages. That trend involved both urbanization and a general rise in the standard of living, which must also have dramatically increased the proportion of white-collar workers, including university graduates. As society became more complex and knowledge-intensive, more "economists" were trained and found employment just as did lawyers, accountants, physicians and other professionals, while business schools, too, became a crucial part of higher education. After the 1957 sputnik crisis especially, the U.S. university system was renovated, so as not to fall behind the Soviet system of equally massive higher education. At that point, the university curriculum in economics became a matter of great importance. It contained no reference to Marx in the first twenty years of Keynesian success, and so bourgeois economics in the framework of the "neoclassical synthesis" was the only economics officially taught during that period. By the middle of the 1960s the situation changed somewhat with the rediscovery of radical political economics, a trend sometimes known as the "Marx renaissance". But, in the end, Marx's economics was never seriously studied, and, thus, was easily forgotten amidst the factional strife of dilettante social theorists and their ideological struggles. It was increasingly thought, on the other hand, that bourgeois economics had become so "scientific" that it needed no longer fear Marxist ideological criticisms. That, of course, was the routine practice (affectation), as I have already pointed out earlier, of the "dominant ideology" in society, which aims at preserving its privileged position by hiding its true nature, i.e., by feigning to be "above ideology".

The mathematical and statistical adornments which now abounded in its exposition made the economics of the neoclassical synthesis more esoteric, and so more appropriate as an ideological weapon to support America's "international strategy" under the Cold War, in which the West was deemed to remain the stronghold of "capitalism broadly understood"[36] which preserved freedom and democracy, against the East that fell under the yoke of Soviet communism. Even though the Keynesian "macro" policy conceded to "large government" in the pursuit of industrial peace, classical "micro" theory still appeared to preserve the traditional creed of a pre-established harmony, in the form of a Pareto-optimal, Walrasian general equilibrium, the existence and stability of which had been mathematically proven under reasonable assumptions.[37] Even the economist's failure to synthesize the micro and macro components of the theory into one single system was overlooked, in view of the fact that the similar division of theory still prevailed in physics. The assimilation of Keynes, however, had to be limited to the multiplier theory of consumption; for, only to that extent did Keynes remain innocuous. Beyond that limit Keynes could have become dangerous, as he, for his part, rejected "classical" price theory altogether, claiming himself to be the inventor of a "general" theory. Actually, his "uncertainty theory of investment" was diametrically opposed to the concepts of pre-established harmony and general equilibrium, since he was obviously aware of the twist that the "production of durable goods by means of durable goods" would cause to economic theory, which could no longer exclusively count on the enforcement of capitalist rationality, as Minsky and other post-Keynesians have later elaborated.[38]

In any case, during the 1970s, the explosion of petroleum prices engineered by OPEC terminated the happy "Keynesian" social-democratic period. As unit labour costs began to rise, no amount of aggregate-demand-policy manipulation à la Keynes helped to circumvent stagflation, while the Minsky-style "financial instability" asserted itself. That was because the "producers of durable commodities by means of durable commodities" borrowed only to meet the previously arranged commitment to pay cash for whatever reason, not (capitalist-rationally) for the production of more surplus value (freely disposable income). They did not necessarily borrow to earn extra income out of which to pay interest and amortize the principal; they often borrowed, instead, by issuing their own debt instruments which were not self-liquidating, thus adding to the overall indebtedness in society. In this way, industrial firms are taken hostage by money-lenders, whose profit cannot be explained capitalist-rationally. If this danger is inherent in the regime of commodity production deeply entangled with durable goods, the liberalization of finance (pressed on by the "innovativeness" of the money-lenders) clinches it. The real economic life of society is exposed to the dictates of investment banking, security finance and the relentless gambling of the money-lenders, who, in pursuit of speculative gains, have no intention of converting their idle funds into real capital. Anyone familiar with the dialectic of capital knows that "money-lending capital" is an irrational (and so self-destructive) form of capital, characterized by its "measurelessness" in the Hegelian sense.[39] It existed before capitalism, which began by taming it. Now its return in the new form of "casino capital" spells the doom of (industrial) capitalism, and, with it, of human society and nature as well. Yet, the rich and powerful in today's society want us all to believe that their unbridled activities in the market are best left alone. Let us see how the new trend in bourgeois economics lends support to their view of the world.

IX

If the unwinding of capitalism is reflected in the loss of coherence and integrity in economic theory, that symptom, interestingly enough, appeared in the 1970s, as the prestige of Keynes plummeted, drawing the curtain on the "neoclassical synthesis". The euphoric view that economics had now grown into an advanced science, and that it was capable of "fine tuning" the economic management of the state, faded away quickly and was replaced by bitter frustration at its inefficacy. Two important trends appeared at this point. One was the introduction of game theory into microeconomics, and the other was the reconstruction of macro theory without Keynes.

Central to the neoclassical price theory had always been a perfectly competitive market (described as anonymous) for commodity exchanges, in which innumerable small firms competed among themselves, by "taking the ruling prices as given", i.e., under the assumption that these would not change in response to whatever way the individual unit acted. With the development of Fordism, however, many industries became "oligopolistic" in the sense that a few large firms in the market competed among themselves (non-anonymously), being perfectly aware that what they would do would affect the strategies of their competitors. To analyze this kind of situation, the theory of games rather than infinitesimal calculus was obviously more appropriate. However, since the theory of games was a new branch of mathematics, of which the seminal contribution dated only from 1944, it took a while before it penetrated to the core of economic analysis. When, in the 1950s, Nash equilibrium (often illustrated by what has come to be referred to as the case of "The Prisoners' Dilemma") was established as a general solution to all non-cooperative games among a finite number of players, it was already clear that Walrasian general equilibrium was but a special (limiting) case, in which the number of players was thought to be infinite. In light of this result, however, the previously known theorem that competitive general equilibrium was also Pareto-optimal (meaning that it constituted a situation in which no one's position could be improved without worsening someone else's position), though still correct within its pre-set logical space, was challenged as "not so realistic" to represent the real world of interactive competition amongst oligopolies.

The thesis that equilibrium resulting from games among a small number of interactive competitors is, in general, not Pareto-optimal has a far-reaching consequence; for, it summarily repudiates the traditional, liberal faith in Pre-established Harmony. From this perspective, the "capitalist" market does not guarantee an optimal allocation of resources, nor does it reconcile conflicting worldly interests into a heavenly harmony, as can be easily surmised from the simple case of The Prisoners' Dilemma. Price theory, in other words, can no longer insinuate the salutary effect of the Invisible Hand. Once that message was learned by the profession (and I believe that occurred in the 1970s), research in microeconomics began to deal with such (apparently more realistic, but) ad hoc cases, as "rent-seeking" as opposed to profit-seeking, "principal-agency" problem which may produce perverse results in the market, and the like. All of these trends suggest a regression of faith in capitalism. Or, to put it otherwise, casino capital[40] today can no longer count on neoclassical price theory to support its apologetic of the existing order. Yet, this outcome turns out to be not quite as fatal to the dominant ideology as it might appear at first sight. The reason is that, today in the third (and final) period of transition away from capitalism, the productive powers of the world economy have been raised so enormously with the successful assimilation of petro-technology, ICT, robotics, new materials and the like, that the gain in use-value production in this regard far outweighs whatever loss that may have accrued from its failure to achieve maximum efficiency. In other words, "scarcity" in material wealth no longer remains the primary concern of economic management in an affluent world, which thrives on increasingly "materialistic and secular values".

It is for that reason, all the more, that the reconstruction of macroeconomics without Keynes is most urgently desired. The currently dominant ideology of the neo-liberal counter-revolution originates in Wall Street, where the powerful financial interest nestles. Throughout the second period of ex-capitalist transition, the latter vegetated under the strict New Deal regulations, which the Keynesian social democracy prolonged, as it aimed at the "euthanasia of the rentiers". Now it wants to preserve the maximum freedom to participate in money games, the lucrative territory that it once lost but more recently regained; to that end, it needs "small government" and mild deflation, rather than "big government" and mild inflation which the aborted social democracy demanded in the past. This being the case, what the dominant ideology wishes to teach is the lesson that the control of the economy by casino capital is both necessary and desirable. Instead of the dubious Harmonist parable of Pareto-optimal general equilibrium with its outdated religious overtones, a "scientistic" and policy-oriented, but non-Keynesian, macroeconomics that endorses both small government and mild deflation becomes more serviceable. In response to this need, the "hypothesis of rational expectations" has surfaced into the blinding limelight. The latter simply means that all expectation errors in the model are assumed to be random, so that the agents in it must, on average or overall, predict the correct future values of economically relevant variables such as long-run equilibrium values, which are already indicated in the model. Based on this theory, some economists thrived in asserting the "policy ineffectiveness proposition", according to which no discretionary macro policy, monetary or fiscal, can be effective, since it is bound to be outwitted by the "rationally expecting individuals and firms" that act to cancel its effect, in order to arrive eventually at the correct future values of the model's long-run equilibrium. Even more interesting to casino capital is the so-called "efficient market theory", which says that the rationally expecting and well informed units in the model would leave no profit opportunities in security prices unexploited, so that, in the end, all prices in financial markets will be correct and will reflect market fundamentals. Thus, the hypothesis of rational expectations appears to have proven not only that the state has no place in the management of the contemporary economy, but also that casino capital acts to stabilize, rather than to destabilize, financial markets!

In this way, today's neoclassical economics has shifted the fulcrum of its ideological support for "capitalism broadly understood" from the semi-religious Pareto-optimal allocation of resources in microeconomics to the more anthropocentric (or this-worldly) hypothesis of rational expectations in macroeconomics. Yet, its "normative" stance in laying down how "capitalism" ought to work, and what its correct state of equilibrium should ultimately be, by simply designing an arbitrary model of the economy, and adorning it with an esoteric aura, remains assiduously invariant. The amazing egotism of the neo-classical model builders and their determined indifference to the extent to which their model may already have vastly diverged from reality is still rampant and out of control. Just as their forefathers in the pre-1914 imperialist age, they, too, tell us how the world economy ought to work, instead of how it in reality does. For, in designing their model, even if some of them may fail to correctly evaluate available information, such errors being "randomly" distributed, the "rationally-expecting" Chicago economists must be able, on the whole, to generate correct and realistic models to justify their pre-conceived idea of what the right "capitalist" economy ought to look like. Thus the navel-gazing tendency of bourgeois economics after Ricardo, which never intended to seek the truth about capitalism (in the true theoretical sense of the word), but merely created the illusion that the good old tradition of democracy is preserved by "capitalism", broadly understood to mean the antipode of all sorts of collectivisms, continues to survive strongly to this day. It is this illusion that should be inculcated as the basic lesson for bright youths, so as to kindle their ambition for an upward-mobile bright career.

X

During the age of imperialism, as capitalism reversed its self-purifying tendency, many forms of intermediate classes had already appeared; this trend, however, was still limited in comparison to what happened later in the Fordist period. As the urbanization of society was accelerated and as social life became correspondingly more complex, a large number of middle-class intellectuals, especially university graduates, became essential. In the present post-Fordist society, often characterized as "knowledge-intensive", many positions require even more advanced professional skills. At the same time, the relation between the economic substructure and the ideological superstructure of society has also become blurred, which implies increased importance in the role played by the dominant ideology, which (without so appearing) vindicates the hierarchy of the existing society. Surely the economic management of society today cannot be entirely left to the commodity-economic logic of capital which survives only in the "private sector" of the economy. For often a national consensus must be sought to warrant a decision that will affect the long-run future of citizens. In order that the national consensus continues to conform to the dominant ideology, all the super-structural institutions of education, culture, entertainment, information and mass communication must be mobilized. The cultural or educational campaign to form and spread national and international consensus with respect to the shared "values" of civilized society now becomes quite systematic and mind-controlling (if not mass hypnotic). Indeed, the economic management of today's society, as of any society, operates on Polanyi's three principles: exchange, redistribution and reciprocity.[41] For the purpose at hand, these may be translated, respectively, into the "market principle of capital", the "planning principle of the state" and the "cooperative principle of people". Although in capitalist society the first principle overwhelms the other two, the present trend points to the restitution and reinstatement of the latter. In fact, it is this fact that is reflected in the blurring of the relation between the economic substructure and the ideological super-structure in the present society.

Casino capital seeks a reversal of this trend and wishes to reassert the supremacy of the market principle (commodity-economic logic) of capital over the others in today's world economy[42] It has tried to reformulate an anti-Keynesian macroeconomics, not only by making use of the hypothesis of rational expectations, but also by claiming it to be "axiomatically true". I have been at pains to argue, however, that axiomatic truth is a pure tautology, just as the truth of the celebrated Euclidean theorem that the three inner angles of a triangle add up to a straight line is true, if and only if the axiom of parallel lines is true. The theorem falls apart in a non-Euclidean space. In just the same way, if the world economy today operates in a way that is misrepresented by the Chicago models, it is the latter that is to be discarded, not the former. The world economy today is already deeply stuck to the combination of "small government and mild deflation". Mild deflation will not, however, turn into a hyper-deflation, since obviously prices cannot approach zero with increasing speed without overshooting its goal and becoming negative. There is, however, always the danger of a mild deflation turning into a "deflationary spiral", in which production and employment contract endlessly, as it did in the Great Depression of the 1930s.

As the foregoing discussion made clear, an increasing stock of idle balances (monetary savings), unable to be converted into real capital (investment), is generated in the private sector. Contrary to the hopes of the neo-conservatives, then, the private sector will not be reactivated by further deregulations and tax reductions. It needs deficit spending by "big government" ($G - T > 0$) to fill in the gap left by the private sector ($S - I > 0$). Yet, this is precisely what the dominant ideology promoted by casino capital prohibits. The tawdry alternative that casino capital recommends is to activate security finance and to abet money games, that is to say, to contrive a "bubble", which can stir up the real economy. For, bubble means asset inflation (as distinct from commodity inflation), which, by giving the impression of plentiful money, entails the expansion of the real economy under the lure of inexhaustible demand, while it mutely aggravates its over-indebtedness. Sooner or later it is destined to burst, unable to support its own weight. Indeed, the bubble-and-bust pattern of the economy repeated itself several times in America, feigning industrially oriented business cycles, until the fall of Lehman Brothers put an end to this doubtful method. Unless another bubble is effectively contrived soon, the world economy is destined to fall into a bottomless deflationary spiral, out of which there is no way out but "huge government" spending. In this context, it is most urgent to inform ordinary citizens on how to discriminate between truth and falsehood in what passes for the teaching of "scientific" economics.

Currently, as the world economy faces an incipient deflationary spiral, a battle is being waged between the dogma of "small government and mild deflation" upheld by casino capital and what true economics teaches. In Japan, USA and Europe, "mild deflation" is already turning into deflationary spirals, because their central governments are inhibited from spending more than their tax revenues, even while the private sector continues to save far more than it invests. That is the surest recipe for aggravated deflation, based, as it is, on the false idea of fiscal discipline. The fact that the national budget works quite differently from family budgets, which belongs to the elementary knowledge of economics, is deliberately ignored, and the accumulation of the national debt is routinely denounced as a sign of profligate government. Fiscal conservatism may have made a good sense in the past, but it only does harm today. After years of campaigning for "small government" the national budgets of most advanced countries are already starved of tax revenues, while they are forced to spend on many public needs, which cannot be easily delegated to private enterprises, so that the fiscal deficit often needs to be covered by borrowing. The stock of national debts consequently increases, adding to the burden of debt servicing, while restricting the flexibility of programme spending in the budget.

Any sovereign nation that adopts a managed currency system, however, has the intrinsic right to issue fiat money, since, after the "demonetization" of the commodity money such as gold, managed currency system means nothing else but a *fiat money standard*. The newly issued money at the discretion of the nation-state can, of course, be used to supplement fiscal revenues when warranted, as the elementary theory of *functional finance* teaches. There is little reason to hesitate or to demur at this move. Yet the dogma of fiscal conservatism, embodied in the dominant and ideologically-charged economics, either deliberately ignores this possibility, or denounces it as "inflationary taxation", which no responsible government should ever even dream of taking recourse to. The reason for this misconception is quite obvious. Unlike the dialectic of capital, bourgeois economics has no dependable theory of money, due to their traditional *dichotomy of the monetary and the real*, sometimes expressed by the belief that *money is merely a veil of the real economy*. Thus, despite the generally held view that money is a "miraculous invention (presumably due to Providence)" that enables the market to function smoothly, bourgeois economics never really understood how a "commodity money" such as gold must be generated of its own accord from the pricing (or the expression of value) of the commodity by its owner, nor does it understand how the gold producing sector automatically regulates the production of gold, monetary or non-monetary, according to the operation of the law of value. All it knows is that, IF there is a certain amount of gold already in the vault of the central bank, commercial banks under its aegis can create credit-money (active money to purchase commodities) up to a certain multiple of that amount of gold. From this bourgeois economics simple-mindedly infers that, even under a fiat money standard, the whole question of the optimum money supply can be left to the discretion of the central bank. Not so. For otherwise, a situation described recently as "the Great U.S. Liquidity Trap of 2009-11" would not have occurred.[43]

This bourgeois view is, in effect, equivalent to claiming that only the central bank (which is supposed to be independent of the elected government) can generate fiat money in the form of "base money", B, on the basis of which the private banking system may create credit money, r^*B, where r^* is the legally prescribed upper limit of the cash-reserve ratio. This claim implies a pious hope that, even under the managed currency system (or fiat money standard), the question of the money supply should be kept as far as possible within the sanctuary of the private sector, supposedly free from interventions of the state. But that is an impossible fantasy, when commodity-money such as gold has already disappeared. For, as mentioned earlier, monetarism errs in believing that the bank multiplier ($r \leq r^*$) is always equal to the legal maximum cash-reserve ratio ($r = r^*$). Under deflation, a bank's power of credit creation always falls short of the legally prescribed cash reserve ratio ($r < r^*$), because, even if reserve money is plentiful, banks cannot responsibly lend for a risky or unsound project. This would mean that, under deflation, not enough active money to circulate commodities is created, even while abundant idle money is held uselessly biding its time, i.e., while waiting for the interest rate to rise. It is necessary then for the government of the sovereign state to regain the power to create fiat money, F, for itself to directly finance its fiscal projects, quite apart from base money, B, which does not lead to sufficient creation of credit money, due to a persistently depressed bank multiplier ($r < r^*$).

When gold (or any other commodity-money) is "demonetized", as it is at present, a sovereign state, which has to adopt a managed currency system, is not only empowered but is also obligated to create fiat money in two forms: first as "base money", B, or cash reserve of the banking system (through the central bank), and secondly as "fiscal money", F. The latter must be created directly into the demand-deposit account which the duly elected government of the sovereign state must hold at the central bank, and that amount must be convertible on demand into legal tender notes, for whatever purpose that it (the duly elected government of the sovereign state) sees fit. In other words, it is the responsibility of the state that operates a managed currency system to supply a "near optimum quantity of fiat money" either as base money, B, or as fiscal money, F. (This part is, in abstract terms, equivalent to the government's printing its own paper money.) The creation of fiat money is not a prerogative of the central bank which is supposed to be "independent" of the state, even though the latter may delegate to the former, under some circumstances, the technical operation of adjusting the quantity of "base money". It follows that, under deflation specifically, supplying an excessive amount of "base money", B, and no (or not enough) "fiscal money", F, will merely end in proliferating idle money (to abet speculation), while withholding the supply of active money (to slow down or block the circulation of commodities), thus perpetuating the deflation of the economy. Given the enormous deflationary gap that currently exists in the economies of the developed nations, there is little risk of inflation as the consequence of printing more active money, F, to undertake necessary fiscal projects.[44] Thus, whether the Great Depression of the 21st century can be averted or not will depend solely on whether or not the public can still wake up from the mesmerizing spell of the currently dominant and ideologically-charged economics to retrieve the sound fiscal tools for arresting the on-going deflationary spiral.

Notes and Reference

[1] Marx himself always talked of "the capitalist mode of production" or of "this social formation" referring to modern (bourgeois) society, and hardly ever of "capitalism", though it is common today to use this latter term in the same sense. This usage originates perhaps with German writers such as W. Sombart and M. Weber.

[2] Herodotus, *The Persian Wars*, Book IV, chapter 196 (Modern Library College Editions), p. 369.

[3] Marx, *Capital*, I (New York: International Publishers, 1987 Printing), p. 91.

[4] The "contradiction between value and use-values" is a recurrent theme throughout this paper. More comments and explanations on this concept will follow.

[5] This expression is often attributed to Engels.

[6] Th. T. Sekine, *The Dialectic of Capital*, volume I (preliminary edition), (Yushindo Press, 1984), pp. 40-45.

[7] K. Marx, *A Contribution to the Critique of Political Economy* (Moscow: Progress Publishers, 1970), p. 52.

[8] Mark Blaug, "Classical Economics", in *The New Palgrave Dictionary of Economics*, Macmillan Press (1987).

[9] Eric Roll, *A History of Economic Thought*, Prentice Hall, the 3rd Edition, pp. 201-211; pp. 335-337.

[10] K. Marx, "Disintegration of the Ricardian School", Chapter XX, *Theories of Surplus Value*, Part III (Moscow: Progress Publishers, 1970), pp. 69-237

[11] The concise statement of this conception by Marx himself is found in the Preface to his *A Contribution to the Critique of Political Economy*, pp. 20-22.

[12] See my *The Dialectic of Capital*, vol. I, Yushindo Press (1984), pp. 12-15.

[13] It is well known that Adam Smith refers to his famous "Invisible Hand" once in the *Wealth of Nations*, and once again in the *(Theory of) Moral Sentiments*. I do not know if Smith was in any way influenced by Leibniz who had lived about a century before Smith. But, the scholar of Smith's calibre and friend of Hume cannot have been totally unaware of Leibniz' idea.

[14] A state of the economy is described as "Pareto-optimal" if, in it, no one's level of satisfaction can be made better off without making someone else's level of satisfaction correspondingly worse off at the same time.

[15] Eric Roll, *op. cit.*, pp. 245-250.

[16] About the "teleological coexistence", see Th. T. Sekine, *An Outline of the Dialectic of Capital*, vol. II (Palgrave, 1997), pp. 129-132.

[17] Marx's term "vulgar economist" applies to these ideologues whose main contribution is to the apologetic of the existing order, not to an objective explication of what makes capitalism.

[18] David Ricardo, *On the Principles of Political Economy and Taxation* (Sraffa Edition 1953), p. 11.

[19] The classical reference for Uno's stages-theory of capitalist development has always been his work entitled *Keizai-Seisakuron*, of which the translation into English by me under the title of *The Types of Economic Policies under Capitalism* will soon be published.

[20] Because of this inherent bias to view theory (or the logic of the pre-established harmony) to be above the (contingent and aberrant) real world, bourgeois economics always uses "reality" only for anecdotal illustrations of theory; it does not consider reality as "the life-world" wherefrom everything begins. In other words, bourgeois economics draws up a map of heaven first, to which it wants the geography of earth to adapt.

[21] Eric Roll, *op.cit.*, pp. 368ff.

[22] Although the first economics ever taught in Japan was believed to be from John Stuart Mill's *Principles* in the liberal tradition, it was soon replaced by the German style economics of Schmoller's school, presumably because the latter's policy orientation proved more useful for the training of bureaucrats in this newly emergent modern nation. However, its influence lasted only for about one generation, before, it was quickly forgotten after WWI, and was replaced by that of either Marx or of the Marginalist school.

[23] Even in that case, winning an ideological battle and taking over the power of the state do not as a rule promise a happy ending. For, as Paulo Freire has cogently argued (in *The Pedagogy of the Oppressed*, 1970), many revolutionaries who once liberated people from the yoke of oppression easily turn into dictators themselves, who, once in power, end by oppressing the same people. Practically no Marxist revolution has so far been able to disprove Freire's exceptionally perceptive observation.

[24] It is the fundamental thesis of this paper that bourgeois economics after the disintegration of the Ricardian school down to the present day lacks altogether any scientific foundation. Trivial technicalities apart, it does not qualify as a body of well-founded objective knowledge. Instead, it constitutes a myth which integrally supports the dominant ideology of modern society, just as theology (in the sense of religious cosmology) used to form the core of the dominant ideology of medieval society. In order to be modern, it must pretend to be "natural scientific" rather than "metaphysical", even though such pretension can easily be foiled. (In several essays in this volume, I have argued that a social science which pretends to be objective by adopting the natural-scientific method always calls for "conformism" to the existing social order as if it were part of the natural order.) Bourgeois economics thus defends itself, not by arguing convincingly that it has objective truth in its command, but by merely reinforcing the institutional apparatus which bestows mythical values to its profession, e.g., by creating exclusive, elite educational institutions or by glorifying some of their brilliant practitioners with a Nobel prize or other worldly honours, regardless of whether they speak truth or not. This, however, has always been the case since time immemorial; society always values the intellectuals who make exemplary contributions towards its stability. The only difference from the time of the Harmonists is that, in today's highly urbanized, mass-consumption societies, the myth must be sold by more than religion and patriotism. The psycho-technology of marketing which appeals to the sub-consciousness of the consumer may have to be mobilized to recruit ambitious, upwardly mobile youths for this purpose. To believe that the Marxist ideology with virulent invectives against the existing social order might be capable of dislodging the neoclassical ideology would be puerile, and would only be playing into the hands of its sophisticated mind-control.

[25] See Uno's 1970 Essay "Capitalist Development after the First World War" appended to his *Keizai-Seisakuron* (translated into English as *The Types of Economic Policies under Capitalism*). About this book, see note 18 above.

[26] Peter Temin, *Lessons from the Great Depression*, The MIT Press (1989), p. 32.

[27] This is how I intend to understand Minsky's world. "Capitalism may very well work best when capital assets are cheap and simple. Instability may very well be exacerbated as production becomes more capital intensive and as the relative cost and gestation periods of investment goods increase, for in such a capitalist economy financing arrangements are likely to appear in which debtors pay debts not with cash derived from income production, but with cash obtained by issuing debt" (Hyman P. Minsky, *Stabilizing an Unstable Economy*, McGraw Hill, 2008, p. 222). His definition of capitalism in the sense of "using capital-assets" in production is different from ours. According to his definition, the more extensive the use of capital-asset (fixed capital) in production, the more capitalist presumably the mode of production becomes. In our view, on the contrary, the "bulking large of fixed capital" in heavy industries (at the stage of imperialism) already begins to adulterate the working of the laws of capitalism. But, if and when the use of fixed capital, which yields periodic revenues in future, becomes even more extensive and pervasive in production, the latter may no longer be adequately subsumable under the laws of capitalism, which means that its disintegration must begin.

[28] See Th. T. Sekine, *An Outline of the Dialectic of Capital* (Palgrave, 1997), volume 1, pp. 206-215.

[29] Mitsuhiko Takumi, *The Great Crash [Daikyôkô-gata Fukyô]*, Tokyo: Kôdansha (1998).

[30] Th. T. Sekine, *Outline of the Dialectic of Capital*, volume 1, pp. 220-224; volume 2, pp. 61-69.

[31] Here it is obvious that, under capitalism, the micro law of value is grounded on the macro law of population. The futile (and never to be successful) attempt at seeking a "micro-foundation of macro theory" in bourgeois economics only shows its upside-down character.

[32] Here, I borrow the expression from Karl Polanyi's justly celebrated book, *The Great Transformation, the Political and Economic Origins of our Time* (Boston: Beacon Press 1944, 1957, 2001).

[33] This asymmetry is due to the fact that banks cannot lend (create bank-credit) unless there is a demand for loans. In the mildly inflationary, Keynesian social-democratic period, commercial banks were normally supposed to be "fully loaned up", meaning that the bank multiplier (ratio of demand deposits to cash reserves) normally went up to the legally allowable maximum limit. However, in the subsequent neo-liberal period, the demand for loans was not always as vigorous, so that banks could not always create as much credit money as the legal limit permitted. Under the circumstances, if the central bank operated to provide commercial banks with increased base money (or reserve cash), the latter did not respond by increasing the money supply in proportion. In other words, the central bank cannot always regulate the money supply by simply manipulating the supply of reserve cash to banks. The central bank can stop inflation but not deflation. In this regard, the interpretation of "bank multiplier" as variable "velocity of monetary circulation" rather than as a constant "Phillips coefficient" may be more apposite.

[34] Knut Wicksell, *Interest and Prices*, 1898 (English Translation, Augustus Kelly, 1962), chapter 7.

[35] See D.C. Colander & H. Landreth (ed), *The Coming of Keynesianism to America* (Edward Elgar, 1996), for many revealing episodes in this connection.

[36] Although the Unoist thesis in this essay is that, after WWI, the world economy is in the phase of disintegration of capitalism, and does not mark any new stage of its development, the word "capitalism" continues to be used abundantly in a more general and superficial sense of "simply being or acting capitalist-like". In the context of international relations after WWII, that word is broadly understood as the economic and political regime of the Western camp under the hegemony of the United States, as opposed to the Eastern camp led by the Soviet Union. The fall of the latter in the late 1980s was thus journalistically touted as the victory of capitalism over socialism, and was duly exploited by the dominant ideology of the day.

[37] There was a period spanning the 1960s and the 1970s, during which the existence and stability of general equilibrium were the hotly debated themes among mathematical economists, and the elegance of the models they used fascinated many in the profession.

[38] Hyman Minsky, *John Maynard Keynes*, McGraw Hill (2008); Paul Davidson, *John Maynard Keynes*, Palgrave (2007).

[39] Th. T. Sekine, *An Outline of the Dialectic of Capital*, volume 1, pp. 101-104.

[40] "Casino capital" is a category that does not belong to the purely logical theory of capitalism, nor does it belong to any theory of its developmental stages. It applies only to the empirical-historical context of today's world economy. Yet, it is closely related to the logical concept of money-lending capital, the salient feature of which has already been described as "the irrational form of capital".

[41] In practically all of Polanyi's writings these three "forms of integration of the economy" recur; however, one finds a most systematic explanation of these forms in chapter 3, entitled "Forms of Integration and Supporting Structure", Karl Polanyi, *The Livelihood of Man* (edited by Harry W. Pearson), Academic Press (1977).

[42] There is clearly an element of the usurpatory ploy to this design. The commodity-economic logic of capital was both meaningful and important when it could most efficiently organize society's use-value production. Today, however, casino capital does not intend to seriously pursue the production of use-values and gain surplus value in so doing. Casino capital wishes only to gamble on it. For this irrational form of capital to claim capitalist rationality on its part can only be a joke from the standpoint of or the dialectic of capital, even though bourgeois economics may be blind to it.

[43] Pollin, Robert, "The Great Liquidity Trap of 2009-11: Are We stuck Pushing on String?", Political Economy Research Institute, University of Massachusetts, Amherst, *Working Paper Series* 284 (www.peri.umass.edu).

[44] Examples of hyper-inflation from the past are frequently quoted to justify the false idea of "fiscal discipline" under deflation, as if an issue of fiat money by the state (in the form of F rather than B) to finance its fiscal programme will always end in an endless hyperinflation. Yet, those self-styled "positive economists" who so argue would never even bother to proffer a credible simulation study in support of their thesis. Under the current state of deflation, where *ex ante* savings far exceed investment, and so abundant stock of idle money (money held to satisfy the speculative motive) fail to be converted into real capital (which also means the presence of a large deflationary gap), a considerable increase of F will not entail an uncontrollable rise of commodity prices, unless there are other concomitant factors leading to such a result. I regret that there is no more space left here for further elaboration of this issue. I wish to be able to discuss it more adequately in another place.

In the meantime, I however, draw attention to Professor Haruki Niwa's important works on the measurement of Japan's deflationary gap: "The Recent Deflationary Gap in Japan: a Quantitative Measurement", *Journal of Asian Economics*, 11 (2000), pp. 245-258; "Deflationary Gap in Japan, 1970-2000: a Quantitative Measurement", *Journal of Economic Policy Studies*, vol.1, No. 1-2 (2003), pp. 79-101; Niwa, Haruki, "Deflationary Gap in the Japanese Economy, 1970-2004", Measurement of Its Scale" in *Foundation of Economic Policies according to New Keynesian Orthodoxy* (in Japanese), Tokyo (2006). More recently, Professor

Niwa applied the same method to estimate that the potential GDP in the 1990 [2000]-price for the year 2008 [2010] amounted to about ¥979 [¥1020] trillion, which, in comparison to the actually recorded figure of GDP, in the same 1990 [2000]-price, of ¥537 [¥545] trillion, shows the gap equal to ¥442 [¥575] trillion, again in terms of the 1990 [2000]-price. The figures updated to 2008 [and subsequently to 2010] have been made available to me by Professor Niwa himself. I wish to thank for his kindness.

Appendix

Bibliography

Introduction by the Editor

I. Methodological Essays

1. "Uno's Method of Marxian Economics", in *Chiiki Bunseki*, Aichi-Gakuin University (1994), vol. 33, no. 2, pp. 73-80.
2. "The Dialectic, or Logic that coincides with Economics", in Albritton, R. and Simoulidis, J. (ed), *New Dialectics and Political Economy*, Palgrave (2003), pp. 120-130.
3. "The Dialectic of Capital: An Unoist Interpretation", in *Science & Society* (Fall 1998), vol. 62, no. 3, pp. 434-445.
4. "An Essay on Uno's Dialectic of Capital" (1977), appended to Kôzô Uno, *Principles of Political Economy* (Harvester Press, 1980), pp. 127-168.

II. Theoretical Essays

5. "Uno School Seminar on Theory of Value", in Albritton, R. and Sekine, T. (ed), *A Japanese Approach to Political Economy, Unoist Variations*, Macmillan (1995), pp. 13-33.
6. "The Necessity of the Law of Value, Its Demonstrations and Significances", *idem* (1995), pp. 34-43.
7. "The Transformation Problem, Qualitative and Quantitative", in *York Studies in Political Economy*, PEY Research Group, 4th Issue (1985), pp. 60-96.
8. "The Law of Market Value", in *Science & Society*, vol. XLVI, no. 4 (1983), pp. 420-444.
9. "Arthur on Money and Exchange", in *Capital & Class* (Autumn 2009), pp. 35-57.

10. "General Equilibrium and the Dialectic of Capital", in *Chiiki Bunseki*, Aichi-Gakuin University (1999), vol. 37, no. 1, pp. 27-51.

11. "Marxian Theory of Value, What We Might Learn from It", in *Korean Journal of Political Economy*, vol. 2 (2004), pp. 1-35.

III. A New Essay

12. "Towards a Critique of Bourgeois Economics", first published in this volume (2013).

Website for this Work and further material:

Towards a Critique of Bourgeois Economics
http://dx.doi.org/10.4444/34.20

www.owlofminerva.net

CPSIA information can be obtained
at www.ICGtesting.com
Printed in the USA
BVHW071101170619
551192BV00018B/465/P